THE RINGMASTER'S TALE

Autism, Asperger's, Anarchy!

Helen Wallace-Iles

Illustrated by Jenny Stout

ISBN: 9781723978388

First published in 2018
by Kindle Direct Publishing

10 9 8 7 6 5 4 3 2 1

'So Matilda's strong young mind continued to grow,

nurtured by the voices of all those authors

who had sent their books out into the world like ships on the sea.

These books gave Matilda a hopeful and comforting message:

You are not alone.'

Roald Dahl, Matilda

Actual conversation with my children...

'Guys, I'm thinking about writing a book on autism and I'd like to include lots of stories about the sort of things that happen in our family. I don't want you to feel like I'm talking about you in public if you're not happy about it. Are you all okay with me writing personal stuff about you?'

A whispered discussion between my children follows,
accompanied by much nodding of heads
and resulting in this wonderfully encouraging reply:

'Don't worry Mum, we don't mind; no-one will read it anyway.'
'Excellent. Thanks for that then, guys.'

This book is therefore dedicated to my four
remarkably honest children:
Christopher, Dominic, Aidan and Isabelle.

You are my life's work.
Each of you is an exceptional, unique and limitless masterpiece.
Thanks to the four of you I can confidently leave this world a far,
far better place than I found it, and whatever I achieve during
my lifetime counts for nothing compared to the genuine honour
of being your mum.
Always remember how much I adore you all
and most importantly remember this, guys:
'Dreams aren't for rookies...*giving up* is for rookies'.

Not that anyone will ever know that,
because no-one will read this book anyway.

Obviously.

Table of Contents

The art of tea making
Pushy parenting
Using your child's special interests
Functioning labels
The spectrum at war
HD humans
Working with a diagnosis

What is bereavement?
Coping with the death of a child
Grieving when your child has autism
PTSD or OTSD?
The cancellation of expectations
Working through the bereavement process
Looking for the positives
Living in the present moment
Taking things gently

Is autism a disease?
Should autism be cured?
Quack cures
Should autistic people be changed?
Should autistic children be aborted?

Why the SEN system will never be perfect
Managing in mainstream
Being actively patient
Suggestions to help your child at school

Meet the Ringmaster

My mother-in-law once told me that when her three boys were small, her father would often shake his head and say 'This family doesn't need a mother, it needs a ringmaster!'

I smiled politely, and raised an eyebrow at his little joke, saying 'Yes, I can imagine...'

As it turned out of course, I couldn't. No-one can.

As my own boys grew up, I quickly realised that her father had not, in fact, been joking after all.

***

Twenty five years later, I'm the mother of three autistic sons and a small daughter with a more than generous sprinkling of Asperger's.

This book is an honest account of some, but by no means all, of the adventures we've shared and is designed to be the first in a series of three books exploring the changes all autistic children and their families experience as they learn and grow into adults. As a result it focuses primarily on the time my children were young, with the teenage and adult years being described in the next two books.

Meanwhile, this one includes lots of useful information about the basics of autism and where to find help and support for anyone who's new to the condition.

Nothing is exaggerated, although a lot of it will be beyond belief to people without children on the colourful and constantly shifting landscape that encompasses autism, ADHD, Tourette's, dyslexia, dyspraxia etc.

Successfully parenting children who are considered 'different' is tough; there's no getting away from that fact. It's hard and exhausting and often completely overwhelming. The sheer logistics of it will chew you up and spit you out without the slightest shred of remorse, and to survive it you'll need to discover parts of yourself you never even knew existed. Fortunately, you will.

There's more courage, patience and strength in all of us than we know, and this book is written for everyone who understands that through bitter experience; equally it's written for those who don't understand it just yet, through no fault of their own. It's not for the faint-hearted, and it shows beyond question how laughing *about* something is very different to laughing *at* it.

Welcome to the greatest show on earth

Roll up! Roll up! May I proudly present the world that passes as 'normal' in my house...

All who enter here do so at their own risk and are advised to find a seat at the back, because things are about to get very loud, very messy and (if you're that way inclined) seriously offensive. Those of a nervous disposition are advised to leave immediately via the nearest exit.

For the rest of you, welcome to the wonderful, terrible, mysterious and often death-defying circus that is **Living with Autism**. Performances run 24 hours a day, 7 days a week, 365 days a year, for the rest of my life.

Stay well behind me, I've got a whip...

Meet the Performers

'We may not have it all together
but together we have it all'
Anon

Back row: Christopher (Child 1), Dominic (Child 2),
Nigel (Boyfriend, Husband & Isabelle's dad)
Front row: Isabelle (Child 4), Me (The Ringmaster), Aidan (Child 3)

Special guest appearances by Pat (Ex-husband & dad to the three boys)

Just some of the performers' many talents:

Christopher has autism, dyslexia, dyspraxia and misophonia
Dominic has autism, hyperlexia, dyspraxia and hypermobility
Aidan has autism, dyslexia, dyspraxia, ADHD and Tourette's syndrome
Isabelle has Asperger's, dyspraxia and sensory processing disorder

Warning - May Cause Offence

"It is easy to be brave from a safe distance."
Aesop

When I was a child, this was a picture of a pirate. He was short, had a wooden leg, a hook for a hand, a missing tooth and a big sword for killing people. He had old clothes, one eye, wore black trousers and had a bald head.

Today, this is a picture of a Professional Sea-Faring Wealth Reliever. He's anatomically compact, has a prosthetic lower limb, is manually depleted, has poor oral hygiene and struggles with anger management issues because he's morally and ethically challenged.

He's economically marginalised, visually impaired, wears trousers which may once have been politely described as 'coloured' but can now fairly safely be called 'black' again depending on the company you keep, and is entirely follicularly independent. The fact that he appears to be male doesn't necessarily mean this is the gender he chooses to identify with, so my use of the pronoun 'he' can safely be assumed to be pretty offensive to some people as well.

The truth remains however, that he's a short, bald pirate with a wooden leg and we all know he is.

Extreme Political Correctness, in all its disapproving, restrictive, joy-crushing glory, is the absolute opposite of life with anyone on the autism spectrum. The idea of somehow explaining ideas like these to people with so little understanding of even the simplest everyday psychological barriers is really beyond laughable, and those who spend their lives paralysed by words like 'should,' 'shouldn't,' 'must' and 'mustn't' could learn a lot from watching the way autistic people make sense of the world.

My suggestion to anyone who's obsessing over this kind of thing is to come and live the life of an autism parent, or indeed of an autistic person themselves, for a week. See how high these things come on your list of priorities then. The truth is we have more important things to deal with and in an autism household it really is a case of 'different needs, different agenda'.

Anyone who's taken an autistic child into a shop and said 'You can't go behind the counter' will know what I'm talking about here. More often than not they'll stroll straight across the shop, duck behind the counter and announce 'Yes I can: look, here I am.' The thing is, they're right. They *can* go behind the counter. The fact it's not socially acceptable and they 'shouldn't' do it, along with everyone else's mysterious ability to understand this weird, invisible rule, is completely beyond them and leads to a lot of anxiety and confusion on their part. Problems arise later of course when you tell the same autistic child 'You can't fly out of the window.' To their way of thinking you were clearly mistaken about their ability to go behind the counter and are therefore most likely to be wrong on the flying front too. Since your power to predict what they 'can' and 'can't' achieve is now highly questionable, my advice would be to skip the arguments and fit window locks.

Political correctness used incorrectly

In theory, Political Correctness is a necessary, useful, well-meaning strategy, introduced to help reduce discrimination and promote equality, and all power to it for that. We all have a lot to thank it for, whether we appreciate it or not. I believe absolutely in everybody's right to equality and choice and have no problem at all with anyone standing up for themselves and saying 'Hey, I'm not like everybody else. *This* is who I am, and who I am is worthy of respect.' In reality of course, the human psyche being what it is, a large number of people will simply follow those with the loudest (and usually the most ridiculous) voices and agree with anything in a desperate bid for public approval, forgetting about their previous ideas on morality and ethics and happily abandoning common sense somewhere along the way. In my experience it's often those same people who sit behind closed doors and snigger up their sleeves at the very things they supposedly find so distasteful. Seriously, I've seen this happen a lot.

No matter how ridiculous the new idea of what's acceptable or unacceptable might seem, people will play the game. There'll always be someone ready to squeeze a few more drops of guilt out of the general population by implying some turn of phrase they've used inoffensively all their lives has suddenly become an outrage to public decency, and rather than seem prejudiced, people will conform. As a result 'extreme Political Correctness', along with its insidious bed-fellow 'unfathomably complicated Health and Safety' have become monsters to be hated or adored in equal measure depending on your point of view.

During my lifetime I've seen these principles, which started as a genuinely positive force for change, being manipulated almost beyond recognition by a very vocal minority. Having hijacked ideas that were designed to improve people's lives and promote acceptance, they've turned them instead into weapons to confuse, control, restrict and divide the general population. The idea that being different entitles you to *better* treatment than everyone else is a very dangerous one if taken to its logical (or illogical) extreme, but there are many people in the world who believe this and set about persecuting anyone who doesn't conform to their ideas in the name of Political Correctness, completely missing the hypocrisy of their own terribly judgemental behaviour.

I often get the impression they're looking for some kind of apology from other members of society who aren't 'different' like they are, and they'd like these 'normal' people to feel guilty for some reason, presumably simply because of who they are. Surely this kind of discrimination is the very thing they're supposed to have been offended by in the first place, isn't it? In case anyone was still wondering, this isn't a viewpoint I share. No surprises there then.

I believe being different is exactly how we're all supposed to be. To me, every human being is unique and valuable, regardless of race, nationality, gender, religion, ability, financial status, sexual preference, political viewpoint or body type. That's *every* human being. In this outrageously confusing world, there are, of course, people who need extra help to let them lead a fulfilling life, but needing to be treated *differently* because you're different to the majority of people in some way isn't the same thing as being entitled to *better* treatment at the expense of those considered 'normal'. Not at all.

Be compassionate, be accepting, be understanding of others, but always remember to apply those same principals to yourself. Whether you consider yourself to be in a minority group or not, you have just as much right as anyone else to be happy, healthy and safe and if someone tells you otherwise, don't believe a word of it.

Having an able body and a capable mind is nothing to be ashamed of, any more than identifying with the gender into which you're born or having a particular skin colour, however light or dark it is. Working hard and enjoying a decent standard of living aren't crimes either, so please ignore the guilt trippers who'd like nothing better than to make you feel there's something wrong with your perceived good fortune or 'privilege' if this is how you've chosen to live your life.

Feelings of anger and frustration are completely understandable when you believe you're being ignored or overlooked, and doing something constructive to help your voice (and the voices of others in a similar position) be heard is something I support wholeheartedly. Be very wary though, of people who take this mind-set to extremes and direct scorn and anger at other people simply for being who they are. Discrimination works both ways, as does respect, and no matter how politically correct someone considers themselves, there's nothing equal or fair about anyone who tells you 'Yes, you can be yourself, but only if you do it my way.'

Different views on being different

Autistic people, you'll be relieved to hear, have no qualms whatsoever about pointing out other people's differences.

They'll usually do it very loudly and publicly, preferably when everyone else is silent. The reason they do this isn't to hurt or embarrass people, but because they see nothing 'wrong' with anyone else. They'll remark on someone having one leg because it's unusual, not because they see it as somehow deficient. Everyone is equal in their eyes, and there's no prejudice or malice behind their words, just truthful observation.

Again, this works both ways: autistic people aren't concerned about whether you're someone society thinks of as privileged; they're much more interested in who you are as a person and, in all honesty, whether you share an interest in dinosaurs, Star Wars, LEGO or whatever else their particular fascination might be. The need for politically correct language only arises when the speaker feels something is wrong and needs extra-sensitive handling, which is pretty patronising when you think about it, implying that a one-legged man will somehow be unable to deal with being reminded that he has one leg, because there's something so terribly lacking about him as a result.

Ridicule is one thing, honesty is something else, and the venom in malicious words comes not from the words themselves, but from the intention behind them. At the very least, you can always rely on autistic people to tell it like it is, please or offend, and when you think about it, since they'll often assign as much importance to a piece of wood or a rubber band as they will to members of their own family, they're society's foremost experts in promoting equality for all the world's inhabitants, both animate and inanimate.

The majority of non-autistic people have little interest in whether or not they're 'allowed' to say or do something they've said or done quite harmlessly all their lives, and simply brush this kind of disapproval off, going about their business laughing at the absurdity of it all. In my day to day life I'm very much one of these people, but I'm all too aware that by writing this book I'm making a public statement, so just for the record, if my thoughts and actions are unpopular with some people it will come as no surprise, nor will it stop me from expressing them; after all, just as treason has been said to be a matter of dates, so is Political Correctness.

Mind your language

If you're new to the world of autism, the following information will come as a bit of an eye opener to you. If, on the other hand, you've been dealing with the condition for any length of time, you'll know no-one can write a half-decent book on the subject nowadays without including this particular little minefield of unwritten rules.

Firstly, when you're talking about living with autism, how should you refer to it? Newcomers might be forgiven for assuming the answer could be as 'living with autism'. No, no my friends, that would just be *way* too easy.

Autism's identity crisis

There are a large group of people who believe in 'Person First' language, meaning they'll frown on you for describing someone as being 'autistic'; they believe describing them this way puts the condition before the person and therefore dehumanises them. When I say 'frown on you' what I mean is 'correct you loudly and usually in public, making you feel like an absolute monster who understands precisely nothing about autism'.

In the same way you wouldn't describe someone as being a 'cancerous' person if they had cancer, this group passionately believe a person's identity should always be separated from their autism. As a result they prefer to use the term 'person with autism.'

Meanwhile, there's an equally large group of people who believe just as strongly in 'Identity First' language. Put simply, they choose to describe themselves as autistic because they see this as their identity. Being described as a 'person with autism' makes them imagine someone carrying a big box of autism around, and since it's separate from them, it's presumably something they can pick up or put down when they choose to, which of course they can't. They believe autism is nothing like cancer (or any other disease for that matter) and shouldn't be thought of in the same way, making it acceptable to describe someone as 'autistic' rather than 'cancerous' because autism isn't something awful they don't want to be associated with. They detest phrases like 'suffers from autism' and 'autism sufferer' for this very reason.

These people will also correct you, very firmly and often in CAPITAL LETTERS (gasp) if you upset them online by saying they've 'got autism' or with a look of quiet disgust if you're speaking face to face.

In my experience then, it often tends to be people who either want to appear politically correct or believe in finding a cure for autism who exclusively use 'Person First' language and autistic people themselves, who accept the condition as simply the way they've been designed, who use the 'Identity First' form instead.

Oh, and also…

Then there are people whose *children* are on the spectrum: Should they be called 'autism parents' or 'autistic parents'? Some people believe by calling yourself an 'autism parent' you're implying you've got the condition yourself. Others believe this is implied by the term 'autistic parent'. But what if you *do* have the condition yourself? If your children also have it, does that make you an 'autistic autism parent' or an 'autism autistic parent'? If they don't but you do, does that make you an autistic (or autism) non-autistic (or non-autism) parent? Oh dear.

The debate rages on, and trust me, as strange as it sounds when there's clearly so much more to worry about, people can get *very* upset about this kind of thing.

In the chaos of our day to day lives where arguing about linguistics is *way* down on our list of priorities, most of us simply use both terms interchangeably, so you might wonder why I'm bothering to describe it all in so much detail.

There are two main reasons: firstly, you *will* meet these people, and they *will* correct you, so it's better you understand their points of view in advance and don't get bullied into agreeing with them just because you haven't been given both sides of the argument. Secondly, as a writer, I realise the language I use is inevitably going to jar with some people, but with the situation being as it is, the only way I could talk about autism without upsetting anyone would be to not talk about it at all. Since that isn't an option, I'll be using the words 'autistic person' and 'on the autism spectrum', plus the expressions 'person with autism', 'autism parent' and 'living with autism' throughout the book because to me none of them are offensive and simply make the most sense in whatever context I'm using them at the time.

Apologies in advance if they bother you (feel free to cross them out in your own copy and replace them with your preferred descriptions – seriously, that's what I'd do) but don't let them put you off, because you'll miss out on lots of really good advice for the sake of semantics and that would be a terrible shame. Remember, you don't have to agree with exactly *how* I say things to benefit from *what* I'm saying.

Awareness vs Acceptance

Something else people can get very upset about is whether it's better to promote 'autism awareness' or 'autism acceptance'.

On 1st November 2007, the United Nations General Assembly passed a resolution making 2nd April 'World Autism Awareness Day', the idea being to make it a focal point of the year when people across the globe could learn about the struggles faced by families living with the condition. They could also use it as an opportunity to raise funds to finance research into the causes of autism and create changes in their communities that would lead to a more accepting, increasingly autism-friendly world. 'What a great idea' you might think.

In reality of course, when it launched on 2nd April 2008, very little was known about the true nature of autism and most people still thought it was a disease. As a result, a lot of the day's focus was put on how terrible it is, how autistic people are a burden to their families and a drain on society and how the condition should be cured by eradicating autism from the face of the earth as quickly as possible. Unsurprisingly, lots of autistic people didn't like these ideas very much.

Over time, the autism community began to see the term 'autism awareness' as meaning being *aware* of autism with a view to *curing* it, leading to the introduction of another term later on: 'autism acceptance'. The idea behind this one is that autism should be accepted as just another part of the diversity of human life, and society should be encouraged to adapt and make things easier for autistic people without patronising or pitying them.

Personally I have no problem with the term 'autism awareness' because to me, being aware of something represents the first step towards accepting it. If you're not aware something exists, how can you accept it? Believe it or not, I've spoken to plenty of people over the years who are outraged at the idea that *anyone* still exists who hasn't heard of autism. People like this spend their time complaining that there's no need for autism awareness because everybody should already know all about it. Since this clearly isn't the case, I prefer to spend my time accepting that many people *don't* know much about it and helping them understand it a bit more so they can make their own minds up about the best ways to handle it.

I discuss this in much more detail in the 'Kill or Cure' chapter, but for now let's just say that with humanity being what it is, there are some pretty extreme views on either side of the debate (understatement).

Functioning labels

Another potential disaster zone if you're new to the condition is how to use 'functioning labels'. Functioning labels are a kind of shorthand used to describe how well an autistic person can perform specific tasks, and since autism is a spectrum condition, they can range from 'high' to 'low' and everything in between. They can describe someone's ability to do anything from hopping on one leg to writing an entire symphony without any musical training. I've covered these in a lot more detail in the 'To Diagnose or Not to Diagnose: That is the Question' chapter, because if you thought knowing whether to be 'aware' or 'accepting' of autism or using the right language to describe people's identities was complicated, believe me, you ain't seen nothing yet.

A matter of life and death

People will always get worked up about whether or not something is politically correct, but I'd like to talk about one specific time and place when being politically incorrect really *was* a matter of life and death.

In July 1933, the Law for the Prevention of Offspring with Hereditary Diseases was passed in Nazi Germany, legalising forced sterilisation of schizophrenics, epileptics, chronic alcoholics and those considered mentally retarded. Hundreds of thousands of people underwent this procedure while worse still, countless others fell victim to the quaintly named 'euthanasia' policy of slaughtering the mentally and physically disabled en-masse.

In Nazi-occupied Austria, a quite extraordinary paediatrician was running a clinic for 'disturbed' children who seemed unable to function in their everyday lives yet showed remarkable talents in other areas. Incredibly, he stood up and publicly argued that being different didn't necessarily mean being inferior, and that the children in his care should be allowed to live, so they could contribute to society in their own unique ways.

Just think about that for a moment: his actions were most definitely at odds with the political views held at the time, making him terribly politically incorrect, and he risked far more than public disapproval by voicing his opinions - he actually risked his own life - yet somehow he found the courage to do so. His name was Hans Asperger and his theories on the treatment of autistic people changed the course of hundreds of millions of lives for the better, something that continues to this day.

The principles behind this book

This book has absolutely *not* been written to deliberately cause offence to anyone, yet I'm perfectly aware that a lot of it will upset the extreme PC and Health and Safety Brigade by nature of its honesty. To write a book about the reality of living with autism and make it somehow quaint and universally inoffensive would not only be impossible but would also mean it was completely useless. Those who've lived this life would find nothing to relate to on its pages, or worse still, would assume they must be doing something wrong since their lives are very far from quaint. Those who have no experience of autism would be no nearer to understanding the true nature of the condition once they'd finished reading, which again seems rather pointless.

This is an open, honest account of my life as a mother of autistic children and some of the challenges I've faced and overcome along the way. It contains plenty of advice from someone who knows exactly what it's like to suddenly find yourself thrust into a strange new world you didn't expect and don't really understand. No-one is obliged to either read it or use its sometimes unorthodox advice, but I hope many of you will do so, and you'll find comfort and support as a result.

I won't flinch from describing some of the hard times, but equally I'm not afraid to celebrate the good ones. Anyone who's parented autistic children knows what it feels like to despair, goodness knows I understand that, but my family and I are living proof that you *can* get through those times and reach a place of peace, one that's all the more fulfilling because of the seemingly endless struggle to find it.

If you can't change your experiences, change the way you experience those experiences. You may have to think differently to other people and act differently to other people along the way, but then, your life *is* different to other people's.

Accepting this fact will allow you to do what you're designed to do as a human being: adapt and survive.

Risk the disapproval of others who don't understand; be honest about your life and tell it like it is. Laugh about the outrageous things that happen in your world; cry about the apparent hopelessness of it all. Whatever you do, hold your head up and remember this: *it's the people who are different that make the biggest difference in this world*. On that you have my word.

My advice then, to those people who've already taken exception to what I've said would be that since this book isn't compulsory reading anywhere just yet, the best thing to do would be to put it down and look for something else to read. Right about now would be a good time, before any more of the inevitable offence is caused.

WAITS

Well, as you're still reading, I'm going to assume you're one of the huge silent majority who still have the courage to venture out into the world in the hope of learning something new without trying to sanitise everything and everyone you meet for fear of causing some imagined offence. In which case, I'll begin my story...

BASE Jumper

Parkour Runner

Free Climber

Autism Parent

Chapter One

A Foreign Country

'There is nothing noble in being superior to your fellow men.
True nobility lies in being superior to your former self.'

Ernest Hemingway

It seems to me that Life always gives you what you need.
What you *think* you need or what you *want* are of no consequence whatsoever to Life. My belief, therefore, is that whenever possible, you should strive to make what you *want* and what you *need* the same thing, then you're absolutely guaranteed to get what you want. It might not be easy, and the truth is it may be almost impossible at times, but finding the positive in a seemingly negative situation is a philosophy that's seen me through countless tough experiences, many of which would no doubt have destroyed me otherwise.
So, what was it that Life felt I needed so badly, yet I definitely didn't want? Let me explain: As a child and also as a young woman, I worried constantly about what other people thought of me. To win the approval of strangers in the street, people I didn't know and would most likely never see again, was an all-consuming pass-time of mine. Their opinions were far more important to me than my opinion of myself; I was firmly and very uncomfortably entrenched in the 'What will the neighbours think?' mentality.
I was born in 1966, into a very different world than the one I see around me today. Political Correctness had yet to be invented, and disability in all its various guises was banished to the shadows and hidden away like a dirty secret. When I was small, mixing disabled and able bodied pupils in schools was pretty much unheard of and the 'slow' or 'retarded' kids (yes, sadly that was a perfectly acceptable term back then) who we mostly referred to in whispered voices in case their conditions were contagious, just quietly disappeared, never to be seen again.
They didn't disappear of course, but to us they might as well have done. If and when their 'poor, brave' parents ever dared to bring them out in public, we'd shy away from them, speaking in hushed voices and feeling justifiably afraid of these unknown and unpredictable little creatures. They existed in another reality, one

where anything and everything could, and usually did happen. It was their world, which we never wanted to visit, because in fairness, why would we? They were there: living, walking, breathing within twenty feet of us and yet these children were farther away from us than the stars; we believed we had nothing to learn from their world and they were definitely not welcome in ours.

This didn't come from a place of hatred or intolerance on our part, but from the simple fact that we accepted this way of thinking because it was the only message we received from the society we lived in. We no more questioned this mind-set than we questioned whether the sky was blue. Thankfully, there were adults somewhere who were beginning to stand up and say 'That's enough! These children are human beings too and they don't deserve to be hidden away!' but who these people were and why they were saying this kind of thing was something none of us had any idea about at the time.

Naturally there were always the 'odd' kids in every mainstream classroom: the kids who didn't mix, the kids who couldn't speak properly, the kids who struggled with reading and writing, the kids with a funny walk. Their lives were invariably an ongoing nightmare of ridicule and exclusion as they became victims of the merciless pack mentality of the playground. It never sat well with me, but as a small child I said and did nothing. Like everybody else, I was silenced by my fear of somehow becoming an outcast too if I spoke up.

On many occasions I witnessed the casual cruelty of both children and adults towards these kids. Fuelled mainly by frustration and a lack of understanding rather than by outright malice, people would humiliate them as a matter of routine. Doing nothing to help as a young child is one of the few regrets I carry with me to this day, which explains a lot about the way I live my life nowadays I suppose, but more on that later. Never was the phrase 'the past is a foreign country; they do things differently there' so thoroughly appropriate.

The odd kids, however, had no connection at all to the retarded ones as far as we could tell. They were like us, only not like us, whereas the others, those whose names could only be spoken in a whisper by our parents and therefore by us too, were simply beyond our understanding. The thought of having 'one of those' children when I grew up filled me with abject terror, and I was far from alone in this mind set. What greater tragedy could a mother experience than to produce something so obviously substandard? I appreciate this seems terribly cruel, but there was nothing cruel about me as a child; in reality I was deeply sensitive, considerate and kind. The simple truth is that when I was small it was made quite clear to me that if your children weren't physically perfect, intelligent, well-behaved and preferably beautiful, then they were unacceptable; and you, as a parent, were a failure. Desperate to conform, I planned for my perfect future, with my perfect children, and Life, as it tends to in these situations, laughed.

The terrible crime of not fitting in

By the age of ten, I was beginning to notice that I had a lot more in common with the odd kids than most of the other children in my school could manage. I wasn't loud or boisterous; I loved to read and study and my thirst for knowledge grew stronger with every fact I uncovered. I was known as a 'brain-box' which was an insulting label for a highly intelligent person. Back then, it was generally accepted that brain-boxes (now known as nerds or geeks), swots, teachers' pets and all the other assorted goody-two-shoes in school were to be despised almost as much as the odd kids, and believe me, we were. Through the years of bullying that followed it dawned on me, slowly but inevitably, that the psychology of the playground was only slightly less restrictive than a strait-jacket.

Standing out, in any way at all, was a sin, and the heinous crime of being either too bright or too dim, too attractive or too unattractive, too popular or too unpopular, too loud or too quiet, too rich or too poor, too happy or too sad just wouldn't be tolerated.

Anything that challenged the accepted idea of 'normal' would lead to jealousy, ridicule and often open hostility, yet there was nothing terrible or even unusual about my school or any of the children in it. We were simply products of our time, our genetics, our conditioning and our environment, in just the same way as today's children are products of theirs.

It's important to remember that although we do our best to live in a civilised and sociable society, on a biological level, we're pretty much still living in caves. Humans are essentially pack animals with deeply ingrained instincts, urging them to reject anyone they consider to be an inferior member of the group, to aid the survival of the species. People who are unfortunate enough to be identified as inferior naturally have the same powerful instinct to belong and they'll often go to unbelievable lengths to be accepted by their social circle. This is potent stuff that's really not easy to overcome.

'Tall Poppy Syndrome' and 'Crab Bucket Theory' are both rather quaint terms used to describe an ugly and destructive undercurrent that runs through many, although not all communities. The widespread desire to 'cut others down to size' like overly tall poppies is still largely tolerated by most societies. It's certainly nothing new, being described many hundreds of years ago by the great philosopher Aristotle, but the intent behind it isn't always malicious.

As Jim Lynn so aptly puts it 'Strange, don't you think, that the ones who love us the most are often the ones who would keep us from reaching the stars?' Sometimes the motive for reminding us not to have dreams and ambitions that are considered 'too big' or 'too unusual' comes from a genuine sense of concern for our well-being. It's simply the same old instincts at work, as our family and friends try to make us as acceptable as possible to 'The Clan', for fear that we'll end up alone and unloved because we stand out too much.

Incidentally, anyone unfamiliar with the niceties of social behaviour in crabs (although I can't imagine such people could possibly exist...) may be interested in the origins of the second term: If you place one crab in a bucket, it can easily reach the top and succeed in climbing out. If you place two or more crabs in the same bucket, something entirely different happens: As the first crab tries to climb out of the bucket, the others will grab hold of it and pull it back down, so they all share in the same fate. The crabs become so engrossed in their struggle that unless they're somehow released from the bucket, they'll all eventually die.

The similarities to human society are obvious, but fortunately for us, unlike the crabs, we have the power to overturn and escape our 'bucket' simply by changing our perspective. In my experience one of the quickest ways to do this is to watch the 'odd' kids and see how those without social awareness make sense of a world half-paralysed by etiquette. Naturally we can also learn a great deal from the 'odd' teenagers and the 'odd' adults too, and there are certainly plenty of them out there to watch. Of course in my case there are plenty of them *in here* to watch too, and you certainly learn quickly when you learn without leaving your own front door!

Today many people believe these attitudes are a thing of the past, especially with the younger generations who've grown up in a politically correct environment, and as much as I'd love this to be the case, sadly it isn't.

Babies and toddlers aren't designed to be thoughtful or patient or kind and they never were. The human race certainly wouldn't have survived this long if our offspring didn't make their needs known in the most urgent of ways: Screaming, punching, kicking and biting are all totally unacceptable behaviour traits or excellent survival skills depending on your perspective. Trust me, the toddler perspective on life is the closest thing to a truly psychopathic world-view that most of us will ever witness. Let me explain:

Toddler Rules of Possession

1. If I like it, it's mine.
2. If it's in my hand, it's mine.
3. If I can take it from you, it's mine.
4. If I had it a little while ago, it's mine.
5. If it's mine, it must NEVER appear to be yours in any way.
6. If I'm doing or building something, all the pieces are mine.
7. If it looks just like mine, it's definitely mine.
8. If I saw it first, it's mine.
9. If you're playing with something and you put it down, it automatically becomes mine.
10. If it's broken, it's yours.

This is in fact only a small excerpt from the Indisputable and Most Sacred Bible of Toddler Law as parents of two year olds are all too painfully aware, although I believe Rule 10 does have a sub-clause which states 'If you look like you're still getting some enjoyment from it, however small, it instantly reverts to being mine.' There are other rules of course, such as 'If I can't carry every toy in the room/shop at once, I would rather drop them than let you help me, because they're all mine.' The list goes on.

Schools and nurseries therefore can still be pitiless places at times, where the raw ingredients of human nature meet society's rules head on, engaging in a grim and sometimes bloody battle to the death; yet this tried and tested process goes on to produce (on the whole) wonderfully happy, well-balanced adults with plenty of finely-honed social skills, and a lot of compassion to offer. It's all too easy to judge these 'normal' kids and find them wanting, but if we do, surely we're no better than those who judge the 'odd' ones. Human nature might be flawed and toddlers may need a lot of guidance as a result, but let's face it, it's all we've got to work with, so we might as well get on with it, and with each other too.

Reinventing the nerd

When I was eleven we moved to a different part of the country which gave me the unexpected chance to reinvent myself. There was no hiding my intelligence as far as I could tell, and I was tired of being bullied for it, so I became, for want of a better expression, a sort of Warrior Geek. I'd come to the London suburbs from Suffolk which drew attention to my accent and meant I was constantly accused of being stuck up. This was a new one on me since everyone at my old school either spoke the same way I did or had such a broad local accent that even a trained ear would struggle to understand it at times. I spoke too slowly for the London kids and could pronounce 'th' instead of saying 'f' which clearly made me the worst kind of snob they'd ever met in their lives.

Try as I might (and believe me, I tried) I couldn't seem to get the accent right, and as my teenage hormones kicked in I thought 'Sod it, these people don't know me, I could be terrifying for all they know' which couldn't really have been further from the truth at the time. I began to stand up for myself and for my right to be clever and unashamed of who I was, and this was a far easier transition for me than for most people, I suspect, since I hadn't had to make the social leap publicly from being the shy, introverted little girl I'd always been at primary school into something entirely different.

As I began to tap into my more assertive side, I clung to the hope that people might believe I'd always behaved like this, and I'm pleased to say that my strategy worked. Most of the bullies backed off and showed me a form of grudging respect, many of them going on to have quite reasonable and even friendly relationships with me.

As a by-product of this, I ended up defending the other nerds, geeks and 'odd' kids as well, and by the time I left school at fifteen I had a serious, yet mostly unintentional, reputation for being a bit of a nightmare if I felt anyone was being singled out and bullied for being different. I found out many years later that I also had a reputation for being someone you could talk to if you had a problem and was hailed as a bit of a hero by some: a person without whom (so I'm told) they felt they might not have survived school at all. Mostly though, I had a reputation for being weird, scary, aggressive and best avoided.

Books however, as we're all aware, should never be judged by their covers. Behind my carefully painted eyes, outrageous hair and highly questionable fashion sense, I was more concerned than ever with what other people thought of me. What if they saw through me? Had I really changed enough to carry it off? What if I let them in and they didn't actually like me? Like most teenagers, I hid these insecurities behind as many masks as I could in the hope that if anyone managed to see through one, there'd be another waiting underneath to send them off in the wrong direction. Every morning the battle armour was meticulously applied: strange clothes, scary make up, half a can of hair spray and most importantly a seriously hostile attitude.

Most people never got past the first layer, and gave me a generally wide berth because I looked like bad news. Those who decided that bullying me was still a good idea would get as far as the attitude and quickly change their minds. The number of people who got past that could be counted on one hand, and that was how I preferred it. If I could've continued to isolate myself and hide behind my scary masks forever I probably would've done, but as usual Life (no doubt largely for its own amusement) had other ideas.

Growing up geeky

The next nine years mostly passed in a lonely, confusing muddle of unsuitable, dissatisfying jobs and terrible relationships as I tried (and spectacularly failed) to fit in and 'be like everybody else', something my family seemed to value more highly than I can explain. Although I have no doubt that blending in made them feel both happy and safe, and their desire for me to do the same was largely well-intentioned, for me it was just impossible and for a while I seemed to lurch from one disastrous friendship group, boyfriend and form of employment to the next. By the age of twenty four I'd become deeply disillusioned with life and had pretty much given up hope of ever finding a place to belong. I'd mostly reverted to my former persona and become withdrawn and isolated again. I much preferred to escape into the endlessly fascinating worlds of fantasy fiction than spend time in the deafeningly noisy bars and nightclubs other people of my age seemed to enjoy so much. There was a great deal of tutting and shaking of heads at my terribly nerdy ways, which of course were seen as weird and anti-social, and the fact that I read and re-read The Lord of the Rings so many times the book fell apart (no, seriously, it physically fell apart) was very worrying to those who knew me: evidence if ever it were needed that I was the most terrible misfit who would never find love or happiness and would simply wither away and die, to be discovered years later as a bleached skeleton, still clutching whatever remained of the book between my bony fingers.

I'm making light of it here of course, but for many years this universal disapproval caused me an enormous amount of pain and anguish. You have to remember, this was long before the invention of the internet, and terms like 'Geek Chic' didn't even exist, so as far as I was aware, I really was 'The Only Geek in the Village' - in fact the only one in the world - which was what I was being told on a regular basis. Everyone else did indeed seem to do things in the same way, moving through their lives feeling perfectly content to do what their friends were doing, but no matter what I did, I just wasn't able to tolerate living that way. At the time there was very little acceptance of being different and virtually no respect towards people's social preferences, something I'm incredibly grateful for in today's society as you can imagine.

At this age I knew nothing about different personality types and simply believed what I was told: being introverted meant you were anti-social and being socially awkward meant you were rude. In reality I'm not anti-social at all, although it would be many years before I really understood this, and it bothered me a great deal to be thought of this way, so I'd do my best to go out with friends as much as I could, spending most evenings feeling awkward, bored, frustrated and wishing I was at home reading instead.

Still, it was on one of these miserable occasions that I met a young man in a bar who, for want of a better description, rather intrigued me. He was tall and handsome (both plus points, obviously) but more noticeable by far was the slightly aloof, other-worldly air he had about him. He didn't seem to have any interest in behaving the same way as the other young men in his group; he wasn't looking for attention or trying to prove himself to anyone, he was simply there, being himself and quietly enjoying the evening. It's a difficult, if not impossible thing to describe, but although he wasn't 'my type' at all (which with the benefit of hindsight was probably a very good thing considering my appalling taste in boyfriends at the time) I was strangely drawn to him and his ability to be so totally self-contained in such a public place.

We struck up a conversation where I quickly learned that his name was Pat and that among many other strange synchronistic life circumstances, we'd been born only a few hours apart from each other. Deciding that fate must have taken a hand in this meeting, I accepted his offer of a date and we began the relationship that was to change my life more than any other, in ways I couldn't even begin to fathom at that point and occasionally still can't to this day.

One lasting memory I have of those early days together is of the first time I visited his flat: to say it was minimalistic would be an understatement. From the magnolia walls to the beige sofa and carpet, everything was quite remarkably muted and there was nothing at all in any of the rooms that didn't have a specific function. Once the front door was closed, Pat lived in a quiet oasis of largely empty space, which I found incredibly soothing after the turmoil of my own life, and I loved it. Pat had no interest in either competing with other people or being drawn into their problems. The everyday dramas and gossip of his friends' lives just didn't touch him, because unlike every other person I'd met up to that point, he simply chose to remain untouched by them. He was largely, I suppose, a closed book, but as always not one which could be judged in any way by its seemingly serious, slightly bland cover.

Almost immediately I realised that Pat had a lot of specific personality quirks which I found very endearing, among them his great sense of humour, which was shockingly inappropriate even by my standards. He was also physically incapable of eating certain foods - chiefly celery (his arch nemesis) - the very thought of which would make him gag. I found him fascinating.

He worked in the City of London and always caught a train several hours earlier than he needed to, so he could avoid the rush hour crowds. Watching him leave for work every morning well before 6am, I'd often think 'Wow! He must *really* hate crowds...' Which of course he did, so this was his solution. If it seemed odd to other people, well that was no concern of his, in fact many of the things *they* did seemed odd to *him* but he didn't mind, he was simply doing his thing in the way that worked best for him, and expected everyone else to get on with their lives and do the same.

After so many years of desperately trying to fit in for fear of getting things wrong and going out of my way to do the 'normal' thing, you can imagine how refreshing I found his approach to life.

Pat had his challenges too of course, as everyone does. Adapting to change was difficult for him, and he'd become easily frustrated if he felt out of control, but these were part and parcel of who he was and I was more than happy to work together to make a go of a relationship I felt had so much promise.

We moved into his flat together and some time later found we were expecting a baby. Although I was hugely excited by this turn of events, at this point the sum total of my experience with children was zero, so naturally I panicked and went all out to study everything I could about pregnancy, birth and motherhood. It's difficult to imagine just how much I read on the subject, because the amount of information I can collect and process when I need to is nothing short of colossal, and at the time, I certainly felt the need to.

If there was *anything* I could lay my hands on that was even vaguely related to child-rearing, I'd devour it. By the time this child was born, I reasoned, with my ever-expanding pile of books, magazines and carefully collected tips from other parents, I'd be the world's foremost expert in both the practical day-to-day meeting of its physical needs, and the loving, nurturing care of its delicate emotional health. Obviously I was too busy soaking up all this fascinating new information to hear Life laughing heartily away to itself, but laugh it did, and to be honest it hasn't stopped laughing since.

Let the performance begin!

Following nine and a half glamorous months of morning sickness, swollen ankles, carpal tunnel syndrome and pre-eclampsia, we finally made our way to the maternity unit.

Sixteen and a half gruelling hours later, our first born son was safely delivered and the systematic destruction of all my carefully laid parenting plans began. Christopher was born on his back, his eyes wide open and his arms and legs perfectly folded across his body, giving him the appearance of a slightly startled ball. Cautiously and deliberately he started to unfold, his face registering complete amazement as his limbs found nothing around him but empty air. Raising his entire upper body clear of the bed, he turned his head from side to side and waved his arms, with a look of growing panic in his eyes. I knew just how he felt. Although I'd longed for a healthy son and was genuinely delighted to have produced such a beautiful specimen, I'd kind of taken it for granted that he'd be at least something like the other new-borns I'd met in the past: small, fragile and a bit floppy round the head end, but here he was: huge, strong and already very well-muscled.

'Are they meant to do that?' I asked the midwife rather feebly. 'Well, they can...' she said, looking every bit as uncertain as I felt. Christopher meanwhile had gone as stiff as a board and closed his hands into tight little fists, which were not to be opened again for more than a few seconds at a time for several months to come. His eyes continued to rove wildly round the room and the terror on his face was becoming more and more obvious. I remembered hearing that if you stuck your tongue out at any new-born baby they would copy you, so in an attempt to distract him, I tried to catch his eye and do just that.

It was in that moment that my life changed forever and I stepped onto a new and unfamiliar path which I hadn't even realised existed. I moved my head from side to side trying to look into his eyes, and each time I did, Christopher's head would do the same, mirroring my movements exactly until we appeared to be doing some strange, hypnotic dance, a bit like snake charming. Even through the pain and confusion of the labour, a dull sense of dread began to gnaw at my insides as I realised he wasn't trying to *make* eye contact with me, but to *avoid* it. What was happening here?

I'd brought a little ball with me with a chime inside and decided to give that a go instead, but every time the toy moved towards him, he'd turn his face sharply away. What I didn't realise of course was that his senses were completely overloaded with the sudden changes he was experiencing and he was desperately trying to process what on earth had just happened to him. At the time, all I could hear was a voice in my head saying 'There's something wrong, there's something wrong, there's something wrong...'

We spent the next couple of days in hospital where things quickly got a whole lot worse for us both. The midwives were adamant Christopher should breastfeed but he had no interest, so they decided to 'make' him feed by pushing his head backwards and forwards against my chest. As soon as they touched him he'd go totally rigid and scream blue murder, his digestive system completely shutting down, and after several very traumatic hours, I decided to bottle feed instead. The midwives were far from impressed that I'd 'given in to my naughty son' as they put it, and this was the first but by no means the last time he'd be described as 'the most stubborn child I've ever met.'

For Christopher, the main problem on the ward was the noise. I was told over and over again that babies are never disturbed by the sound of other babies crying, and it was good for him to get used to noises like the tea trolley and the sounds of visitors arriving and leaving. I'm sure this is true for the vast majority of new-borns, but no-one seemed to have told *him* any of this and the sound of something as harmless as a curtain being drawn back would send him into hours of rigid, screaming hysterics.

Every time I managed to settle him, a baby would cry somewhere; his head and shoulders would appear above the top of the cot and the most awful ear-piercing wails would start up again, setting off the other babies, which in turn would upset him even more. With the added problem of some very unpleasant smells and the terribly harsh overhead strip lighting, the place was constantly attacking our senses and we both felt like we'd landed in some kind of Autistic Baby Hell. After 48 hours with no sleep at all, both Christopher and I were feeling exhausted, overwhelmed and more than a little terrified.

Nature versus nurture

Lots of people believe autism isn't present at birth and only develops around the age of eighteen months to two years. This is definitely not the case, and on that you can trust me 100%. Like anything 'new' that human beings experience, everyone will have an opinion on it until autism is more fully understood, and its origins and treatments will be debated, tried and tested. Many will prove correct and many will be discredited along the way, and that's all as it should be, but since this is my book, it naturally contains my opinions and ideas at the time of writing. Both are based on many years of extensive research and much first-hand experience, and I offer them to you not as medically proven facts, at least not as I write this today, but simply as my own personal truth. Science might not be able to prove exactly *how* these traits are present from birth, but being involved with this condition on a day to day basis, I know beyond any question or doubt that they *are*.

I can tell you this much with absolute certainty: true autism is a highly complex, all-pervasive genetic condition - one that affects every part of the individual concerned - and is as obvious as skin or eye colour if you know what you're looking for. The effects of autism might be *noticed* more at around the eighteen month stage, so the confusion is perfectly understandable, but it doesn't mean they weren't already there. Autism doesn't magically appear in a child; it's already within every part of their genetics and has been since the day they were conceived.

Which parts of these genes activate and how the individual's brain makes sense of the signals it's receiving as a result are affected by all kinds of things including their IQ levels, life experiences and environment, but the genes are still there right from the beginning.

Although there's no doubt that many factors can trigger underlying autistic traits, if they're not already present, there's simply nothing to trigger. Autistic people are born autistic, but lots of well-meaning people feel that if they accept this fact, they'll simply have to accept the suffering autism can bring as well and will therefore be unable to help relieve it. To my way of thinking, nothing could be further from the truth. Acceptance of people's natural differences is the easiest way for any of us to find peace, but the path to accepting autistic people as being simply another part of the diverse spectrum of humanity is going to be a long one. It would be lovely if everyone could agree, but as with most things in life, that agreement will take time.

It's worth bearing in mind that genetic conditions as complicated as autism aren't always obvious simply by looking at a person's immediate family. Sometimes a gene can be masked, staying hidden for a generation or so before finding the right conditions to surface and express itself. Interestingly, one of the best analogies for this situation I've ever heard came from Christopher himself when he was seven. He described a masked gene as being like a computer: you can switch it off and it seems like everything's gone, but press the right button and you'll find all the information is still there and that it quickly reactivates.

Autism is a way of being rather than a disease, and if families can find the courage to look at themselves and their relatives honestly and openly, putting aside any feelings of anger, guilt or shame, they often see the autism there, alive and well, happily running back through the generations.

It may have gone largely unnoticed in the past and will almost certainly have gone undiagnosed, but look closely enough and there it will be nonetheless. The question that springs to my mind is 'So what if it is?'

There's so much we still have to discover about the physical, emotional, psychological and spiritual elements that combine to make every human being who they are. Surely only the most arrogant and short sighted of people would claim to understand everything about human nature or physiology. We're all human, yet each of us is a unique combination of all our experiences, our interpretation of each one of them, and of the DNA we inherit. In reality, how much do any of us really know about ourselves? We use only a percentage of our brains; what else are we able to do but have yet to discover? What might we achieve if we simply change our perspective? Autistic people's behaviour can certainly seem very different from what's considered normal but when you think about it, even 'normal' is still largely unknown to us.

Our true potential is greater than any of us can imagine, and we can either allow that fact to scare us or excite us. We can look at our limited self-awareness as something frightening and run away from it, or see it as an opportunity for adventure and explore it. The bottom line is that we're all here, we're all different, we're all just learning as we go along, and we all have the ability to not only push ourselves, encourage ourselves and surprise ourselves, but also to do the same thing for others. An autistic person's potential and their idea of normal is naturally going to be as unique and individual as they are, so it's vitally important to understand that autism isn't necessarily something terrible, restrictive or frightening. Put simply: it is what it is; we're just not sure exactly *what* that is yet.

Beliefs at the time

I remember several specialists telling me with absolute conviction that autism couldn't be a genetic condition because it sometimes affects one child in a family where no-one else is autistic, and therefore it must be learned behaviour. It never did much for my popularity with the health professionals when I asked 'If there's no-one else around them exhibiting any traits of autism, who on earth is the child learning their behaviour *from?*' It may not have made me very popular, but at least it made more than a few people stop and think.

Just for the record, their answer was always the same: 'We don't know yet, that's still being researched.' As comical as this might sound, I do understand that they could only give out the information they'd been given and weren't supposed to speculate on it or express their own opinions. In truth I suspect there were (and still are) a huge number of specialists who were just as frustrated as I was by the lack of official answers, but there were (and again still are) always going to be one or two know-alls who expect you to blindly accept anything they tell you just because their job title differs from yours.

In fact, in my experience, there are usually two kinds of health professional you'll meet when you deal with autism: The first are the ones who've read it all in a book and are convinced they know everything about the condition. Often they won't have children of their own, let alone children on the autism spectrum, and these ones are quite simply a nightmare to deal with. They believe that when you become a parent your brain is instantly removed, so you lose all ability to reason, and as a result they're incredibly patronising. Nine times out of ten they'll have a clipboard permanently clutched to their chest and a sickeningly soft voice, so they're very easy to spot, if not all that easy to stomach.

The second kind are the ones who've also read it all in a book and say to you 'Look, I don't have autistic children myself so I can't possibly know what you're going through, but I have read lots of books and I know a lot about which strategies have helped other people and the support that's available, so maybe we can work together to deal with all this.' They'll treat you with respect, ask your opinion on things, and most importantly of all, they'll *listen* to you. Again they're very easy to spot: they're the ones who don't take themselves too seriously and are actually prepared to smile and laugh with you about your situation.

It's these people who'll hold you up when you're sinking and bring you back from the brink of madness when it all gets too much, and believe me it will, so whatever you do, make sure you stick with these ones - they're worth their weight in gold.

I'm very much aware that those of you reading this book in years to come will be thinking 'What on earth is she going on about? Of course autism is genetic...' and yet this is the depressing reality autism parents of my generation face.

The best place to meet is on common ground

So what's it like being an autism parent? Well, firstly being a parent to *any* child is something you just can't hope to understand unless you live it yourself, which is obviously really annoying if you're not a parent yet and are trying to get an idea of how it all works. I'll do my best throughout this book to describe it, but inevitably my descriptions will fall woefully short of the all-consuming experience of parenthood. It's worth pointing out of course that the experiences I'm describing are my own, so even if you were living the same life, in the same family as I am, your experiences would still be different because you and I are different people. That doesn't really make my job any easier, does it?

In good news, there is one thing that's pretty standard with all forms of parenting: whoever we are and whatever our circumstances, on a deep, instinctive level, every fibre of our being is intensely aware of the fact we'll never have a more important job than being parents, even if society's current trends happen to be telling us something different.

Our in-built biological desire to create a tiny, somewhat improved version of ourselves to carry on our genetic line is so deeply ingrained in us that should we be fortunate enough to succeed in our quest and actually produce one (or indeed, several) we will, as long as we're neurologically healthy, do everything within our power to maintain its well-being and happiness.

Clearly there are exceptions to this rule as we all know, but the vast majority of people, regardless of gender, belief or geographical location, strive with an almost super-human effort to provide their offspring with the best physical, emotional and psychological environment they can muster.

All new parents therefore suffer from perfectly natural feelings of 'performance anxiety' when dealing with the avalanche of emotions that suddenly overwhelm them after having a child. They wonder, as they compare their offspring with the mythical (and imaginary – trust me on this one) 'perfect child' if they're really doing enough; if they're giving their child the best start in life or whether, in their darker moments of self-doubt, they're actually damaging them in some way by not being 'perfect' themselves.

Understandably then, this is a highly vulnerable time for *all* parents, not just those whose children have additional needs, when the opinions and approval of their friends, family and society in general suddenly become incredibly important. After all, they themselves are novices – the learner drivers of the parenting world – and as you'd expect, they turn to people who have more experience of all this chaos for the reassurance they so desperately need.

Unlike most other species, our offspring are born utterly defenseless and completely dependent on us for their survival, so becoming a parent is a scary business and without the hugely heightened sense of danger that suddenly floods us when our children arrive, many would never have survived beyond infancy.

According to an old proverb 'it takes a village to raise a child' suggesting that to successfully bring up a well-balanced youngster is invariably a communal effort, and never is this made more clear than when you suddenly find yourself raising a child who simply refuses to play by the rules of your village (or society), in fact one who doesn't even appear to realise there are any rules it's supposed to play by in the first place.

Autistic children don't think like other children, nor do they react like them, or even see, hear, taste and feel things the way others do, and for your 'village' this can be both frustrating and confusing. Well-meaning advice becomes useless and the tried and trusted methods of child-rearing that have produced so many happy, healthy young people across the generations seem, quite inexplicably, to have the opposite effect on these strange, unsettled little beings.

Inevitably your parenting skills will be called into question and you'll struggle to answer people when they ask you why your child behaves in such unusual ways, but don't panic, knowledge really is power here, and that's why I'm writing these books. These are the books I wish someone had given me to read when I was a new autism parent. These are the books that say 'It's okay', 'I know how you feel' and 'I get it' but most importantly these are the books that show you how to handle whatever situations this extraordinary lifestyle decides to throw at you, with as much grace, dignity, inventiveness and humour as you can muster; something every person in every village in every corner of the world could definitely benefit from.

Parenting as an extreme sport

In some ways then, I'd be very happy if there were times when people reading this book thought 'Are you sure that's an autistic thing?' or 'that sounds like normal family life to me...' or even 'surely all children do those kinds of things...' My intention here isn't to make families living with autism seem so abnormal that no-one else can relate to their experiences; my intention is, in fact, the exact opposite.

What I hope to achieve by writing these books is to describe the kind of scenarios *all* families can recognise on some level or another, whether they're already battle-hardened autism warriors reading from the front line trenches, or they're new to the whole thing and are still finding their way around the wonderful, terrifying world of autism, step by cautious step.

Even though I find myself inside a daily performance that makes a routine by Cirque Du Soleil look uninventive, if we look for them hard enough, there'll still be plenty of common threads to connect our experiences - you just might not need to put on your red coat and top hat and crack your whip quite as often as I do!

author's note No actual red coats, top hats or whips were used in the rearing of my children.*

So, first and foremost, children are children, parents are parents and people are people, and whether or not autism has been thrown into the mix, there's no question in my mind that in the end, as families, we're all far more alike than different. What we experience as parents of autistic children takes nothing away from the very real stresses and strains *all* parents experience, and if any parent tells you that they never feel tired, overwhelmed or unhappy, don't you believe them.

Parenting any child is a hard, draining and sometimes frightening experience, and one no amount of research or planning can ever truly prepare you for. Autism parenting is the same, only a much more extreme version. I suppose living in a family touched by autism is a bit like living life on full volume with no mute button. Navigating every day with only a sketchy fragment of map and regularly being pushed far beyond your limits quickly becomes your 'normal'. You need quick reactions, super-human endurance and above all else, you need to hold your nerve.

Autism parents live in a permanent state of fight or flight - on full time red alert - where life becomes a restless, sleepless jumble of continual emergencies to be sorted out, or better still avoided. Priorities change beyond all recognition, with the tiniest incidents taking on the kind of importance only other parents living with autism can really appreciate.

For example: 'What do you mean they've changed the packaging on his favourite food?' To understand the horror of this particular situation, you'll really need to have experienced autism first hand. You see, when someone is profoundly affected by autism, not only does their food have to be a particular brand, but the packaging has to look a particular way, otherwise the food will taste different and you're guaranteed to run into some serious problems. I know it sounds strange, but I'll explain it later on in the book, I promise.

So how can I describe the reality of life with autism? The honest answer is that there's nothing I could write that would fully explain what it's like to parent an autistic child. The sheer weight of responsibility which comes with being a parent to *any* child is nothing short of mind-boggling, so that in itself would be impossible to put into words, but if you add to it the uncertainty of developmental delays, behavioural issues, learning complications, social anxieties and a world that's largely unaware of the challenges your child is facing, then imagine these concerns stretching out ahead of you across the years, seemingly without end, you might get some idea of the magnitude of what it means to find yourself parenting a child on the spectrum.

Oh, and there's also the fact that you're now expected to not only successfully work around these issues, but to solve them too, without having the slightest idea how, and with precious little information available to help you do it. That being said, I'm hoping these books will give you at least a flavour of what it's like, because having *some* idea of what autism parents cope with every day has got to be better than having no idea at all.

If I had to sum autism parenting up in one word, it would definitely be 'relentless'. Autism itself has no interest in whether you're tired or ill or unhappy; there's nothing malicious about it, it's just totally oblivious to who you are. It has no appreciation of time and simply requires you to meet its needs, day and night, 24 hours a day, 7 days a week, 365 days a year, and believe me, its needs can be brutal. It's very important to remember that I'm talking about *autism* here and *not about your child*, but it can be hard to make that distinction while they're small, as you can expect to be punched, kicked, head-butted, scratched, screamed at and spat on many times every day. Your property and possessions will be regularly destroyed; you'll experience frequent disapproval from friends, family and strangers alike and existing without sleep (or even rest), although seemingly impossible, will quickly become your only option.

Lying in bed at night bruised, aching and emotionally exhausted, longing with every fibre of your being to be able to simply relax and go to sleep, yet instead lying wide awake as your brain struggles to process the chaos you've experienced during the day, is something you'll soon come to recognise. The realisation that tomorrow will only bring more of the same means that rather than unwinding, you'll invariably become even more anxious as you wait for the next assault on your senses.

Within twenty minutes of going to bed your brain is likely to register one or more of the following: banging, crying, screaming, running footsteps, vomiting or the unceremonious removal of a nappy. If you're not up and ready for action within three seconds of the first wave of noise, the next thing you'll inevitably hear will be the splintering of glass, plastic, china, wood or (God forbid) bone, as Unsupervised Autistic Mayhem breaks loose!

This is a very real part of bringing up children with autism. It can seem never-ending and unchanging, and hope can be an elusive thing to keep hold of after a few days, let alone weeks, months and years of it.

'Parenting as an extreme sport' is the best way I can describe it: tough, dirty, exhausting and dangerous but ultimately fulfilling in ways most people would never consider possible. Think BASE jumping with a healthy dose of sleep deprivation. It's safe to say I'll never need to sky dive for thrills. Believe me, if I wanted an adrenaline rush when the boys were young, all I had to do was let two food groups touch on their plates. An hour and a half of screaming, punching and stomach-churning self-harm was a pretty standard reaction to such an unforgiveable mistake, and although at the time I had absolutely no idea why they were reacting that way, I learned really, *really* quickly not to allow it to happen.

To this day people still comment on how particular I am when I make food for my guests: 'Would you like a specific brand of bread? Brown or white? Would you like your sandwiches cut into triangles or squares? Can you have butter and peanut butter touching in the same sandwich? Butter or margarine? Smooth peanut butter or crunchy? Any particular brand? Crusts on or off? Cut with a knife or kitchen scissors? Patterned plate or plain? Drink? Cup or mug? China or plastic? Would you like a straw? Red or blue? We have multi-coloured if you prefer...' Well, when I say 'comment on' that generally means 'laugh at' as you can imagine, but after more than 25 years of living this way, these are very hard habits to break, and anyway, when it comes to making sandwiches for my children, these rules are still just as important as they ever were.

Finding joy in the little things

From my description so far, I'd understand if right now you were beginning to wonder exactly what was so fulfilling about this way of life. The important thing to remember here is that *you're not the only one living an extreme lifestyle*. Your child has been living in a world that's too loud, too bright, too confusing and too overwhelming since the second they were born, and this isn't something that's going to change for them, no matter how much you might wish it would.

When you see your child suffering, even if you don't fully understand why, your parental instincts will kick in and scream 'Do something! Make it better!' and boy will you try, because achieving this will suddenly be the most important thing in the world. Here's the challenge though: People say that no child comes with a set of instructions or an operating manual, and they're right of course, but when it comes to autistic children, we're talking about a whole new level of confusion, with considerably fewer written directions available to guide you through the maze.

It's not something I can easily put into words, but in essence I suppose it's a case of the higher the stakes, the bigger the rewards. When the tiny steps forward that the majority of parents rightly take for granted become enormous obstacles to your child's happiness that need to be battled with on a daily (and nightly) basis, overcoming them is cause for huge celebration. No matter how insignificant they seem to other people, your child's achievements take on a whole new level of importance, and watching them expand their skill set one excruciatingly difficult step at a time can, if you allow it to, open your eyes to a whole new way of viewing the world.

This incredible sense of accomplishment and the unique perspective on life it gives me are just two of the reasons why I chose to have not one but four of these beautiful, unique, exhausting and inspirational children. Seriously, isn't this partly why anyone chooses to have more than one child, whether they're autistic or not? I think so, and let's face it: no parent does it for the beauty benefits.

So why *do* we do it? More importantly, *how* do we do it? The answer, like so many things involving autism, is both startlingly simple and immensely complex. The answer is love.

Love is not love...

The flowers and cuddly toys used to represent romantic love are a wonderful way for people to express themselves, but since they're such a tiny part of something so much bigger, love itself is often misunderstood and seen as something a bit fluffy and pathetic. In reality of course, nothing could be further from the truth, and if you ever want to see pure love in action, watch an autism parent successfully handle their child during a crisis or meltdown.

Take a step back and observe any parent whose child is in danger and you'll catch a glimpse of the all-consuming power of real love. For autism parents, danger comes in many forms: some subtle, some all too obvious, but whether our children are in danger of breaking their necks thanks to their legendary lack of risk-assessment skills, or in danger of having their hearts broken because they're unable to grasp the finer points of making friends, the effect love has on us is always the same.

Love is the force that drives us on when our bodies are broken and our brains are screaming for an end to the relentless chaos we're experiencing, allowing us to exist without sleep on a heady mixture of adrenaline and sheer willpower. This isn't the love of fine weather and sunny days, but the deep, raw Shakespearean love which 'looks on tempests and is never shaken.' It makes no sense, knows no end and is utterly fierce in the face of the overwhelming terror we fight on a daily basis. It's the force before which all hate and anger, all confusion and doubt, all exhaustion and fear simply fall away. Coursing through us with the sudden ferocity of a lightning bolt just when we're sure we've reached our limits, love urges us to delve deeper than we ever thought possible, to find answers we never knew we had, to questions we never dreamed we'd have to ask.

It's love that prompts us to change our perspective on parenting: to alter our expectations beyond anything we could have imagined and to find genuine delight in the smallest of victories - from the successful tying of a shoe lace to the first invitation to a classmate's birthday party.

Love holds us together while we clean up the seemingly endless stream of wreckage, clutter, vomit and poo that goes hand in hand with raising autistic children.

In short, it's love that allows us to see past the chaos and connect with our child. Autism brings with it a whole different set of needs, and as a result we develop a very different agenda to the majority of parents, yet in the same way all healthy parents do, we love our children just as fiercely, just as completely as we possibly can. We don't do it because we're heroes or martyrs or because we're super-human in some way (although I've often been called all three). We do it, quite simply, because our children, like all children, are 100% worth it.

A Day at the Circus

October 1998

- Child 1 (age 6) decides to dress himself for school. Full instructions have been given the previous evening, so am feeling confident of his success.
- 7:30am: Hear dreadful choking sounds coming from bedroom. Discover Child 1 strangling himself with school tie. On further investigation, realise my direction to 'slide your tie up until you reach your top button' have proved useless as his top button is in fact missing.
- Hastily explain that reaching one's neck is also an excellent time to stop tightening. #AlwaysCheckTheButtons
- 8am: Child 2 (age 3) has recently started returning from nursery each evening with dirt under his fingernails. Ask nursery staff why, and am told he plays in the same muddy spot outside every day, saving his place each night with a specific stone.
- 6pm: Collect Child 2 from nursery. Frazzled nursery teacher informs me Child 2 has in fact been digging *escape tunnel* under fence for some time, using stone as entrance marker once loose soil has been replaced.
- Having finally completed tunnel, Child 2 has today led daring band of small children out onto pavement, getting three toddlers through fence before staff noticed anything was amiss.
- Teacher assures me playground is now scheduled to be tarmacked.
- Explain Child 2's latest obsession is Chicken Run (film about group of militant hens constantly plotting escape from farmyard prison).
- Conclusion: Child 2 may not have any speech yet, but has plenty of imagination, leadership and strategic planning skills. #ProudMummyMoment

When they change the packaging
on your child's favourite foods...

Chapter Two

The ABC's to Elemenopee's of Autism

'Nothing in life is to be feared, it is only to be understood.
Now is the time to understand more, so that we may fear less.'

Marie Curie

Now would seem like a good time to explain what autism actually is. I'll be discussing lots of these issues in more detail elsewhere in the book, so this is just a brief, easy to read outline of some of the basics. Obviously lots of you reading this book will already know a lot of this information from first-hand experience, but if you're anything like me you'll still find it reassuring to see things explained clearly and correctly for a change. Tired of reading the apparently endless media articles depicting autistic people as either cold-hearted serial killers or life's tragic victims who need to be patronised and pitied? Me too.

The first thing I need to point out here is that no-one (and that really does mean *no-one)* knows exactly what autism is, whether they say they do or not. During my lifetime I've seen some really big strides being made in the fields of science and education which have gone a long way towards explaining both the causes and the successful management of the condition, but believe me, there's no description that will ever truly explain everything about what autism is, because trying to explain it would be like trying to explain what it means to be human.

From the time when humanity first asked itself 'What am I and why am I here?' the human body, mind and spirit have been three of the most thoroughly researched subjects on the planet, yet we still know only a fraction of what they're capable of achieving. That's actually really cool when you think about it, because it means we still have *so* much more to discover about just how incredible we are. Autism is a highly complex condition that affects every part of an individual, but what makes it so unique is that the way it develops is also affected by the feedback it receives from the outside world. It's safe to say therefore that even if science one day cracks the pattern of genetic factors involved, or if the world's great philosophers suddenly line up and agree on the lessons that autism has to teach us, there will still be more unanswered questions about what the condition is than I'll ever live to see answered.

This chapter, therefore, sets out to describe what we *do* know (the ABC's) and what we'll probably never fully know (the Elemenopee's). In case anyone doesn't understand this reference, 'Elemenopee' is that mysterious letter between K and Q that so many primary school children are confident they've grasped, only to find out with a shock some time later that this sound is in fact made up of five entirely separate letters: L, M, N, O and P. Understanding something and *thinking* you understand it are two very different things, and although I certainly know a lot about autism, I most definitely don't know everything. Nowhere near.

A brief history of autism

I need to be very clear about something here: what we now refer to as 'autism' is something that's been around as long as humanity has existed. There have always been people who've fitted the profile so perfectly that if they were born today they would definitely be diagnosed before they reached school age. Seriously. Always.

Before 1908 though, when Swiss psychiatrist Eugen Bleuler first created the term, there was no specific word that could be used to define autistic people and as a result they were persecuted, celebrated or integrated into their society alongside everyone else - pretty much like they are today!

Bleuler first used the term to describe a schizophrenic patient who seemed to have withdrawn into his own world. He took it from the Greek word 'autós' meaning 'self', which he felt was a pretty good description of a person who was both obsessed with their own interests and somehow locked inside their own mind.

The true pioneers in autism research (and the ones most people have heard of) were Austrian-American psychiatrist Leo Kanner who worked with profoundly affected children, and Austrian paediatrician Hans Asperger who worked with children who could speak fluently and function more independently. Although both men worked on the same subject at the same time during the early 1940's, surprisingly they never actually met.

In 1943, with the full support and agreement of Kanner, Austrian-American child psychologist Bruno Bettelheim put forward the spectacularly unhelpful idea that childhood autism was caused by a lack of warmth shown by the children's mothers, giving rise to the long-since discredited theory of the 'refrigerator mothers'. I shudder to think of the anguish these poor women and their children must have suffered. They were often separated from each other, supposedly for the child's own good, and as you can imagine, this caused untold amounts of heartbreak and devastation.

Fortunately for future generations, American research psychologist and *autism parent* (of course) Bernard Rimland strongly disagreed with Bettelheim on this point and in 1964 he published his ground-breaking book 'Infantile Autism: The Syndrome and its Implications for a Neural Theory of Behavior'.

By now Leo Kanner had realised that the 'refrigerator mothers' theory was a mistake, and to his everlasting credit he wrote the foreword for Rimland's book. By doing this he gave the book a great deal of credibility which in turn was extremely helpful in changing people's ideas about the origins of the condition. His ability to put the welfare of autistic children above his own ego and publicly state 'Hey, I got it wrong, now I believe that *this* might be a more accurate explanation...' definitely qualifies Leo Kanner as one of my personal heroes.

Autism goes worldwide

Autism began to be more widely recognised throughout the 1970's and in the 1980's Asperger's work was finally translated into English and published, which was when research into the condition really took off.

The wonderful Dr Lorna Wing was one of the scientists who made enormous strides towards unravelling the mysteries of autism at the time. Not only was she the first person to describe it as a spectrum condition, but she also popularised the term 'Asperger's syndrome' recognising that there were specific differences in behaviour between the separate groups of children assessed by Leo Kanner and Hans Asperger.

Norwegian-American clinical psychologist Ole Ivar Lovaas also made a huge contribution towards the treatment of young autistic children, encouraging early intervention as a key strategy in helping to improve the quality of their lives. Lovaas's work, along with that of numerous other anonymous pioneers in the field, continues to shape many of the successful methods used to manage the condition today.

Autism or Asperger's?

One of the questions I'm asked more frequently than almost any other on this subject is 'What's the difference between autism and Asperger's?' This is a tricky one to answer because when it comes to diagnosis, the differences between the two conditions will vary depending on when you've been assessed, whereabouts you live and which specialist you see.

As Tony Attwood so accurately puts it: 'It is important to recognise that the diagnostic criteria are still a work in progress.' Somehow I suspect that statement will always be true and he's certainly not wrong when he says it's important!

In very general terms though, the differences are that people diagnosed with Asperger's tend to be viewed by their specialist as being more intelligent than those diagnosed with autism (although that's very often far from the truth, but more about that later). People with an Asperger's diagnosis tend to have no apparent speech delay, while people given an autism diagnosis will mostly have great difficulty learning in the same way as the majority of the population and will have delayed (or sometimes non-existent) speech. As you can see, the boundaries are a bit vague and that's perfectly understandable since these specialists are trying to diagnose something which affects every person in such a unique way.

As if this wasn't uncertain enough, in March 2013, Asperger's syndrome was removed from the American Psychiatric Association's Diagnostic and Statistical Manual (DSM). Since then, people presenting with these same issues have been given a diagnosis of 'autism spectrum disorder' (ASD), although people diagnosed before March 2013 still keep their original diagnosis of Asperger's syndrome.

Oh, and there's more: Although American doctors swear by the DSM, doctors in the UK prefer to diagnose using the World Health Organisation's International Classification of Diseases (ICD) instead. This manual still recognises Asperger's as a separate condition, so at the moment some UK doctors continue to diagnose it as such. Great, so that's all very simple then...

I've seen many people waste a lot of time and energy worrying about the ever-changing terminology associated with being on different parts of the spectrum and trust me, it's not a good idea. I really do understand how frustrating it is when you just want to know, once and for all, *for certain*, exactly what's going on, but autism just isn't something you can categorise too precisely.

It's a way of being, and has a unique, fluid and somewhat elusive quality about it that defies all attempts to pin it down and explain it completely. Categorising autism is something like trying to define the human spirit.

I hope you won't be too hard on those professionals whose job involves diagnosing people by working out the differences between autism and Asperger's: Anyone tasked with fitting the entire autism spectrum into a series of tick boxes has my utmost sympathy; they really do.

The best approach I've found is not to concentrate on the semantics, but to focus instead on how autism affects you or your child as an individual - the challenges it brings, the talents it enhances - and act accordingly. The trick is to keep working on the difficult stuff and celebrating every success along the way, just as all decent parents do.

What autism isn't

As strange as it sounds, I think the easiest place to start when describing what autism *is*, is to describe what it *isn't*. This is a basic list of some of the most common misconceptions you'll face when you've got autistic children (or indeed, if you're an autistic person yourself) and some information that I hope will help you come up with a quick, polite response if you ever have to deal with them in your day to day life. As much as you might like to smack some of these people in the head with my book and scream 'Educate yourself!' in the heat of the moment, I really wouldn't recommend it, so using some of this information to reply politely but firmly is definitely a better option.

Top Ten Myths about Autism

There are so many myths and misconceptions about autism that it would be impossible to list them all, but here are my top ten favourite (or least favourite) myths and why I can understand people believing that they're true. As frustrating as it can be, there really is no point in getting angry with people who still believe these things. The road to autism awareness and acceptance is a long one, but small steps are made along it every day.

I always find it's a much better use of my energy to focus on how much more 'normal' it's becoming to see autistic people's needs being given the recognition and respect they deserve nowadays, and to hope that as this continues, these uninformed opinions will gradually become a thing of the past. Tough, I know, because the temptation to lash out when you're under stress and being publicly criticised is a strong one.

There have been many times when I've longed for a t-shirt that says 'Oh, you think my child has a bad temper? Let me show you where he gets it from...' and have visualised launching myself at the crowds of self-righteous women who were busy judging me while I struggled to buy some groceries with a child who was emitting the kind of ear-piercing scream that could bring an entire shopping mall to a standstill (and frequently did). As gratifying as this sounds to a severely sleep-deprived brain, I can promise you it's not the answer. How did I cope with this kind of situation? More on that later.

The good news is that during my lifetime I've already seen changes I could never have imagined years ago, and the society you're living in now is a world away from the one where I brought up my eldest sons, so don't lose heart. Seriously, don't ever lose heart. Autism-friendly cinema and theatre performances, vast social media support networks, Special Educational Needs departments in mainstream schools and custom-designed toys, clothing and equipment to help make life easier for families living with autism are just some of the positive steps I've noticed and celebrated along the way.

So, while we wait for the day when everyone understands everything there is to know about the condition (which could possibly be a bit of a long wait, I feel...) here are society's ten most common myths about people on the spectrum:

1. Having autism means you're retarded (yes, I know, it's the 'r' word!)

Believe me, I loathe the word 'retarded' as much as most decent people do nowadays, but there's no guarantee that someone won't say it to you, so it's best to be prepared for this kind of comment.

The truth is that most people on the autism spectrum tend to have either average or above average intelligence levels, and any diagnosis of an autism spectrum condition will have nothing whatsoever to do with how intelligent they are. Autism is simply a difference in the way the neurons in the brain communicate with each other, which leads to complications with social interaction, communication and a need for rigidity in behaviours.

So why do people believe this myth?

Well, because of the specific difficulties that autistic people deal with, they can perform poorly in certain types of test, while excelling in others. This can be mistaken for a general lack of intelligence in all areas, and can often lead autistic people to believe that they're stupid when they're actually far from it. Some autistic people also have mild to severe learning disabilities, but most don't. They may experience complications when trying to learn in the same way as the majority of people, but that's due to the different learning styles autistic people have rather than any specific inability to learn.

The other reason people believe this one is because of autistic people's unusual movements and behaviours. They can look very, very strange if you don't understand them, so it's easy to see why this myth persists, but that doesn't make it true.

A diagnosis of autism means only one thing: you're autistic; intelligence is something entirely different.

2. Having autism means you're mentally ill

Even though autism is currently listed in the DSM-V (Diagnostic Statistical Manual) which covers all mental health issues, it's *not* classified as a mental illness. Autism is a *neurological* condition which makes the brain process information differently. This is due to a specific pattern of wiring that's caused by a complex set of genetic and environmental factors.

So why do people believe this myth?

Again, it's easy to see why people would think someone whose behaviour is so unusual has some kind of mental illness, but there's also another reason this myth continues: psychological disorders such as depression, anxiety and obsessive compulsive disorder (OCD) can very often accompany autism and can be made worse by a failure to recognise the underlying cause of a person's behaviour patterns. Autistic people are very often misdiagnosed as suffering from mental illness when in fact they're simply overwhelmed by their environment. Being autistic doesn't automatically mean you'll have any of these other issues, but a lifetime of being misunderstood can certainly make them more likely to develop. That doesn't make them the same thing as autism though.

A diagnosis of autism means only one thing: you're autistic; mental illness is something entirely different.

3. Bad parenting causes autism

There's been extensive scientific research into the causes of autism, leading to many theories as to its origins. Years ago, before the condition was properly understood, many people assumed that inadequate parenting skills had something to do with the difficulties associated with the condition. The latest evidence all points towards autism being a genetically inherited condition whose effects are shaped and influenced by each individual's life experiences. It's been proven beyond doubt to affect the functions of various parts of the brain, regardless of the way children are parented, leading to the very specific ways in which autistic people behave.

So why do people believe this myth?

Many autistic children find being in a public place totally overwhelming and will go into instant meltdown: screaming, running away, head banging, wrecking shops etc. and the majority of people seeing this kind of behaviour would expect parents to be angry and discipline their child. Parents of autistic children understand that shouting at or even smacking their child can't change the way the child's brain is wired, and will in fact make the situation far worse than it already is. As a result they appear to be simply allowing the behaviour to continue, or even 'encouraging' it by trying to pacify or distract their child, leading to all kinds of disapproval from uninformed passers-by.

Another reason is that although everyone behaves differently when they're in different places (their private and public personas), with autistic people this trait can be far more extreme. An autistic person's brain learns a specific set of rules in one environment and has great difficulty applying those rules to another situation because the surrounding information being taken in by their senses in this new place is entirely different. For instance, they may enjoy eating certain foods at school or at work, but refuse them at home. If they're able to understand the social rules, autistic people can try very hard to follow them even if they don't understand why they're so important to other people, but the strain of trying to fit in and follow these rules outside the home can take its toll, and many autistic people therefore become overloaded both emotionally and physically, having massive outbursts or 'meltdowns' when they finally reach somewhere they feel safe, such as their home.

This distinct difference in behaviour is a classic sign of an autism spectrum condition manifesting itself, but it's very often mistaken for naughtiness and lack of parental discipline since these same children can be immaculately behaved in public or when other people are looking after them.

A diagnosis of autism means only one thing: you're autistic; bad parenting is something entirely different.

4. Autistic people can't speak

Autism is a spectrum condition, meaning that the difficulties autistic people face vary hugely from person to person. One of the main areas affected by autism is the ability to speak, because autistic people find processing and interpreting language very tricky. Expressing what they feel using words can be a real struggle, but autistic people are autistic, not stupid, so many of them will find ways to compensate for this, allowing their spoken language skills to improve hugely over time. In fact, one of the recognised characteristics of autistic people with higher functioning language skills is their enormous vocabulary and their tendency to speak for far longer than is generally acceptable about the things they find interesting.

So why do people believe this myth?

The answer to this is very straightforward: unless someone is profoundly affected by their autism, the vast majority of people simply don't realise the person they're speaking to is on the spectrum at all. They might find them odd or a little obsessive, but if the only people they actually recognise as being autistic are those who are unable (or unwilling) to communicate with spoken language, it's no wonder they assume autistic people can't speak. Asperger's syndrome (or high functioning autism - HFA) is often referred to as 'the invisible disorder' for this very reason.

One important point to remember here is that there are other ways that profoundly autistic people can communicate, for instance using body gestures or sounds, and once you get to know these signals, you quickly realise that not being able to speak doesn't mean they have nothing to say!

A diagnosis of autism means only one thing: you're autistic; the ability to communicate with spoken language is something entirely different.

5. Autism only affects boys

Male and female brains are wired differently, and the areas affected by autism are those most closely associated with typically 'male' behaviour traits.

Without stereotyping anyone, girls' brains are generally better at communication, learning social skills, anger management, flexibility and multi-tasking than boys', simply because they're designed that way. Boys tend to have a harder time learning these skills even without autism thrown into the mix, so when it is, its effects are far more obvious, hence boys are much more commonly diagnosed than girls because the autism is holding their development back to the point where intervention is needed.

So why do people believe this myth?

At present many, many more boys are being diagnosed with an autism spectrum condition than girls, which is understandable considering the differences in their brain wiring but that's not the only reason. Girls with autism behave in a variety of very specific ways, just as boys do, but their behaviour patterns are different. Since diagnosis is based on the *male* signs of the condition, girls often don't seem to fit the recognised criteria, so they miss out on their diagnosis.

As a result, when the majority of people hear about someone being diagnosed, that someone is usually a boy. Also, girls are simply better at fitting in socially, and autistic women will go to extraordinary lengths to compensate for their difficulties or move attention away from them, so they appear 'normal' on the surface, while suffering greatly underneath. Sadly, in today's society there are a very large number of unhappy women and girls on the spectrum who haven't been diagnosed and probably never will be.

Whether they need a formal diagnosis or not will depend on how much the autism affects their day to day life, but the fact is that they're definitely out there, and there are a lot of them. At the time of writing, I'm genuinely delighted to see that a huge amount of progress is being made towards developing a specific set of criteria for the diagnosis of female autism, and am hoping that if you're reading this book some years after I've written it, you'll be thinking 'What on earth is she talking about? No-one thinks that anymore!'

A diagnosis of autism means only one thing: you're autistic; being male or female is something entirely different.

6. Children can grow out of autism

Every parent of an autistic child whose symptoms have improved has heard this one! Autism is what's known as an 'all pervasive' condition, which means it affects every part of the person. In other words, there's no part of the way they think, feel or exist that isn't coloured by autism to some degree or another. It's there from the second of conception to the end of their lifetime, and absolutely, categorically does not go anywhere. To 'remove' the autism from an autistic person would change everything they are, which is why the search for a 'cure' is such a controversial subject.

So why do people believe this myth?

Well, put simply it's because the outward symptoms of autism do, in many cases, change as the people themselves grow and change. Autistic people are *people*, first and foremost, so they'll develop and mature just as everyone else does. The rates at which they mature may be different, but it will still happen. They might learn new coping strategies or find a group of supportive friends and colleagues who accept their quirks and allow them to live an outwardly 'normal' life. If you don't understand the condition then of course you're going to believe they've grown out of it, that's to be expected. What goes on under the surface though is another matter, and the sheer hard work of fitting in (known in the autism world as 'passing') like this can lead to all kinds of other problems, which is why recognition and diagnosis are so important.

A diagnosis of autism means only one thing: you're autistic; having a condition you can grow out of is something entirely different.

7. All autistic people have 'savant' skills

Many autistic people have amazing talents and skills in certain areas, yet struggle with basic things like tying their shoe laces. A large number have particular gifts in art, science or maths, but many others don't, having a more generalised skill set instead. In extreme cases, the difference in skill levels from one subject to another is really big and this led to the wonderfully insulting term 'idiot savant' being applied to autistic people in the past. It means 'idiot genius' and refers to people who struggle to function in everyday life yet show flashes of genius in their specialist areas of interest.

It's widely believed that the term 'mad professor' comes from the high number of university lecturers who are on the spectrum, although they're mostly undiagnosed as yet. Being able to speak in depth and at length about quantum physics while wearing odd socks and making no eye contact doesn't necessarily make you autistic, but if you also have anger management issues, frequently walk into doors, avoid social engagements and prefer atoms to people, you might want to give it some thought!

So why do people believe this myth?

Many autistic people have either average or above average intelligence levels, and since the human mind is a remarkable and mostly unexplained thing, the truth is that none of us know how much we're really capable of. People on the Spectrum don't usually cram their minds full of things they consider unnecessary like wearing the latest fashion, following gossip or being popular, they simply focus on what interests them and give it their full attention. What would be achieved by 'normal' people if they did the same? We can only guess.

Autistic people also think differently to others who aren't on the Spectrum, giving them insights into new concepts and inventions others might never have discovered. As a result they very often become recognised experts in their chosen field, the case of Albert Einstein being one of the most famous. Having an autism spectrum condition doesn't guarantee any specific talents though, because again, autistic people are all different, just like everybody else!

A diagnosis of autism means only one thing: you're autistic; being a genius is something entirely different.

8. Autistic people have no empathy for others

In actual fact, this couldn't be further from the truth. Autistic people can feel enormous compassion and empathy for others, often way too much (something known as hyper-empathy) but what they struggle with is giving out the right signals so that people understand this about them. Expressing emotions outwardly is hard for autistic people, and coupled with their difficulties in reading and interpreting other people's emotions based on non-verbal clues, this is a very tricky area for them. However, not being able to easily pick up clues as to how others are feeling and not being able to easily express how you are feeling either, is *not* the same thing as not feeling these things at all. Narcissists, sociopaths and psychopaths have an actual lack of empathy for others, but these conditions have nothing to do with being on the autism spectrum.

So why do people believe this myth?

Mainly it's because autistic people appear to ignore how others feel and tend to override their wishes and replace them with their own. In fact, this is down to another area where autistic people struggle, that of 'theory of mind' - the ability to understand that others think differently to you, and know different things than you do. For instance someone on the spectrum may stand you up for a date because they've had to work late, but not let you know they're not coming because they assumed you already knew since they already knew.
When challenged and asked 'How do you think that made me feel?' they'll most likely become very defensive because they're confused by this: you feel the same way they do, and they're not upset because they already knew they wouldn't be there.
It's easy to see why people would believe this myth, but with a little understanding, this aspect of their behaviour makes a lot more sense.

A diagnosis of autism means only one thing: you're autistic; having no empathy for other people is something entirely different.

9. Autistic people can't have loving relationships

People on the autism spectrum process many things differently to 'normal' or neuro-typical people, especially their emotions, so the way they make emotional connections with others is obviously going to be different as well. Autistic people might actively avoid interaction with people they have a close connection to, or become more agitated and distressed around them than around other people, because they find it too hard to process the intense emotions that go with relationships like this. They often make little or no eye contact and refuse to be hugged or kissed for the same reason, and naturally it can be very hard to feel loved by someone who doesn't return your outward expressions of affection. With time, patience and a bit of creative thinking though, it's entirely possible to interact with autistic people in a way they can tolerate and once you do, you'll find the majority of them are wonderfully loyal, loving people to share your life with.

So why do people believe this myth?

Well, there's no getting away from it, being in a close relationship with someone on the spectrum can be very, very hard work. Without the right level of support and encouragement, many people become discouraged when it seems like they're failing to connect with their own children or other family members, and start to believe it's impossible. An autistic person's apparent lack of interest in the people around them and insistence on doing things in a set pattern or routine can make them appear to be unreachable, but this is far from the truth. The mistake many people make is in trying to change the autistic person's behaviour to fit in with their own expectations. Insisting on how the relationship 'should' work, rather than accepting the person as they are and interacting with them on their own terms, often leads to a total breakdown in communication, when a small change of perspective could have led to a wonderfully fulfilling relationship instead.

A diagnosis of autism means only one thing: you're autistic; being able to enjoy loving relationships is something entirely different.

10. Autistic people don't want to make friends

One of the main signs of an autism spectrum condition is difficulty processing social situations because they're filled with unwritten rules and etiquette that autistic people find almost impossible to understand.
Social gatherings are usually held in unfamiliar environments too, filled with new sensory information (sights, sounds, smells etc.) that they also struggle to process, and this combination can quickly become overwhelming. Having difficulty expressing emotion and being unable to make 'small talk' can make fitting in and feeling comfortable very hard, and this is why social anxiety is one of the biggest challenges for so many people on the spectrum.
Even when interacting with other people on a one-to-one basis, autistic people often miss both verbal and non-verbal clues as to whether the other person wants to be friends. Despite being desperate to join in, and even being welcome to do so, unless they're specifically told 'I want to be your friend' they won't necessarily understand what's expected of them and will stay by themselves. Autistic people are often loners as a result of these difficulties, while inside they can be yearning for the connection and interaction with others that most people take for granted.

So why do people believe this myth?

Being able to make friends is such a basic human characteristic that when an autistic person appears to reject offers of friendship by not making eye contact or returning a friendly 'hello' people will naturally assume they're rude or aloof and simply don't want to be friends. Someone who avoids parties and other public events will be considered anti-social, so it's perfectly understandable for people to think this way about those on the spectrum. Autistic people are also well known for saying the wrong thing at the wrong time, often managing to offend others entirely by accident, and again this can lead people to assume the autistic person doesn't like them, when in fact the opposite is true.

A diagnosis of autism means only one thing: You're autistic; the desire to make friends is something entirely different.

A perfect example of this happened shortly after Dominic started school. We were walking through the playground together and met several children who smiled, waved at him and said 'Hello, Dominic.' He completely ignored them. After this had happened a few times, I asked him 'Don't you like those little boys?' He looked puzzled, thought hard about it and said very slowly 'Yes, I like them.' Realising what was going on, I said 'Okay, when someone says hello to you, it's good to say 'hello' back, because then they know you want to be friends with them.' I was relieved to see his face light up as he took in this new information. 'Brilliant,' I thought 'He's got it!'

It was obvious he wanted to be friends, and the following morning when the same boys said hello, he fixed them with a perfectly blank expression and said 'Hello, Back' to each one of them in turn. Definitely one of those times I fought back tears in public, went home, sobbed and wondered where on earth I was going to find the strength to get him from where he was to where he wanted to be.

Help came not long afterwards when his teacher went on a two week residential course at a specialist autism school. She came back full of enthusiasm and ideas about how to help him feel more settled and accepted (at this stage he was still running away from school and walking home alone several times a week - fortunately we lived very nearby). She introduced 'social stories' to the class which helped the children understand how others might feel in certain situations; Dominic was fascinated. The break-through moment though was when she made him the 'Star Child' for a day. Each of his classmates was asked to write down why they liked him and came up with answers like 'When I hurt my knee, Dominic was kind and took me to the office' and 'Dominic is always gentle when we play together' which they read out to him one after another.

When I collected him that afternoon he was literally shaking with excitement and looked like he was ready to burst. His speech was still very limited, but he threw himself at me and shouted 'Mum! MUM! Children LIKE me!'

'Of course they like you, darling!' I said, plastering my best 'Isn't everything wonderful?' smile on and listening intently as he did what he could to explain what had happened. Inside, my heart was splintering with grief as I realised that until today he'd had no idea whether anyone liked him or not, simply because they hadn't told him. Talking to him, playing with him, sharing jokes with him: everything those children were doing said quite clearly 'I'm your friend', yet until they said the actual words, why they were behaving this way had all been completely beyond him.

Back then I knew hardly anything about how autism worked and I was overwhelmed with guilt that I'd somehow managed to miss something so important. Nowadays I realise there was no way I could have been expected to understand that he couldn't read social cues, but at the time I felt like a complete failure.

Dominic used to sneak a Buzz Lightyear costume into school in his bag and put it on at playtime despite being told over and over again that he wasn't allowed to. Something suddenly clicked and I asked him 'Why do you like wearing your Buzz costume at break times?' He answered with no hesitation at all and said 'Children like play with Buzz, not like play with Dominic.' Another knife to the heart. What kind of parent doesn't realise something that basic about their own child's idea of themselves? Catching my breath and fighting back tears, I gently explained to him that in fact it was *him* the children wanted to play with, because of who he was. There was a particularly nasty bully in his class - we'll call him Scott - so I said 'Dominic, if Scott wore the Buzz Lightyear costume, would children play with him?' He thought about it for a while and said 'No. Scott hurts children.' 'Exactly,' I said 'but Dominic doesn't hurt children, does he? Dominic is kind and gentle and children like him.' He thought long and hard about this and I could see the conflict on his face as he struggled to work the idea through, but eventually he said 'Yes, children like Dominic.'

He never smuggled the Buzz costume into school again.

So what IS autism then?

Right now I'm having to resist the temptation to launch into a full-on, painstakingly detailed explanation of autism as currently understood by each individual field of science, because as I may have mentioned, I'm an enormous nerd and I've done a *lot* of studying since those early days. Luckily, rather than turning this book into an encyclopaedia and simultaneously boring most of you to tears, I've resisted the temptation and instead I've listed some of the best books I've come across on the subject of autism in the 'Further Reading' section. For now though, here's a very basic outline of the condition and how it affects people:

Autism is a neurological condition which affects various parts of the brain and leads to a different kind of 'wiring' or communication between some areas. The way each specific brain responds to (and makes up for) these differences is as unique as the individual themselves, but there will always be similarities in certain behaviour patterns in autistic people because their brains gather and process information from the environment in similar ways. Autistic brains communicate differently to non-autistic brains, which are often referred to as 'neurotypical' brains because their neurons process information in a more predictable or typical way. A person with autism can therefore struggle with some things other people find easy, but can also excel at things others find difficult.

Autism is currently believed to be the result of a number of different genes combining in very precise ways when a child is conceived, although the causes of this particular combination aren't fully understood yet. As an autistic person grows up, the way these genes express themselves can be affected by all kinds of factors in their environment. This is great news for anyone living with autism because it means that in the same way a neurotypical brain can be positively influenced by its experiences, so can an autistic brain, giving *all* brains just as much potential for development, no matter how they're wired. Autism isn't made up, nor is it 'just a theory'; it's a real, genuine physiological condition that affects every part of a person's physical, mental, psychological, emotional and spiritual well-being and is totally inseparable from the person themselves. It causes difficulties with far more than just speech or learning to fit in, and its many physical effects - including hypermobile joints, allergies and problems with digestion - are well documented.

Do vaccines cause autism?

There's still a huge amount of debate about whether or not you should have a very young child vaccinated against measles, mumps and rubella using a triple vaccine known as the MMR, because some people believe it can make them autistic.
The vaccination is usually given within a month of their first birthday so this is a really emotive subject as parents are naturally (and rightly) concerned about doing what's best for their children when they're so tiny. It's therefore understandable they're going to think something which could give their child autism is a bad idea and want to avoid it.
Other people believe the MMR triple vaccine is completely safe and has nothing to do with autism whatsoever.
Having done lots of research on it myself, my understanding of the subject is this: *true* autism is absolutely, 100% *not* caused by the MMR because it's present from the time a baby is forming in the womb.
Autism is a way of being: a specific pattern of brain wiring that's with a person right from the start of their existence, so to suggest a child isn't autistic then 'becomes' autistic when they're given an injection at just over a year old is simply not true.
The thing with autism though, is because it's a complex genetic condition that's affected by environmental (outside) factors, and because it's a spectrum condition which affects every child differently, there are going to be cases where a child's autism may not have been spotted until they start to fall behind developmentally, which is often around the same age the MMR is given. If this is the case, perhaps they were going to develop more noticeable autistic traits whether they'd been vaccinated or not. It could also be argued that they might have had an adverse reaction to the MMR vaccine and started exhibiting more autistic symptoms than before as a result, but the fact is that if this is *true* autism then it *had to be there in the first place* for anything like a vaccination to trigger it.
If someone says 'My child is perfectly healthy, progressing normally and there's no autism in my family whatsoever but I'm worried about giving them the MMR in case it makes them autistic' I'll always reassure them their child won't suddenly become autistic as a result of the injection because that's just not how it works.
If, however, they've already got concerns about their child for whatever reason: a history of autism in the family, severe allergies, a compromised immune system, obvious developmental delays etc. then they're right to question anything and

everything they expose their child to at such a young age. It's important to take these concerns seriously and perhaps think about getting the three injections done separately to put less strain on their child's delicate system.

I have four children on the spectrum as you know and Christopher did have the MMR but was clearly autistic from birth (trust me on this one!). He didn't show any signs of regressive behaviour after he was vaccinated, although it did make him quite poorly. Because at the time there was a huge scare about the MMR causing autism, Dominic and Aidan didn't have it, yet Dominic was described as 'the most profoundly autistic child we've ever seen' by various specialists. Aidan is also autistic, has ADHD, Tourette's syndrome and dyslexia, again all without having had the MMR.

Isabelle *did* have the MMR at around eighteen months because although her brothers all had bad reactions to their first baby injections like polio and diphtheria (swelling, fevers, rashes etc.) she absolutely sailed through them without missing a beat, and sure enough she did the same with the MMR. She's by far the least profoundly affected by autism of all my four children, so simply from a personal perspective, I can say the MMR doesn't cause or even worsen autism as far as I can tell.

Interestingly, I've noticed when people's children have the MMR and suddenly 'become autistic' they never start developing amazing maths or art skills, or turn into top level physicists like 'real' autistic people can. They seem to become withdrawn, rocking, self-harming, mentally incapable children who don't appear to recover, which makes me wonder this: does the MMR trigger an adverse reaction in certain vulnerable children which produces *autism-like* symptoms? The simple answer to this question is: I don't know. What I do know, though, is that there've always been a small number of children who react adversely to injections. I remember a number of children actually *died* after their injections when I was young, but without the internet you just didn't hear about it in those days.

Evidence that the MMR is linked to autism, when looked at with an unbiased eye, is flimsy to non-existent, and in my opinion, the benefits of being vaccinated outweigh any risks there may or may not be, but the number one thing I'd say is that ultimately, the choice is yours, because this is *your* child, no-one else's, so it's got to be your decision. I'd suggest you speak to your GP if you're worried and avoid all the scare stories you'll find online.

Although some children have undoubtedly had adverse reactions to the MMR over the years, there are an enormous number who haven't, so although that doesn't diminish the suffering they and their parents are going through or make their experiences any less valid, they really are the exception rather than the rule. I'm not a doctor so I can only give you my opinion based on my own experience but for what it's worth, all three of the boys have since had the MMR as teenagers without showing any adverse reactions at all.

The autism spectrum

You'll often hear people describe autism as a 'spectrum condition' but most people have no idea what's actually included on the autism spectrum. As well as autism itself affecting people in lots of different ways, there are also several other diagnoses that qualify as being 'on the spectrum'.

Some people are very profoundly affected by their autism and find it impossible to cope with everyday life, needing specialist care and support at all times. Others are perfectly capable of functioning in society and often pass as 'normal' people with a few odd personality quirks.

Conditions that are currently classed as being part of the autism spectrum are classic, childhood and high functioning autism, Asperger's syndrome, pervasive developmental disorder (PDD) and pervasive developmental disorder not otherwise specified (PDD-NOS). In some cases, depending on the health professionals involved, others such as childhood disintegrative disorder (a.k.a. Heller's syndrome) and Rett's syndrome will be included as well.

Related conditions

There are also a set of conditions very closely related to autism which often manifest alongside it. Attention deficit disorder (ADD), attention deficit hyperactivity disorder (ADHD), dyslexia, dyspraxia (a.k.a. developmental co-ordination disorder or DCD) and Tourette's syndrome are all considered to be related conditions as they affect the same areas of the brain as autism. Other conditions such as depression, obsessive compulsive disorder (OCD) and heightened anxiety often occur alongside autism but aren't listed as being directly associated with it as they're psychological conditions and not neurological ones, which is an important distinction. They're also very often the result of misdiagnosis or of individuals struggling through life not realising why they're so different in the first place.

The triad of impairments

To qualify for a diagnosis of autism you have to show certain characteristics that stem from three areas of difficulty which are known, rather discouragingly, as 'the Triad of Impairments'. I know that sounds a bit negative, like there's something lacking in a person because they have trouble in these areas, but looking at what the term means rather than how it's phrased and thinking of them as being *complications* rather than *impairments* will give you a much more positive approach to dealing with them.

There's no denying that they're part and parcel of being on the spectrum, so whatever you call them, the important thing is that they're identified and that you're able to get the right support as a result without feeling like there's something wrong with having them in the first place.

The Triad is defined as follows:

1. Difficulties with social interaction

2. Problems with verbal and non-verbal communication

3. Lack of imagination and creative play leading to rigid, ritualistic behaviours

This doesn't mean any actual lack of imagination or creativity - on the contrary, lots of autistic people are talented writers, musicians and artists - it means having difficulty predicting what might happen next in certain situations due to missing the subtle clues other people instinctively notice.

It's vital to remember that the Triad can show itself in countless different ways, and some people will struggle far more with one part of it than another. It doesn't mean someone is any 'less autistic' if they're more social than another person, it simply means they're dealing with the three aspects differently, in the same way that every person on the planet deals with things differently, depending on their personality, intelligence levels and environment.

What does autism look like?

The most important thing to remember about autism is that it's a *spectrum* condition. It covers a huge range of abilities, which is why there are so many different descriptions of it, so many myths about it and such a variety of diagnostic terms for all the different ways it presents itself. As a general rule though, people on the spectrum will show either some, or all, of the following characteristics:

* Having speech and communication difficulties: not developing speech at all, learning to speak but choosing not to, speaking in an overly formal way or even speaking too loudly or too much

* Using echolalia or palilalia: Repeating what they've heard in a conversation, on television etc. (echolalia) or repeating what they've just said themselves, either aloud or under their breath (palilalia)

* Displaying awkwardness in, or avoidance of, social situations: difficulty understanding social rules

* Walking round and round the perimeter of play areas rather than joining in with actual play because they have no idea what they're supposed to be doing if their playtime isn't structured and explained to them

* Suffering acute distress when their routines are changed without notice

* Enjoying specialist interests in one or more subjects, about which they'll happily gather vast amounts of knowledge

* Demonstrating a great affinity with animals, nature or spirituality

* Having a fascination with numbers or patterns of information such as train timetables

* Showing an intense interest in dinosaurs, history, space, science or LEGO (the list is endless!)

* Walking on the tips of their toes

* Having a tendency to speak about their special interest at length, whether it's an appropriate time to do so or not

* Having trouble understanding cause and effect which leads to difficulty in learning from previous mistakes: often repeating the same behaviours yet expecting a different result

* Having little or no sense of danger or alternatively having very high anxiety levels

* Turning their head and using their peripheral vision to look at objects

* Making repetitive body movements and/or sounds when excited, anxious or tired – known as self-stimulatory behaviour or 'stimming'

*Flapping their hands, twirling their fingers or rapidly bouncing one of their legs when they're excited or under pressure

* Self-harming by head banging or clawing at their skin when upset or excited

* Skin-picking, hair-pulling, nail-biting or biting the skin around their nails

* Having an unusual reaction to analgesics or other forms of medication - it's often difficult to sedate autistic people for operations

* Having poor, inappropriate or non-existent eye contact; not liking to be looked at too directly

* Finding it difficult to express and handle emotions - all emotions, not only those considered negative

* Having explosive or implosive anger issues leading to outwardly aggressive behaviour or self-harm

* Struggling to understand body language, facial expressions, tones of voice and gestures in other people such as winking or pointing

* Disliking cuddles or kisses and/or enjoying rough play and tight hugs

* Experiencing sleep disorders: inability to settle, restless movements during sleep or sleeping only very briefly

* Being over or under-sensitive to specific noises. Covering or rhythmically slapping their ears if a sound is considered too loud, or not responding at all to loud noises such as crashes or bangs

* Being over or under-sensitive to light. Squinting and covering their eyes if a light is considered too strong, or looking directly at bright lights without any apparent discomfort

* Having the ability to see, hear and smell things others can't, leading to stress caused by the flickering of overhead strip lights or by the presence of strong fragrances

* Being fascinated by 'white noise' made by machines like vacuum cleaners, hair dryers or washing machines

* Finding it difficult to understand sarcasm, irony or figures of speech like 'sitting on the fence'

* Tending to take things very literally and follow instructions to the letter

* Showing less challenging behaviours when they have a high temperature

* Refusing to eat a variety of foods or to try new ones due to a dislike of different appearances or textures

*Having gastrointestinal (GI) disorders including chronic constipation or diarrhoea, irritable and inflammatory bowel conditions and gluten intolerance (known as Coeliac Disease)

* Having unusually flexible joints, particularly in the upper body: bending the fingers into unusual shapes is common, as are difficulties with hand writing, getting dressed and brushing teeth (known as hypermobility)

* Showing a lack of spatial awareness (not understanding where they stop and something else starts) making them appear clumsy or even destructive

* Having over or under-sensitive fingertips and toes, leading to difficulties with nail cutting

* Having an over or under-sensitive mouth. Resisting having their teeth brushed or using a pacifier for much longer than usual

* Constantly needing to fiddle with, destroy or chew inedible objects

* Eating and drinking things that aren't safe, such as small toys, insects or washing-up liquid - a condition known as pica

* Displaying unusual responses to pain or temperature: apparently not noticing some types, while overreacting to others

* Expressing an intense dislike of certain environments and/or types of clothing

* Refusing to wear shoes, socks, coats, gloves or hats due to sensory issues

* Insisting that all tags and labels are removed from their clothes

* Having unusual styles of walking or running: walking on tiptoe is very common as is hand or arm flapping when running

* Finding it difficult to ride bicycles, paddle canoes or do anything requiring bilateral co-ordination (the use of both sides of the body together to complete a task)

* Becoming obsessed with unusual objects that are collected and arranged in very specific ways, often in straight lines with boys or in colour/size order with girls

There are many more characteristics that people on the spectrum share and *even more unique differences between each of them too* which is why autism is so notoriously difficult to diagnose. These are just some of the most common behaviour patterns you're likely to notice when you interact with a person on the spectrum, and like all autistic traits, each of these can be linked directly back to one or more of the Triad of Impairments.

What causes these behaviours?

Again, resisting the temptation to subject you to a detailed lecture on brain science, I'm going to cut out a lot of the technical terms and focus on describing the basic procedures that *all* brains follow when they're making sense of their world. I'll then highlight what we understand so far about the differences between how an autistic brain and a neurotypical brain go about it.

How brains learn (a very simplified explanation!)

From the moment your brain begins to develop, its most important function is to gather and process information from the outside world, collect feedback using its senses (sight, smell, hearing, taste and touch) and match it to the data it's already got (its memories) so it can keep you safe, healthy and happy. In this way we all create our own unique versions of reality and use these to handle the different situations we experience. As we advance and learn new skills, our brains build new pathways for this information to travel along and our reactions and responses to life change each time this happens.

Okay, here comes the sciencey bit: This process is achieved using a large number of highly specialised nerve cells which are constantly transferring information in both electrical and chemical forms. These cells, called *neurons*, come in several different types which are responsible for different jobs: *Motor neurons* carry information from your brain to your muscles, *sensory neurons* carry information from your sensory receptors (nerve endings associated with your senses: sight, smell, hearing etc.) on through your body to your brain, and *interneurons* are in charge of transferring information between all the different neurons in your body. Your neurons communicate with each other using chemicals called *neurotransmitters* and create *neural pathways* for them to travel along, which are built between one part of your nervous system and another.

How 'normal' brains learn

If you have a 'normal' or 'neuro-typical' brain (i.e. one whose neurons communicate in a way that's pretty much like most other people) your neurons collect their information and quickly transfer it around. Once this information finds its way in, your brain decides what it's all about and connects it to any information it already has on the same subject, fitting it all together like the pieces of a jigsaw. In other words, the feedback your brain gets from whatever it's experiencing is matched against its memories, gradually building a kind of individual reference library just for you, filled with information on everything you've ever encountered. Amazing, but true!

The information in this library is then organised and prioritised according to your experiences, but because the world is so impossibly full of things to see, hear, touch, taste and smell, a certain amount of generalisation takes place during this process. Your brain groups together things it considers to be similar, then automatically sends you the appropriate message telling you how to react to each of these similar things, because if you reacted to each one as if you'd never seen it before, your senses would quickly become overwhelmed and you'd find it extremely difficult to function. A great way to understand this concept is to think about how babies learn.

The wonder of dogs and ducks

When you see a baby watching a dog or a duck for the first time, you'll notice how utterly fascinated they are by this strange, unknown creature. There was a time when this same experience was just as interesting to you, and your neurons went whizzing around processing all this fantastic new information and filing it away for future reference in just the same way. Now imagine what would happen if you felt this same sense of absolute, jaw-dropping wonder every time you saw a dog or a duck; literally every single time. It wouldn't be a major issue if you lived in a world with a severe shortage of dogs and ducks, but suppose you didn't, or suppose we were talking about trees here, or blades of grass, or even people.

In order to stop this happening, as I said, your brain groups together the things it finds similar and classes them as either dangerous, safe, or somewhere in-between which lets you react to them in an appropriate way, and to make sense of the constant stream of information your brain is trying to decode and sort into categories, it uses a process of matching the patterns it already has (its memories) to the new information it's receiving.

Once an acceptable match has been made, your brain's response to anything it thinks is similar will become more and more automatic, and it will prioritise your responses *for you* without you having to think about them consciously any more. Changing your response from 'OH WOW!!! A FROG!!! THAT'S AMAZING!!!' to experiencing a quick, unconscious 'frog' leaves you free to focus your attention on processing new and more useful experiences, which is what your brain wants: it wants you to learn. The easiest way to show you how this process of pattern matching works is by showing you (unsurprisingly) a pattern!

The ingenious image below was designed by a lady called Jackie Bortoft to illustrate the theories of her husband Henri, a celebrated author and lecturer.

At first, second and even third glance, this appears to be no more than a group of randomly arranged shapes, but what if I told you that there's an animal hidden in there somewhere? Have a good look and see if you can find it.

For anyone who can't (and that's going to be the vast majority of us) there's actually a giraffe's head sitting among the markings.

Now go back and look at the first image again. Can you still see the giraffe? Yep. More importantly, can you *un-see* the giraffe? Cover it over, take a moment, uncover it and try again. Can you look at the image and *not* see a giraffe? Nope. Your brain has successfully matched the pattern hidden in the shapes to something it already recognises, and now it's solved the puzzle, it's not going to let you waste time missing the answer in future, so it responds *automatically* and lets you know it can see a giraffe.

If you'd never seen a giraffe before, your brain would only see a jumble of shapes; it wouldn't mean there wasn't a picture of a giraffe's head in there somewhere, just that you wouldn't be able to see it yet, and that's a really important thing to understand. It's the same with everything in life: the more you learn about something, the more you can appreciate it for what it *really* is, not just what it first appears to be. Autism is a prime example of this: although it can seem overwhelming, distressing and downright scary to begin with, once you understand it a bit more you can start to appreciate what's below the surface, and often what you'll find hidden inside its complex patterns can be quite beautiful.

Why are brains so annoying?

Your brain is a learning mechanism, designed to experience as much as it possibly can during your lifetime, so now that it's found the giraffe, it wants to be off finding other interesting things to experience instead. As much as *you* might want to recreate the feel-good 'Eureka!' moment you experienced when you first realised what was hidden inside the pattern, your brain is having none of it. It will reward you with just *one* shot of dopamine (the 'reward hormone') when you solve the puzzle, then tell you to find it something else to get excited about instead.

I know it seems like your brain's being a bit annoying here, because we'd all love to experience and re-experience something that makes us feel good, but if we did, we'd end up getting stuck in our most pleasurable moments and eventually we'd fade away and die, and that's not something your brain is going to allow to happen if it can be avoided.

As a side note, it's by hijacking this natural reward system that addiction gets hold of you because the more you get of whatever is giving you pleasure (alcohol, nicotine, heroin etc.) the more your brain will adjust and get used to whatever dose you're taking as it tries to move you forward to the next learning experience, so you end up needing more and more of the same thing just to achieve the same high.

Meanwhile, back at The Dog & Duck...

Okay, let's continue with our example about dogs and ducks: Assuming everything is working in a typical way, having recognised a dog as being referred to as 'dog', any object a child's brain encounters from then on that makes a barking sound, has four legs, fur, a waggy tail, a wet nose, sharp teeth and pointy claws (or even something which represents this object, such as a painting, drawing, sculpture or toy) will be correctly identified as 'dog'.

If you listen to toddlers when they begin to speak, you'll notice that all birds will generally be referred to as 'duck' and all four legged animals, from goats to donkeys, will be identified as either 'cat' or 'dog' depending on which one they've been introduced to first. This is a clear sign that their brains are working beautifully and are starting the long process of sorting different species into groups based on their own unique characteristics.

How autistic brains learn

One of the main differences in how an autistic brain processes information can be found in the area of generalisation. Rather than seeing an object and automatically

73

grouping its individual parts together to identify it as something recognisable (four legs + fur + waggy tail = Dog) then being able to transfer this information into other recognisable forms (pictures, sculptures etc.) which are supposed to represent a dog, an autistic brain makes no *automatic* connection between similar things, which means it's still got just as much information in its reference library, but the library itself has a very different kind of filing system. This system categorises every detail it receives on separate sheets of paper, and gives each one of them the same amount of importance as the next.

Just give that some thought for a moment: An enormous reference library made up of single sheets of paper with one individual detail written on each of them, all mixed together with nothing prioritised and no defined sections where any of the sheets can be filed. Could you make sense of it? Well, maybe you could *eventually*, if you had enough time to sift through each piece of information in turn, every time you needed to make a decision about something, but could you function in your day to day life that way?

Remember we're not just talking about dogs or cats here, but about *everything you encounter,* from food to weather conditions to using your motor skills or tolerating pain, and from processing sounds to regulating your sleep patterns; not to mention the most unfathomable, illogical mystery of them all: human behaviour.

Learning in this disjointed way makes it almost impossible to understand the concept of cause and effect, because the vast majority of things we encounter every day don't follow absolute, unchanging rules. Gravity is one thing that's fairly consistent: if you drop something heavier than air it will fall, whereas something lighter than air will float, but mostly we have to rely on something that's *implied* before we can work out how to act accordingly – i.e. it's *implied* that if I cross the road without looking I might get run over; it's not a *definite*, it's just a distinct possibility. Once we've learned this and started to look both ways before crossing, it's once again *implied* that the same rule will work on *every* road, all of which are different and have different types of traffic travelling on them. An autistic brain will interpret each of these roads as new experiences and have to learn to apply the rule to each one individually so as you can see, not being able to generalise can be a serious issue when it comes to safety. It's also why so many autistic children (and adults) appear to have no sense of danger.

Conversely, people on the spectrum can also suffer from hugely elevated anxiety levels for exactly the same reason. Having realised the world is potentially a dangerous, unpredictable place, being unable to work out what might happen next in any given situation can leave them feeling incredibly vulnerable and lead to an increase in rigid or self-soothing behaviours.

Autistic brains process their whole reality this way, yet people on the spectrum can still learn to make sense of their world and often achieve quite remarkable things, which actually makes them pretty amazing in my opinion.

Learning in fragments

So how do they do it? Well, as with so many things in life, it's all in the details. Autistic people analyse their environment one fragment at time, then use a process of deduction to work out what it is these fragments might add up to and how to join them together. Into this process they'll add what something looks like, smells like, feels like, tastes like and also its environment, meaning that two identical things can appear quite different to an autistic person if they come across them in different places.

If they eat a certain food at home, that doesn't mean they can eat it somewhere else because what they can see, hear and smell at the time will have changed, and for them this can change the way the food looks, smells and even tastes. Seriously. They're not just being 'picky eaters', this is a real part of the condition. This perhaps explains why so many autistic people become fixated on particular foods (in very specific packaging) and refuse to try anything new. Having something safe and familiar to eat when everything else around you is chaos must surely be very reassuring.

What I'm describing sounds difficult to handle, I know, yet this is only a tiny part of what people living with autism deal with every day. If I wrote about everything that's affected by this form of brain wiring, this would be the longest chapter in history, so instead I'll give you an example:

Imagine learning about several different species of birds. It's a simple enough process if you've accepted a general reference point telling you that if something has wings, a beak and feathers and it also lays eggs then it's most likely a bird. It wouldn't be too difficult to add some more information to your reference library by learning about the huge variety of shapes, sizes and colours that make up the bird kingdom, and to have plenty of fun while doing it.

Imagine now that you're learning about them in an autistic way: detail by detail. How is an owl, with its huge yellow eyes, nocturnal hunting habits and grey feathers, anything like a kingfisher, with its striking blue colouring, elongated beak and ability to catch fish during the day? Is a hummingbird or an ostrich really very much like a peacock or even a penguin? Do they share the same habitat? Can they all fly? What about shape, size or colour? Do they tweet or whistle or squawk? They may all lay eggs, but do any of their eggs look exactly the same? Autistic brains are immensely logical, so to them, something is either the same or it's different, there's no instinctive recognition of 'similar' and when you experience it this way, the breath-taking diversity of life on our planet, rather than being something beautiful and engaging, can become something frightening and overwhelming.

Just for a moment, think about how much you have to *assume* about things you encounter every day in order to make sense of them.

This learning process has to happen consciously rather than automatically, a bit like the difference between speaking your native language and learning to speak a new one using a phrase book. Remember that autistic people have no ready-made phrase book to refer back to, and because things aren't prioritised in the same way as you'd expect when they're learning, they're constantly trying to process everything at once too.

It's understandable then that they often become confused and distressed by things other people deal with as a matter of course. *This isn't a sign of low intelligence* as was once believed to be the case, but simply of becoming overwhelmed by the enormous amount of information they have to consciously process just to make sense of things.

Once you understand this, the desire to create some kind of logical order in an ever-changing, irrational world by collecting, organising and categorising objects becomes perfectly reasonable. As a result, behaviours like arranging items in long straight lines and refusing to accept changes to their routine (often the only things they feel they *can* predict and understand in an otherwise terrifyingly unpredictable world) suddenly make a lot more sense.

So that's a bad thing, right?

There's no doubt that the confusion and anxiety that's created when your brain processes information in this way isn't an easy thing to deal with at all. Learning to speak when you apply this same thought process to understanding language makes it nothing short of baffling, and the frustration that goes with being unable to communicate in the usual way is truly heart-breaking to witness, let alone to experience.

Handling emotions becomes a major challenge (and that's an understatement) while social interactions - where you're expected to interpret not only people's spoken language but their body language too - can become so frightening that it seems like they're best avoided altogether.

Add to this the physical complications it brings to perfecting your motor skills, regulating your tolerance to pain, temperatures and noise, and the countless other challenges autistic people deal with every day, and it certainly seems like having this type of brain wiring has got to be a bad thing, right?

Well, it's certainly a *difficult* thing, but does that necessarily make it an entirely bad one?

'Suffering from' autism

As you can see, it's fair to say that autism does indeed cause a lot of suffering, so I can understand why so many people refer to those on the spectrum as 'suffering from autism' or 'autism sufferers' but personally I'm not a fan of either of those expressions. My problem with them is the way they focus solely on the difficulties autism creates. They leave no room for the positives it can bring too. Both expressions conjure up images of 'suffering from Ebola' or 'cancer sufferers' making autism sound like a disease that needs to be cured. If they're used around people who are new to the condition, they can definitely give a one-sided view of how a person's life might be affected by being on the spectrum. That doesn't mean for one second that people with autism (and their families) don't suffer, because they do, it simply means there's lots more to the condition than just the suffering it causes and that's *such* an important distinction to make when you're discussing it.

What on earth is so great about autism then?

If you're suffering from severe sleep deprivation, watching your child's intense distress without having a clue how to help them and are terrified about the future, this sounds like a perfectly reasonable question to me. I know from experience how autism can seem like a never-ending nightmare of anxiety and chaos, but it really does have a positive side, even if it can be almost impossible to find at times. Luckily for you, after over 25 years of looking on the bright side, I've found so many things to be optimistic about that they'll fill a whole chapter all by themselves. Everything from autistic people's ability to find intense joy in the smallest of details to their loyalty and lack of judgemental behaviour is covered in the 'And the Good News Is...' chapter, so keep your chin up and keep reading. Autism really isn't all about doom and gloom, it's about so, *so* much more.

Top Ten Rules of Autism

1. If it's important, lose it.
2. If it's moving, fall off it.
3. If it's marked 'unbreakable' don't believe it.
4. If it's clean, drop food on it.
5. If it's too small for you, get stuck in it.
6. If it's on the floor, trip over it.
7. If it's essential, forget it.
8. If it's stationary, walk into it.
9. If it's stuck, force it.
10. If it's full, spill it.

Sometimes Helen wondered where on Earth her children's autism came from...

Chapter Three

Playing the Generation Game

'Family: like branches in a tree, we all grow in different directions,
yet our roots remain as one'
Anon

I'm quite sure that somewhere in the world there are families who've welcomed the arrival of an autistic child and given his or her exhausted parents nothing but positive, helpful and supportive advice right from the start, but I can honestly say that in all the years I've dealt with the condition I've never actually met a family like it myself.

Instead I've found one of the biggest causes of anxiety for new autism parents is the stress created by their extended family's refusal to accept the situation for what it is. Their own parents and grandparents will often try incredibly hard to convince them there's nothing unusual about their child's autistic behaviour, saying they'll either grow out of it or would behave perfectly if they were just given a bit more discipline. They'll often point out how everyone in the family behaved the same way when they were children, so things must be okay because there's nothing wrong with any of them now they've grown up. Sound familiar? You're definitely not alone.

Assuming families have your best interests at heart which I'm sure the vast majority of them do, why can they be so strongly opposed to the idea of your child being on the spectrum? The answer is often a mixture of two hugely powerful emotions: love and fear.

A new performer enters the ring

By the time Christopher was two and a half I felt he'd made fantastic progress and was longing to have another baby both for myself and to give him a younger brother or sister to love. While everyone else saw a naughty, hysterical, aggressive, non-verbal whirlwind of a child, I saw a sensitive little boy with hugely heightened anxiety who was trying his level best to learn and make sense of an overpowering world. I'm not saying he was easy to look after because he absolutely wasn't, but once you understood him it was obvious he had a huge amount of love to give, so I really felt he was ready to welcome a new sibling, and I certainly felt ready to love another little person, one I assumed (quite wrongly of course) would be a bit like Christopher only different in his or her own unique way. Naturally the family thought I'd lost my mind when I announced I was expecting again, but being considered insane was nothing new, so I kept my own council and carried on regardless.

I had the most appalling migraines and sickness through the entire pregnancy which led the doctors to believe I might be carrying twins as my hormone levels were so high. In fact I was carrying an absolute giant of a baby who had to be delivered three weeks early by caesarean because he was too big to fit through my pelvis. Babies lay down their fat stores in the last few weeks, so when Dominic arrived he was nothing but skin and bone and looked like a tiny, toothless old man - a very handsome one, I might add. As predicted, he was enormous and at a fraction under ten pounds he weighed more than most babies do at full term. Although Christopher hadn't been formally diagnosed yet, I was convinced by now that he was indeed autistic, so when Dominic behaved in a completely different way as a new-born I breathed a sigh of relief and congratulated myself on producing such a placid, calm, co-operative and thoroughly 'normal' baby. As always, Life laughed merrily away to itself, but at the time I was far too delighted to notice.

The baby who couldn't cry

Unlike his brother, nothing in the ward – and I do mean nothing – disturbed Dominic in the slightest. He slept peacefully through all the noise and also through most of his expected feeding times. When he did eventually wake up some twelve hours later he opened the most intense pair of sapphire blue eyes I've ever seen and instead of crying, he sang. His voice was hauntingly beautiful and he communicated using a soft, lilting melody I still remember to this day.

The tune would stop as soon as I gave him a bottle, then he'd fall straight back to sleep for anything up to eighteen hours at a time. The midwives thought he was adorable and called him The Little Mermaid, describing him as the most perfectly behaved baby they'd ever seen. You can only imagine how proud I felt.

By the age of two months Dominic was still sleeping anything up to twenty-three hours a day, waking only for the occasional bottle when he'd sing his little song and instantly fall asleep again. At first, rather than being concerned, I was relieved I didn't have another baby like Christopher to contend with, but after a while I did start to wonder if this was the way babies usually behaved. We seemed to have gone from one extreme to the other: Dominic would happily cuddle anyone and could be taken anywhere without complaint, unlike his brother who'd always become hysterical at the very idea of going out or meeting other people. His attention span was remarkable and he'd get lost for hours in things like coloured cotton reels, which he'd grab one after another and examine in minute detail through the corner of his eye. His brother meanwhile had a shorter attention span than a goldfish with ADHD and needed constant interaction and stimulation to prevent meltdowns. Thank goodness Dominic wasn't autistic too, I thought, as Life sniggered up its sleeve.

At the time I had no idea autism was a spectrum condition so it seemed obvious to me that if Christopher was autistic then clearly his brother wasn't. As it turned out, Dominic was about as far towards the profound part of the spectrum as you can get, and what I'd thought of as contentment and co-operation was in fact total indifference to anything and anybody outside his own all-consuming thoughts. It did occur to me that a baby who didn't cry wouldn't have survived long in the wild, but what didn't occur to me was that he *couldn't* cry because his neural circuitry was so jumbled he had no idea how to manage it. I didn't dwell on this at the time because to be honest I was just thankful he wasn't screaming the place down like his brother, but when I think back on it now it's obvious something was a bit unusual right from the word go.

By the time Dominic was eighteen months he was every bit as violent as his brother, only instead of being aimed at the world around him, his aggression was turned firmly inwards. When he was upset (which was pretty much all the time) he'd bash his head so hard on the glass front door that we had to have it replaced with a wooden one to stop him smashing straight through it and causing himself some grievous injury.

Despite the endless screaming, sleeplessness and gruesome self-harm, the family assured me that firstly there was nothing wrong with him, and secondly, since he'd started off so well, his behaviour, like his brother's, was once again down to my complete lack of parenting skills.

The specialists disagreed and several paediatricians described him as the most profoundly autistic child they'd ever encountered. When I mentioned this to the family they refused to believe a word of it and decided I'd somehow managed to convince *all* the health professionals (health visitors, GP's, paediatricians, speech therapists etc.) that he was on the spectrum just to excuse my own failure to raise him correctly. Incredibly, when I asked them why on earth all these people would waste their time working with Dominic if there was nothing wrong except my own inability to parent him, they said 'Well it's obvious: they want to justify their jobs and it's people like you who keep them in work.' It's laughable, I know, when you consider how overstretched the special educational needs (SEN) system is, but the family were utterly determined to cling to the idea that there was no autism involved here, only the most useless parenting imaginable. People will fight tooth and nail for their idea of reality despite overwhelming evidence to the contrary, and this was a classic example of not so much being *unable* to see what was going on, but being *unwilling* to.

He's not autistic because…

Over the years I can honestly say the single most common cause of disagreements with family and friends regarding my children is a discussion about whether or not they're autistic at all. In some cases it's not so much that people *can't* see the situation for what it is, but that they *won't* see it because, as I said before, they simply don't want to. I've genuinely lost count of the number of conversations I've had with well-meaning people who tried to reassure me that everything was fine in my children's world because:

- Their husband and/or sons behaved in exactly the same way as mine when they were young: 'That's not autism, that's just men.'
- There was nothing wrong with my children (I agree!) so if they did have autism, which was highly questionable anyway, they must have it in such a mild form that it was invisible: 'Well, if you're right then they're only a little bit autistic.'
- When they got older, my children functioned so well their autism must have magically disappeared somewhere along the way: 'Maybe they used to be autistic but they've obviously grown out of it now.'

When parents and grandparents get together it's perfectly natural for them to discuss their children and if any parent is struggling, to look for common ground where they can build some solutions together. This is a healthy part of belonging to a civilised society and can lead to solid friendships and support networks both inside and outside the family that become invaluable over the years. Bonding like this is so instinctive that people will often make lifelong friends with a whole variety of personalities based purely on the fact their children are in the same class at school.

It's worth remembering then, that when people offer you the strategies they found successful, their advice is generally well meant - sometimes not, and believe me, I've met those people too - but as a rule they're simply trying to help. While I can see how people might think this advice would make autism parents feel better, the truth is it does the opposite.

If there's nothing different about our children then by implication we must be the most terrible parents (as my family were always happy to point out in my case). Obviously we're the sort of people who spend their lives making endless excuses for their children's behaviour while still failing to correct it. Despite the enormous amount of freely available advice and literature on the subject of how to raise well-balanced children, we just can't seem to manage it. Clearly we're just not trying hard enough. If you've ever given advice like this to an autism parent, I realise that might not be what you meant to say, but if you stop and think about it for a moment, it's a bit insulting, isn't it?

All autism parents are familiar with brilliant advice such as 'Can't you just *make* them eat/sleep/speak/concentrate/whatever it is they struggle with?' Oh yes of course, we could just *make* them do it - if only we'd thought of that: when all else fails, apply brute force. Unfortunately, this approach of 'Oh, I can fix that for you' will only annoy and frustrate parents who are all but tearing their own hair out trying to bring some kind of order to the chaos of their daily lives, and only parents living with autism on a day to day basis really understand the implications of following the 'just make them do it' route.

Playing the long game

Bringing up autistic children means playing the long game. It means running the gauntlet of disapproval and social isolation and putting your child's needs firmly ahead of your embarrassment, loneliness and frustration.

There are no quick fixes, no compromises and no instant results. Nothing you do will be forgotten. Ever. It's cause and effect in its most brutal form: for every action that causes your child distress (whether you understand why or not) there will, inevitably, be a reaction so intense, prolonged and devastating that the results will engulf you both like a tidal wave. This one initial act of 'making' them behave as you'd like them to could quite easily set off a chain of events that destroys any progress you've made together, which is why autism parents are so often accused of spoiling their children. We're not, in fact, pandering to our child's every whim and raising a spoilt monster who believes the world should bend to its will or face the consequences, we're loving, nurturing and teaching them in a way that's as unique as they are.

When you see a parent soothing and comforting their angry autistic child rather than scolding them, it's because there's a whole different ball game being played than the usual parent/toddler power struggles we're all so familiar with. Their child is overwhelmed by anxiety and needs as much reassurance as possible, not more stress because they're being told off for their 'bad' behaviour. It's a terrible injustice the way so many loving, dedicated parents of autistic children are considered lazy, stupid and incapable by people with no idea of the impossible demands this kind of parenting brings.

Anyone who cares about their children has a natural desire to guide and nurture them, to protect them and make them happy. No-one wants to see their children suffering and self-harming through sheer desperation at finding themselves in a terrifying world they can't make any sense of. Autism parents will go to extraordinary lengths to make sure this doesn't happen and as a result, when it comes to their children, they're often the *least* lazy, stupid or incapable people you'll ever meet.

Believe me, we know what our children are *supposed* to do if we treat them a certain way, but for some inexplicable reason they don't. Not only did they not get the memo, but if they *had* got it they'd most likely have eaten it anyway. Parenting 'by the rules' simply doesn't work for us and the natural order of things seems to have evaporated, along with our peace of mind and all our hopes and expectations for the future.

The reality is however, that in public our children will sometimes display almost identical behaviour to that of children whose parents genuinely don't care. As frustrating as it is, I can understand the thinking behind those judgemental tuts, sighs and eye rolls that every autism parent has experienced from passing strangers.

In my case I'd read the literature, I'd listened to the advice, and for a long time I despaired that Christopher still didn't seem to respond 'correctly' to anything at all. These strategies seemed to be working just fine for every other parent, so why didn't they work for me? Today I understand exactly why of course, but at the time it was a complete mystery to me.

Going for a drag round the shops

Taking the boys shopping was about as much fun as you'd expect, but we had no money for childcare and this was before the days of internet shopping so inevitably they had to come with me at some point. By the age of three it was almost impossible to get Christopher into a buggy. He was huge and ridiculously strong for his age, and would go as stiff as a board with his arms and legs sticking out at right angles to his body which became affectionately known as 'doing the starfish'. After much screaming and manoeuvring, the straps would eventually start to be fastened, at which point he'd instantly be gripped by a mysterious paralysis which made him shoot out of the bottom like a collapsed puppet; this was known as 'doing the ninja slither'. In a split second, every bone in his body had turned to jelly; remarkable really considering only a moment before they'd been like reinforced iron bars. It seemed my son had talent after all.

Never one to give up easily, I'd spend the next ten minutes heaving his lifeless body (by now a total dead weight) into the correct position while listening to the tuts, sighs and stage-whispered comments of the disapproving passers-by, and he'd sit, floppy but defiant in his wheeled nylon prison with a look of murderous rage on his face, plotting his escape. As a rule, he'd remain passive just long enough to lull me into a false sense of security, and the second I took my eyes off him he'd revert to his former state of rigidity, sliding forward and thrusting his legs as hard as he could into the pavement, which had the effect of a ship dropping anchor and sent me - handbag, shopping and all - flying over the top of him in an exasperated heap.

After three and a half years of constantly carrying, wrestling and man-handling Christopher, I had the neck muscles of a silverback and the biceps of a power-lifter but he was still far too wriggly and heavy for me to carry along with the shopping while also pushing Dominic in a pram, so someone suggested reigns. Oh dear. These worked superbly for about three minutes until he realised the idea wasn't for *him* to lead *me* along, but the other way around.

This was clearly a complete infringement on his freedom, so in true militant style he staged a sit-in, or rather a sit-down. Unfortunately I made a serious mistake at this point and pulled on the reigns to give him the idea of moving forward. As he felt his body glide along without any effort on his part, a look of sheer delight crossed his face and from then on, no matter where we were, as soon as the reigns appeared he'd instantly lose the use of his legs, raise one arm in the air and sit perfectly still waiting for my next move.

If I didn't seem too willing to drag him along for some reason, he'd encourage me by saying 'Su-man mum-mum' which to the uninitiated means 'I want to be Superman mummy, and fly round the shops on my magic strings.' Wonderful. If I still refused to drag him, he'd start the dreaded ear-piercing scream which was guaranteed to bring any shopping mall to a complete standstill, and would continue indefinitely until he either went into a full meltdown and started vomiting, or felt himself start to move.

I'd love to tell you there was some miraculous solution to this problem, but as I said, this was before the dawn of internet shopping, so until I got him a free nursery place we'd regularly go for a drag round the local shopping centre. Every time he'd gradually collect a large pyramid of dirt up his back; his trousers doing a superb impression of a floor polisher. It's amazing the lengths you'll go to when you have no support and you're out of nappies and milk.

The reaction of the Great British Public was on the whole less than encouraging: narrowed eyes, folded arms and general avoidance were the order of the day, along with horrified exclamations of 'Oh for God's sake!' and 'Disgusting!' Life's perfect training ground for what was to come in the following years really. Oh, and couldn't I just *make* him walk? Sigh.

I prefer to remember the people who came towards us, smiled and said 'Hey, good for you! I've never seen something like that before but at least you're getting your shopping done.' And the ones who actually offered to help us. They were the little bursts of light that shone through the endless darkness of disapproval for me, and to this day I'm grateful for those small acts of kindness.

When Dominic started walking it was suggested I get them each a wrist link - a long strap that attaches to your wrist at one end and theirs at the other. What a great idea. I bought the flexible version to give the boys a bit more freedom to move around and asked myself quite seriously 'What's the worst that could happen?' Well, they worked wonderfully for at least half an hour until Christopher managed to unclip both straps from my wrist and somehow attach himself to Dominic's strap, at which point the pair of them took off at a run, found a huge pillar in Marks & Spencer and ran round and round it on their ever-shortening strings until they both smashed into it face first. Undeterred, I carefully unwound them and tried again, but following a trip to Tesco when they once again attached themselves to each other while I was busy paying at the till then raced along opposite edges of the frozen food aisle with the straps stretched between them like a trip wire, taking out several passing pedestrians in the process, I decided perhaps wrist links weren't such a good idea for us after all.

Personally I thought it showed initiative on Christopher's part and fantastic manual dexterity but my health visitor was quick to point out that I was clearly just a bad parent: that I expected too much from my sons or not enough; that I talked to them too much or too little; that I was inexperienced and uninformed or a complete know-it-all...I could go on. The point is that for years I was told everything about the boys' unusual behaviour was in some way my fault, and it was at this stage I actually wished, many times, for them to have some visible difference which could stop these endless, pointless and totally demoralising conversations. Everyone I met seemed smugly convinced that I was just making excuses for their behaviour, never wondering for a second whether there might be an actual reason behind it.

Remember the younger me? The one who didn't want to end up with one of 'those' kids? It was absolutely my worst nightmare at the time, and yet here I was realising that if my children had something visible like cerebral palsy or Down's syndrome it would be so much easier for society to understand and accept them because there would be something everyone could actually see. The irony was not lost on me, I can promise you that.

The double edged sword of success

So when my children finally did make some progress you'd think it might be cause for celebration within the family, wouldn't you? Sadly, as we all know, families just aren't that simple. Whatever they achieved, even when they exceeded all expectations, which they did on many occasions, I wasn't met with praise for all my hard work and perseverance but by the hugely unhelpful phrase 'See? I *told* you there was nothing wrong with him...'

To the family's way of thinking my children's progress was proof there was never anything different about a close relative of theirs, and it was just my lack of parenting skills that were to blame all along. What a relief for everyone. Except me of course. If you recognise this scenario then I feel your pain; I really do.

No matter how reasonably you explain that accepting something was different about your child is precisely *why* you've managed to support them in achieving so much, some people won't believe you, so my advice would be to invest in a large pillow and scream into it for as long as it takes to feel better, or use the techniques I talk about in the 'There Is No Magic Wand' chapter. I did and they really saved my sanity. Accepting you're unlikely to ever win on this subject can be enormously frustrating, but if it's any consolation, you're in very good company.

Shaking the family tree

As a therapist I've always specialised in the treatment of autistic children and their families and the first question I'd ask any new client was 'Is anyone else in the family autistic?' The vast majority of people would assure me that no, they had no other relatives with the condition, so why their child was on the spectrum was a complete mystery. My next question would always be 'Is anyone in the family a bit eccentric?' 'Oh yes,' they'd say, 'there was Uncle Charlie who had a shed full of jars that all had to be exactly half filled with dirt, and Aunty Elizabeth who lived her entire life believing she was a fairy, but they weren't autistic, they were just weird.' When I'd suggest that, you know, maybe they might not have been 'just weird' after all, but might in fact have been autistic, their answer would usually be 'But they can't have been; they were never diagnosed.'

People of previous generations tell me all the time that 'there was no such thing as autism/ADHD/dyslexia etc. in my day' and they genuinely believe it. They're certain that since the terms used to describe these conditions are relatively new, the conditions *themselves* must be new as well. The truth is of course that these conditions have *always* existed, and the people affected by them have suffered horribly as a result of being either wrongly diagnosed or not diagnosed at all. The likelihood is that if your child is on the spectrum and you start shaking the family tree a bit, people with autism, ADHD, dyslexia and all manner of other 'modern' conditions will fall right out. The trick is to recognise them rather than just writing them off as the family oddballs, which is probably how everyone has thought about them up 'til now.

Back in the good old days

Lots of older people look back on their childhoods and remember a happier, simpler time when the world didn't always seem to be in such a hurry. For autistic people though, the 'good old days' as they're affectionately known, weren't actually very good at all. Generation after generation, autistic people's lives have been ruined by the misery of misdiagnosis, with many of them either ending their lives in prison (due to undiagnosed anger issues), in so-called lunatic asylums (having been misdiagnosed as dangerous or mentally deficient), or by committing suicide (believing they'd never fit in no matter how much they tried and eventually giving in to loneliness and despair).

Thankfully things have changed a great deal now, but the fear of being identified as 'different' runs deep in the older generations, which explains a lot about why they're often so resistant to the idea of their grandchild or great grandchild being diagnosed as autistic.

Many of them (myself included) still remember the 'lunatic asylums' which were later renamed 'mental hospitals'. They were dark, forbidding places run more like prisons than treatment centres, where the most appalling abuse was inflicted on vulnerable people almost as a matter of course. It wasn't until the 1980's that the last of these institutions were shut down, and only a little earlier in 1978 that the term 'special educational needs' was introduced along with changes that meant children who learned in different ways could be taught in mainstream schools alongside regular pupils.

Going back a bit further, even the NHS didn't exist before 1948, so it's important to remember the older generations lived in a much less enlightened and far harsher world than the one we see today. People who were different were considered deficient and as I've mentioned before, parents whose children had developmental disorders would often feel intense guilt and shame. Is it any wonder that grandparents can be afraid of acknowledging autism in their much loved grandchild? It goes against the natural order of things to still be looking after your child when they're an adult, and this could be all a grandparent can imagine happening if they don't know much about autism being a spectrum condition.

Another reason they might object is if they recognise the behaviour in themselves and are afraid to admit it, fearing your child's struggles might somehow be their fault. What they've seen and lived with will be the undiluted version of your child's behaviour, so their quirks might seem quite mild by comparison to what they're used to. They'll look at their own children and say 'they're alright now' because perhaps they're successful in their chosen careers, even though they might be deeply unhappy people. It's highly likely they'll be introverts who haven't shared their feelings with their own parents, so these grandparents won't necessarily realise their own children are so miserable. Lack of communication will feature heavily within the family, and explosive outbursts of anger will be considered normal. They'll tell you it's 'just the way he/she is' and that 'he/she will calm down eventually if you leave them alone long enough'. The older generations tend to measure success in terms of career and finances rather than happiness and contentment and this isn't because they're unfeeling, it's because talking about your emotions, seeing a therapist or working on your personal development just weren't things people did when they were young.

Education, education, education

The good news is that as a rule, getting older makes people more accepting, understanding and patient, so there's every chance that with some honest discussion and a bit of re-education about the way the world works nowadays, your older relatives will become useful allies who'll support you in raising your child, even if they've been resistant to the thought of autism being present to start with. I'm not saying it's going to happen in every case because as we all know some people just get grumpier, more argumentative and more cantankerous as the years go by, but assuming your family are acting out of love and concern for your child, with a bit of luck they'll be willing to listen to, and take on board, some new ideas.

First of all, explain what autism is, what it isn't and how it's a *spectrum* condition so they don't jump to any conclusions about what might happen as your child grows up. Talk about how much support is available nowadays in both mainstream and special needs schools and how the emphasis in the education system is on mixing children of all abilities together rather than hiding some away like they did years ago.

Make sure they understand how much attitudes have changed towards disability these days and discuss the huge online support network that's freely available for autism parents and grandparents to use. Encourage them to ask as many questions as they like and if you don't know the answer to something, look it up together so you can put their mind at rest. It might be a good idea to watch some autism-related films or TV shows together where they'll see the kind of behaviour they recognise in your child and you can talk about it together – I've listed lots of these in the 'Post Diagnosis Survival Pack' chapter.

Show them examples of people on the spectrum who've successfully managed their condition and now enjoy life in the public eye like Susan Boyle and Chris Packham, and point out that many people from previous generations would be diagnosed as autistic if they were born today, including Albert Einstein, Vincent Van Gogh and Lewis Carroll. Use this to remind them that autism is nothing new and has always been a natural part of the spectrum of human behaviour, often leading to brilliance in the fields of science, maths and the arts. They're most likely to have heard how autism is now an 'epidemic' or seen it described as 'autism spectrum *disease*' which can be very upsetting and worrying for them, so reassure them that having autism doesn't mean there's anything *wrong* with someone, just that they're different.

It doesn't mean they have to exclude your child from everyday activities they enjoy with their other grandchildren, just that they'll need to make a few adjustments to how your child is treated so they feel confident enough to join in. Definitely stress the fact that although autistic people may be different, they're certainly not *less* than neurotypical ones and that your child will benefit just as much from their love and support as any other child, as long as it's delivered in a way they can cope with.

Suggest they read some positive books on the subject including this one (well, I would say that, wouldn't I?), plus some books specifically written for grandparents of autistic children like the ones I've listed in the 'Further Reading' chapter - they're full of great tips to help bridge the generation gap. In the meantime here are a few of my own:

- Make sure everyone has very clear roles when it comes to bringing up your child and understands the boundaries so they can help you without appearing to interfere. Your parenting agenda will be very different to theirs so they might find it confusing unless you explain what you're doing and why you're doing it.
- Put together a sensory box they can keep at their house and explain why your child likes playing with these kinds of toys so much.
- Explain that although there are countless different terms for everything connected with autism nowadays, they don't need to know them all by heart unless they want to, because it's better to focus on *who their grandchild is* rather than a string of letters and complicated phrases. I've included some of the most common terms in the 'Abbreviations' list at the back of the book which they might find useful - another reason they need you to buy them a copy of this book!
- Ask them to focus on what your child *can* do rather than what they can't manage just yet, and explain that what you need from them is calm, consistent support and encouragement rather than worry, because you're doing enough of that for everyone already.

- Remind them autistic children progress in different ways and at different rates than neurotypical children, so it's important they don't compare your child's behaviour to that of any other children of the same age. Helping their other grandchildren or your child's siblings to understand how everyone is unique and different can be very useful and really helps grandparents feel involved.

- Prepare them for the fact that your child could behave very differently when you're not around, and that their behaviour might suddenly become very erratic when you turn up to collect them. Rather than meaning you're a bad parent who spoils their child, it actually means the opposite. If your child has been behaving impeccably all day and suddenly goes into meltdown when you arrive, it's a sure sign you've brought them up to understand what's expected of them when they're visiting their grandparents and they've followed your instructions to the letter even though it's been overwhelmingly hard. Since you're the person they feel most strongly connected to and also safest with, seeing you can trigger an outpouring of all the day's difficulties and frustrations because they trust that you'll be able to handle whatever they throw at you (sometimes literally). I used to feel like my children hated me at times because they would behave so aggressively towards me after a day with their grandparents, but it turned out they saw me as their soft place to fall in the world and they were expressing that in the only way they knew how. It certainly would have saved me some tears if someone had told me that at the time.

- Acknowledge that years ago people were made to feel guilty and ashamed if their child was born different, and explain that today those same differences are often celebrated and encouraged.

- Reassure them that if your child does have a Statement of special educational needs, this isn't necessarily a permanent thing, it's just a helping hand to get them the support they need to progress. Point out that SEN Statements continue up to university level nowadays, so the academic expectations for autistic people today are very high.

- Understand they're acting out of love and if things get a bit heated, remember that ultimately all anger comes from fear. In this case it's the fear that their grandchild will be written off and not given the chance of leading a fulfilling life. People only fight with their families because they feel the relationships are worth fighting for, so do your best to look past the arguments and think about the underlying feelings that might be driving these differences of opinion.

Bridging the gap

My dad was born in 1923, and the way I treated the boys when they were small was completely beyond him. He was certain they lacked discipline and just needed more structure in their lives and we disagreed all the time about how best to deal with them. We never really found much common ground until many years later when a package arrived in the mail, quite out of the blue. It was a copy of The Curious Incident Of The Dog In The Night-Time by Simon Stephens (a book about a boy with all the symptoms of autism) and attached was a Post-it note from my dad saying 'Look at this. Someone's written a book about your boys!' After that he made it his business to find out all about autism and became one of the best sources of support I've ever had. My mother-in-law (the original Ringmaster) went through a similar process and is now my children's greatest advocate, telling people that yes, her grandchildren are autistic and what that means is that they're gifted. I couldn't agree more.

Playing the generation game can be annoying, frustrating and downright crazy-making at times, but never give up. Love is way more powerful than fear, and your family can, and often will, surprise you just when you least expect it.

Doing the Donkey Work

Long ago, a man and his young son entered a large city with their much-loved donkey; the man riding cheerfully on the donkey's back while his son led it along using a rope.

A passer-by stared at them and said loudly "That's outrageous! Look at that lazy man sitting up there like a king while his poor son runs along trying to keep up!" Feeling ashamed of his thoughtlessness, the man dismounted and told his son to ride the donkey instead. They walked a little further, feeling very relaxed, with the man leading his donkey by the rope and his son enjoying a ride on its back.

Later on, another passer-by announced "Look at that young scoundrel, sitting in comfort while his poor father trudges along in the dust. Disgusting!"

The boy felt instantly embarrassed and asked his father to join him on the donkey's back.

They rode along like this for a while, both feeling very proud of themselves until another passer-by cried "Look! That's animal cruelty! The poor donkey is bent almost double carrying those two layabouts."

The man and his son were horrified; they both jumped straight down from the donkey's back and began to lead it through the town together.

Soon they came to a market laden with all manner of goods from far off lands. After a while they realised that a laughing crowd was gathering around them. They became very self-conscious and asked a stall holder what was wrong. With a broad grin, he said "Well, I thought I'd seen some stupid things in my time, but this is ridiculous! What's the point in having a donkey when it doesn't do any of the donkey work?"

After a little thought, the man patted his donkey kindly on the nose and said to his son "Whatever we do, someone disagrees with it. Perhaps it's time we made our own minds up about what we believe is right and did what's best for us!"

"Even for parents
of children
that are not
on the spectrum,

there is no such thing
as a normal child."

Violet Stevens

He's working on his bilateral
coordination today!

Chapter Four

To Diagnose or Not to Diagnose:
That is the Question

'Being diagnosed for any difference, it's not about the label
no-one need know, it's about true identity'

Alyson Bradley

The autism spectrum is as wide and varied as the 'human being spectrum' (and twice as colourful) so for some parents, getting a diagnosis for their child isn't an optional thing, it's just common sense. If your child is unable to function on a day to day basis and needs constant care well beyond their infancy, then of course you're going to look for professional advice about the best ways to support them throughout their life.

In many, many cases though, autistic children are not only able to function, but able to shine in certain areas, even though they might be struggling horribly in others. No rational person has a child and thinks 'Oh, I really hope my child has problems; I'd love to spend my time running between endless doctors', paediatricians' and speech therapists' offices trying to work out how to help them cope at school without smashing their head into a wall when they get home.'

Let's face it then, if you can look at your child and think they're doing okay most of the time, or even *some* of the time, it's perfectly reasonable to want to hang on to the idea that they're *actually* okay for as long as possible before you take the plunge and admit to yourself that they might need some extra help.

Making the decision to have your child assessed for autism is a big and often terrifying thing. If you know someone whose child is obviously on the spectrum yet they refuse point blank to accept it, please don't be too hard on them. As I've said before, as parents we're hardwired to protect and nurture our offspring at all costs, so the idea of exposing them to something so totally unknown - something which will change their life forever and put the whole family into wildly unfamiliar territory - can leave even the strongest of parents paralysed with fear. Being gripped by self-doubt and indecision about what's best for your child is all part of the deal for anyone who becomes a parent, not just autism parents, but when the stakes are this high, living in a state of denial can seem by far the best thing to do. Saying 'she'll be fine, she just needs to try harder to make friends', 'boys always develop later than girls', 'don't worry, she's shy, she'll grow out of it' and 'there's nothing wrong with him, he's just stubborn' are all very common ways a lot of parents avoid the issue of taking their child for an assessment.

The best advice I can give here is this: if you're wondering whether or not to get your child diagnosed, just ask yourself, quite simply 'Is my child suffering?' If you've done everything you can reasonably be expected to do and the answer is 'Yes' then it's time for some decisive action.

You're going to have to be brave and determined and persistent, and I'm not going to lie to you, sometimes it will be very, very hard. Tears will be shed, but if your child *is* autistic and you ignore what's going on, they'll only suffer more in the long run. Ultimately it comes down to this: you love your child and you want what's best for them, but at this point you're not sure exactly what *is* best for them, so where do you go from here?

Taking the first small steps

First of all you need to ask some questions: What kind of support is available for my child if he's diagnosed? How will that actually help her? Will he *always* need support? What's the thinking behind her seeing all these different specialists? The list goes on. Explaining what happens during and after diagnosis could fill several books all by itself, so for now I'll just say this: having an autism diagnosis is a bit like using a booster seat. It's there to provide you with some help, and to start with you're going to use it all the time, but if the time comes when you don't need it any more, or you need a different, smaller version to keep your child safe and happy, you can just adapt it to your needs.

So many people think that having their children diagnosed is like a prison sentence, like they're putting them into some kind of box with a lid on it, whereas the reality is that nowadays it's more like offering them a stepping stone to help them move forward to where they'd like to be in life.

Remember, a large number of children who are diagnosed with autism are later discharged from the special educational needs (SEN) system because (unsurprisingly) giving them that extra bit of specialist help early on actually does work! That doesn't mean they're not autistic any more, just that they no longer need any extra help to cope with the day to day business of living their life.

Autistic children need a very specific kind of support to do well both educationally and in their personal lives, and the sooner they get this, the sooner things will get better for them. Think of it as putting stabilising wheels on their bike: there's a bit of extra support when they need it, which can easily be removed later on once they're ready it go it alone. The truth is that the longer you ignore the issue, the more help they're going to need to catch up, both at home and at school, and the longer it's going to take for them to understand themselves and be happy. Believe me, if they're not made aware of the reasons why they're struggling, they'll soon start to believe it must be because they're not as clever as the other children, and their self-esteem will take a nose dive.

But I don't want my child to be labelled

This is the number one reason parents give me for refusing to have their children assessed for autism, even when their child is obviously suffering as a result. It's easy to judge them but let's be honest here, who would want their child to be identified by *any* label that might make certain people think they were lacking in some way? Surely it's got to be better if they learn to cope and can get through life without people pointing and staring at them because they're different, hasn't it? I understand their thinking on this one; I really, genuinely do.

To any parents going through this process at the moment, my advice would be to take a breath, steady your nerves and accept that your child *is* different, and as much as you might not want it to be the case, the world *will* notice, and it will point and stare and insult them for it anyway, whether they're diagnosed or not. I know that's tough to hear and it's an upsetting thing to think about if you're just getting to grips with the possibility that your child might be on the spectrum, but the bottom line is that parenting can sometimes be a very tough business, and dealing with autism can be even tougher. When you live in a difficult situation you're going to need to face some difficult truths, and it will take time, energy and courage to get to grips with what's happening to your family, so don't expect to be okay with everything all at once, because this stage can be pretty overwhelming. Ultimately though, your role as a parent is to stand up for your child and help them conquer their challenges, so you're going to have to be braver than you've ever been and learn how to fight their corner.

The good news is that there's plenty of help available and lots of information out there too, and a well informed, determined parent with a child who understands

101

themselves and is proud of who they are, can grow into a team far tougher than *anything* the world can throw at them. Trust me, I know.

Is 'autistic' the worst way to be identified?

Educationally, the vast majority of autistic children will struggle because of the complicated way they process information. Without a diagnosis, your child will almost certainly be labelled as some or even all of the following:

- Lazy
- Careless
- Stupid
- Naughty
- Rude
- Disruptive
- Oversensitive
- Aggressive
- Spoilt
- Anti-social
- Humourless
- Belligerent
- Clumsy
- Hopeless

How do I know? Because all these labels (and more) have been attached to my own children before their diagnoses were complete. So were they lazy, careless, stupid etc.? Nope. They were autistic. Once their diagnoses came through, each of them had access to help, understanding, support and compassion at school, college and university that they'd never have received if I'd refused to have them 'labelled' as autistic, and believe me, it was their diagnoses that made *all* the difference to the paths their lives have taken.

Being the odd one out

Another concern I often hear from parents is that if their child is 'labelled' with an autism diagnosis, it will make them a target for bullies. 'No-one wants to be friends with the autistic kid, so why give them a reason to pick on him?' seems like a perfectly reasonable argument, but being autistic is far from the worst way a child can be identified. Take a look at some of the other wonderful 'labels' my children have been given over the years:

- Mental
- Mad
- Eccentric
- Odd
- Geek
- Nerd
- Weirdo
- Spaz
- Downie
- Flid
- Mong
- Freak
- Nutter
- Looney
- Idiot
- Moron
- Retard

Aren't they a delight? If your child is undiagnosed, what are they supposed to say to this kind of cruelty? 'No I'm not', 'Stop being mean' or 'I'm telling on you'? These responses won't have anywhere near as much impact as 'Actually, I'm autistic.' Not only does this informed answer allow your child to walk away with their head held high, it also allows them to make sense of the abuse they're suffering in a rational, logical way, by recognising it for what it is: ignorance. There will always be bullies, in every environment and every walk of life, so learning how to deal with them is a hugely important lesson for every child, not just those on the autism spectrum.

It would be lovely to think that having heard the word, your child's tormentors might take the time to look autism up and realise how hurtful their behaviour has been. I've actually seen this happen on a few occasions as unlikely as it sounds, but in truth most bullies won't really care enough to spend any time educating themselves, because all they're really interested in is picking on someone they consider an easy target. This kind of casual cruelty means far more to your child than it does to those who are dishing it out. Autistic children can be hugely sensitive and will take unpleasant things very much to heart (especially things they can't make sense of) so it's your child's wellbeing and ability to cope with what's happening to them that has to be your focus here.

Knowledge is power

My advice would be to empower your child with the knowledge that they're autistic. Get them diagnosed and focus as much as you can on the *positives* the condition can bring, while working hard to overcome the challenges. You can bet they've already been asking themselves why people are calling them these awful things, and that they're secretly starting to wonder if there's something wrong with them.

To be able to explain to your child that the reason it's happening is because some people just don't understand what autism is yet (rather than just telling them to ignore it or tell their teachers) is incredibly empowering for them because it solves the mystery and makes perfect sense to their logical mind, without making them feel like they're somehow less than their peers. Your child isn't stupid: they know they're being singled out and rejected for some reason, and if you don't tell them the truth about why it's happening, you're leaving them wide open to more abuse, not just at school but at work and even in their social life because try as they might, they're not suddenly going to be able to fit in and be like everybody else, no matter how much you wish they would.

No-one wants to see their child's self-esteem damaged like this, so get in there early and start giving them some tools to build their confidence back up again. Remember, autism isn't a behavioural condition, it's a neurological one, so even if you've seen hundreds of stories about autistic people who struggled to cope as children then went on to become highly successful adults, it's their *behaviour* that's changed, which will be the result of things they've learned over the course of their lifetime, not the fact that they're autistic.

Being autistic never changes, so the idea that if you ignore your child's autism and put them around non-autistic people long enough they'll somehow magically become the same as everyone else is a myth. They might *seem* to be like everyone else on the outside, but on the inside they'll still be autistic.

Putting your child around other people who know nothing about autism is a really important part of helping them to cope in the outside world, so personally I'm all for it. By all means introduce them to as many autistic and neurotypical people as possible, and gradually teach them to behave in a more and more reasonable, respectful way towards their peers, just as all decent parents do, but be careful not to do it at the expense of who they are. Expecting your child to copy everyone else without understanding why, and live their life pretending to be someone they're not just so they can fit in, will lead to all kinds of emotional and psychological problems for them when they're older. Depression, eating disorders, self-harm and even suicide are *way* too common amongst autistic people in today's society. It's no surprise that more often than not these difficulties stem from a person's strongly-held belief that no matter what they do, they're never going to be good enough to fit in.

Recognition & self-discovery

Telling your child they have a diagnosis of autism in a positive, proactive way can help them understand themselves as the unique individual they are and allow them to find their identity within the bright, vibrant and breathtakingly wonderful world of autistic people. They won't suddenly lose their identity or become like anyone else, because they are, at the end of the day, still themselves (which is part of the beauty of being autistic) but they will see similarities in other people on the spectrum and that can be the most enormous relief after spending years and years believing you're the only person in the world who thinks and behaves the way you do.

They'll identify the things they thought of as their own little peculiarities; the things other people may have tried to stop them doing or made them feel ashamed of, and they'll understand the reasons behind them.

They'll see heroes who've achieved greatness against the odds and perhaps they'll be inspired to do great things too. Maybe they'll forge their own path and do something no-one else has even dreamed of yet, or maybe they'll just feel less alone, which is really the most important thing of all in many ways because it gives them permission to be themselves and to flourish in their own unique way, at their own pace, while not feeling like an outcast any more. If your child is autistic and you refuse to have them diagnosed for fear of them being labelled, I can guarantee that the world will identify their differences very quickly, and label them a lot less accurately than a specialist can.

But I believe that 'to label is to limit'

Now, as much as I understand the sentiment behind this phrase, it's not one I agree with in this case or in fact in many cases at all. To put it simply: a label is only limiting if you believe what it's describing is limiting too. Realistically you could describe any word that identifies something in a way most people can understand as a 'label' so the truth is that without 'labels' we'd live in a state of utter confusion. 'Tree' is a label I've never heard anyone describe as 'limiting' and 'Cat' is another, yet as far as I'm aware, neither trees nor cats have any problem with being identified that way, and simply carry on doing whatever it is trees and cats do.

Labels applied to people are different of course because those same people have an understanding of what the label *implies* about them, and this is where their label can become either a positive or a negative thing. Complimentary labels like 'genius' or 'superhero' can inspire and uplift people to achieve more than they'd ever imagined, but as we all know, there are many other kinds of labels, and some of them are nowhere near as encouraging, so I can see where this idea of limiting labels comes from.

Does a label really limit what someone can do?

The short answer to this one is: only if they believe it does.

Take the label of being female for example: Nowadays, women of all ages achieve incredible things. I see them succeed every day in the kind of extreme physical feats, academic breakthroughs and creative triumphs that would've been considered impossible for them not so long ago; impossible, I might add, for no other reason than the fact that they were born as women.

I remember a time when being labelled a woman was most definitely considered a restrictive thing. Women were expected to 'understand their own limitations' (whatever they were supposed to be) not challenge them, and to accept they would never be allowed to do some of the things men did because they simply weren't capable, so there was no point even trying. Women were considered unable to vote, serve on a jury, work while pregnant and even get a credit card by themselves, but were they really incapable of doing these things? Of course not. Those supposed limitations were just ideas that people associated with the word 'woman' at the time and really had very little to do with what women themselves were able to achieve.

These ideas had *everything* to do with what women were *expected* to achieve though, and as a result, society put so many restrictions on them that it was almost impossible for women to do anything other than what was expected of them: a potential self-fulfilling prophecy if ever there was one.

Yet women, who as it turned out weren't actually incapable at all (hey, who knew?) did what women always do: they overcame the restrictions, they persevered through the prejudices and they succeeded. In fact, they *exceeded* every limitation society had placed on them and they fought, each in their own way, a slow and sometimes bitter struggle to change society's ideas about what it meant to be female.

I appreciate that for many women across the globe the struggle is far from over, but things here in the UK have certainly changed a great deal since I was a child. I had a conversation with Isabelle a while ago about why an older female relative had never followed her dream of becoming a dancer. When I explained that during the 1950's the majority of women were brought up to believe they couldn't do anything else but be housewives and mothers, it literally stopped her in her tracks. She took a while to process what I'd said, then a huge grin spread across her face, followed by a fit of uncontrollable giggles. 'But Mum,' she said 'that's just so stupid! How could anyone believe that about themselves? Women can do anything!' I smiled back at her and said 'I know, right?' leaving her to shake her head about just how ridiculous people were in the 'olden days' as she calls them. Being one of the golden oldies from the olden days myself of course, I can completely understand why so many women believed it.

As I look at today's society I can see a lot of autistic people facing a similar struggle when it comes to being labelled. Just as society in general needed to acknowledge what women were capable of, women *themselves* also had to realise that however much negative and discouraging feedback they received from the world in general, they really were every bit as ingenious, creative and incredible as men. Not only that but because they were different, they brought new ideas to the table which, once given a chance, helped to create and shape a better future for everyone.

Different, not less

The ongoing battle for worldwide gender equality isn't a pretty one. Nor has the process been fast or fair or easy, but you know what? It's happening anyway. It's happening because women aren't just going to disappear if they're being treated unfairly or their lives are difficult since the bottom line is that they simply don't have the option to all suddenly transform into men. Women are here, they've always been here and they always *will be* here, and despite society's best efforts to keep them down in the past, they've proven time and time again that being different to men doesn't mean they're worth any less.

By the same token of course, men are also worth every bit as much as women, which is something that can often get overlooked nowadays, I feel. When it comes to this kind of thing there will always be extreme views on both sides, but true equality can never be achieved while either side is trying to dominate the other. Being equal isn't about competing to see who's the best, it's about recognising and celebrating each other's differences and being brave enough to wonder whether combining them might lead us in new and more positive directions.

Autistic people have been fighting a similar struggle for recognition and acceptance for as long as anyone can remember. They may not have been called autistic in the past but, just like women, autistic people have always been there, and in the future they always will be. They're not suddenly going to transform into neurotypical people, which is a good thing of course, because the best way for them to gain the acceptance they deserve is to carry on being themselves and achieve things anyway, whether society expects them to or not. Autism really does bring some incredible gifts with it, but for them to be recognised as such, autistic people need to be diagnosed, otherwise it will always be assumed that it's only neurotypical people who are out there living successful lives.

I would love to think that maybe in years to come my daughter will have a conversation with her own child about when she was a little girl and most autistic people accepted they couldn't do what other people did because that's what society told them, and that her child will giggle uncontrollably at how silly people used to be. Society's attitudes won't be changed overnight, but hopefully they *will* be changed, and I think more than anything they'll be changed by ordinary people witnessing the small, everyday triumphs of those on the spectrum who are busy living happy, productive lives in their own unique ways.

I post uplifting, inspiring stories on my charity's Facebook and Twitter feeds all the time about autistic people exceeding everyone's expectations (even their own) so believe me, these things really are happening out there, and thanks to social media, we can read stories from all over the world about just how astonishing autistic children and adults can be.

Of course, by the same token, we can also read about all the awful, dire predictions some people would have us believe regarding autism. We can focus on the bullying, torture and even murder of vulnerable autistic people and live in fear of the future as so many people do, but this is nothing specifically to do with autism, and more to do with the general wickedness of a small percentage of the human race. Whether your life is touched by autism or not, my advice would always be to decide the future you'd like to create and get busy focussing your energy on that kind of information, and this is the key message of all my charity's work. Enter 'Autism All Stars' on Facebook, Twitter, Instagram and Pinterest to find out more.

But I don't want my child using autism as an excuse

I've been accused many times of making excuses for my children's behaviour, and they've been accused many times of using their autism as an excuse for not picking up new life skills quickly enough. That doesn't make either of these accusations true.

Lots of parents have told me they don't want their child diagnosed because it will give them an excuse to be lazy and to under-achieve, so I think it's important to make something very clear here: no matter who tells you differently, autism is absolutely not an *excuse* for anything; not for difficult or distressing behaviours or for struggling to understand instructions. Why? Because it's the *reason* these things happen and that's a different matter entirely.

While we're on the subject, autism isn't an excuse *or* a reason for being deliberately anti-social, rude or malicious either because there's no need to be that way whether you're on the autism spectrum or not. Autistic people can sometimes come across as rude or anti-social but that's usually quite unintentional and not what I'm referring to here at all.

You'll sometimes see stories about criminals using a diagnosis of autism as an excuse for their negative behaviour, as if having the condition meant they couldn't stop themselves from viciously trolling someone on Twitter or even stalking and murdering them, but these people aren't behaving that way because they're autistic, they're doing it because they've got serious personality disorders that the vast majority of autistic people simply don't have.

On the whole, autistic people are honest, compassionate and often vulnerable people who are far more likely to be the victims of crime than the perpetrators. Being autistic is no guarantee that you'll be a nice person of course and there's no denying that some autistic people are just plain nasty, but please don't make the mistake of thinking that's a direct result of their autism because it isn't.

Having autism means finding it difficult to process information including sights, sounds, fragrances and particularly language (both spoken and body language). It also means taking directions very literally and not necessarily understanding things that aren't *said* but are *implied*. As a result autistic people will inevitably make mistakes and they'll struggle to master things other people think of as obvious, but in my experience they don't use this as an excuse not to learn new skills unless they've been taught to behave that way.

I've heard disruptive children say 'My mum said I can't be quiet because I'm autistic.' Believe me, if they're able to grasp that idea then they're more than capable of learning how to behave appropriately as well. I've also seen lots of parents who, having become frustrated at not being able to teach their young children to button their shirts or brush their teeth independently, have simply given up and are still automatically doing everything for them several years later, without stopping to wonder whether their child might have matured enough by now to give them another go.

The key to teaching your child new skills if they're on the spectrum is to break each one down into the smallest steps you can think of, then tackle each step one at a time until they've learned the right sequence and can complete the whole action successfully. This can be a long, complicated and hugely frustrating process for you both but if you stick with it you're giving your child the best possible chance of making progress at their own pace and in their own way. Having a sense of humour about these things can be very useful here. Teaching your child to see the funny side of the learning process can really help them relax and enjoy it; just make sure they know you're laughing together about what's going on and that you're not laughing at them for making a mistake.

The art of tea making

I've heard it takes around twenty steps to make a cup of tea. This may well be true, but if you're autistic, instructions like 'put the milk in the cup' which obviously *implies* pouring it out of the carton first but doesn't actually *say* it, really aren't going to help much.

If you're practising this particular skill together and you end up with a carton of milk wedged inside your best china mug, your child isn't being deliberately difficult; they've taken what you said literally and done exactly what you asked them to. Make sure you take responsibility for having given them an incomplete instruction rather than saying 'But that was obvious' because clearly to them it's anything but.

For an autistic person, learning life skills is made up of a series of very tiny, logical steps, so assuming you want to make a mug of tea with sugar, have an electric kettle that turns itself off when it's finished boiling, keep canisters of tea bags and sugar sitting on the counter top, keep your spoons in a drawer and your milk in the fridge, this is the sort of sequence you're going to need to teach them:

1. Find kettle
2. Pick up kettle by the handle
3. Carry kettle to sink
4. Open lid
5. Put kettle in correct place underneath tap
6. Turn on tap
7. Fill kettle with correct level of water
8. Turn off tap
9. Close lid
10. Carry kettle back to counter top
11. Place kettle on its base
12. Put kettle's plug in wall socket
13. Turn on plug
14. Flick kettle's switch to 'on'
15. Allow kettle to boil
16. While kettle boils, locate mug cupboard
17. Open cupboard door
18. Choose mug
19. Take mug out of cupboard
20. Close cupboard door
21. Carry mug to counter top
22. Place mug on counter top near kettle
23. Find teabag canister
24. Open canister
25. Remove one tea bag
26. Close canister
27. Replace canister in original position on counter top
28. Place teabag in mug
29. Find spoon drawer

30. Open drawer

31. Find correctly sized spoon

32. Remove spoon from drawer

33. Close drawer

34. Find sugar canister

35. Pick up sugar canister

36. Open sugar canister

37. Dig spoon into sugar granules

38. Lift spoonful of sugar granules out of sugar canister

39. Transfer spoon of sugar to mug

40. Tip spoon forward to allow sugar to fall into mug

41. Close sugar canister

42. Replace canister on counter top

43. Place spoon inside mug without spilling sugar granules

44. Once kettle has boiled, grip handle

45. Lift kettle from base

46. Position kettle above mug

47. Tip forward to pour boiling water into mug

48. Fill mug with correct level of boiling water

49. Tip kettle upright again to stop flow of water

50. Replace kettle on base

51. Pick up spoon

52. Stir tea until sugar is dissolved and flavour is released

53. Find fridge

54. Grip handle of mug

55. Carry mug to fridge

56. Place mug on countertop near fridge

57. Find handle of fridge door

58. Open fridge using handle

59. Locate milk

60. Pick up milk

61. Remove milk from fridge

62. Close fridge door

63. Place milk on counter top

64. Open milk carton

65. Pick milk carton up

66. Position milk carton over mug

67. Tip milk carton forward to pour milk into mug

68. Tip milk carton upright again to stop flow of milk

69. Close milk carton

70. Open fridge door

71. Replace milk carton in fridge

72. Close fridge door

73. Stir tea

74. Remove tea bag from mug

75. Remove spoon from mug

76. Place spoon in washing up bowl

Be honest, did you manage to read every one of those instructions before your mind started to drift a bit and you skipped to the end of the list? Probably not. That's fine when you're reading them here, but when you're following them in real life, missing one can lead to all kinds of chaos.

You might be thinking 'Isn't it *obvious* you need to position the kettle under the tap to fill it, or close the fridge door when you've put the milk away?' The simple answer to that is 'No; not if you're on the spectrum.' Often the things that are immediately obvious to you but not to them will be the things that are *implied* rather than being said directly, and autistic people simply don't get the concept of something that's implied without having it explained first.

They have to consciously break everything down into these tiny logical steps and they don't automatically understand why the sequence works the way it does because again, it's *implied* that for instance you have to boil the water before it will draw the tea from the teabag, so they'll take your instructions literally and if you miss a step out, so will they. They're not being naughty or difficult and it most definitely doesn't mean they're stupid; they're just following your instructions to the letter. It can take a while to memorise all the steps, but give them a bit of extra time and once the sequence is anchored in, they've got it for good.

Eating an elephant

So what's the best way to help your child learn when the world is such a confusing place for them? Well, my advice would be to use this expression as your guide: How do you eat an elephant? One bite at a time.

In other words, the number of skills you can potentially teach your child is enormous and overwhelming, so if you're working on a new life skill together, forget about teaching them anything else for a while and focus on just that one thing until they've mastered it completely.

As you can see from the tea making instructions, what might appear to be one simple action is really a string of various different directions followed in the right order, so make sure they've got the mental energy to process all this new information by giving them plenty of down time. Don't worry if you have to let other things slide a bit, there'll be time to reintroduce the usual rules when they've got the hang of things.

Working out which parts of the process might be a bit flexible (i.e. if you forget to put the sugar in before the milk you can always put it in afterwards) is something autistic people can really struggle with, so at first all these steps will be competing for your child's attention at once; all appearing to be the most important and all demanding to be followed in exactly the right way. To an autistic mind, something is either right or it's wrong, and if it's wrong then literally *anything* could happen. They won't have much perspective about their new skill to start with, so if every last detail of the process doesn't go exactly to plan it can make them feel completely out of control. If this happens they might become agitated and refuse to carry on, and it's important to realise that they're not just overreacting or being dramatic; they're genuinely distressed and afraid of what could happen if they've made even the tiniest mistake.

Something else to be aware of is how difficult it can be for an autistic person to switch from one part of the sequence to another. If you interrupt their thought process before it's finished, believe me it can cause mayhem. Give them plenty of warning that you're moving on to the next step and if you can, put together a series of pictures to help them see where one stage ends and another begins. Autistic people often process images much more easily than spoken instructions so something as simple as a small visual timetable can make all the difference in the early stages.

They'll also need time to process not only each step individually but the pauses between each step as well (think of it as swallowing one mouthful of the elephant and stopping to catch their breath a bit before taking another bite), so you're going to need to be *really* patient here.

Give them lots of positive reinforcement when they master something new, but keep your reactions nice and calm because too much strong emotion of any sort, positive or negative, can overwhelm and upset them while their brain is busy learning new skills. Give them time to digest every new idea, and let them go at their own pace to start with, but remember to push them a little bit too because as a parent, being patient is never the same thing as being passive.

Pushy parenting

We've all heard of pushy parents who force their children to achieve outstanding academic, musical, theatrical or sporting results without stopping to wonder whether their child is actually enjoying the process or benefitting from it in any way. They're the ones busy waiting to turn *any* conversation into one about how 'Jemima just passed her Grade Eight piano exams at seven' or 'Tarquin has been accepted into Cambridge at eleven' while their child hangs back, awkwardly shuffling their feet and looking at the floor in embarrassment.

Let's be honest, no-one likes a pushy parent, but when you're an autism parent, if you're going to do the best for your child then you're going to have to be prepared to push a little.

There'll be lots of pushing involved in bringing up an autistic child: pushing yourself past the point of exhaustion to make it through the sleepless nights, pushing to get them a decent education plan, pushing for acceptance from people who reject them, but those aren't the types of pushing I'm talking about here. If you're not happy for your child's autism to be the reason they don't fulfil their potential, you're going to have to push them - gently, kindly and consistently - outside their comfort zone every now and then, and the truth is that it won't be easy for either of you.

It's absolutely vital to remember that as autism parents we're not pushing our children to over-achieve just to impress other people, we're pushing our children to achieve things the majority of parents quite rightly take for granted because we want to give them the chance of living a happy, fulfilled life to the very best of their abilities.

Now, I know there are people who think there's no such thing as autism because I've met them. They believe autism parents are pushy attention seekers who want everyone to treat their children as 'special little snowflakes' and give them preferential treatment for no other reason than because they're badly behaved. Make no mistake, parents like that *do* exist – again, I know because I've met them – but they're very, *very* much in the minority and are really nothing to do with genuine autism parents, most of whom would give anything for their children *not* to need any extra attention.

When my children were small I had a fearsome reputation for refusing to accept anything less than I felt they deserved, to the point where teachers would often look quite terrified when they saw me coming. Most of them had given up on my boys and thought I was living in complete denial about how much they could achieve. At best they'd tolerate my insistence that the boys be given the chance to make progress, usually with much tutting, whispering and rolling of eyes, and as hard as it was to feel so rejected by them, I persevered against the odds. I've lost count of the number of times teachers have told me the boys couldn't do something because 'We don't want to set him up to fail.' My reply was always the same: 'Have you ever thought you might be setting him up to *succeed*?' Goodness only knows what they thought I was aiming for, but the truth is that I had the same five ambitions for all *four* of my children, believing what mattered wasn't where they started but where they might finish.

Unsurprisingly, none of these ambitions involved inventing inter-planetary space travel or finding the cure for cancer; they were purely things I felt they were all capable of achieving and to this day I stand by my belief that anything else they've achieved since has been a bonus. I don't know your child personally which means I can't have any idea what they're capable of, so please don't feel I'm implying you should have the same list as I did. These are just the five things I felt would give *my* children the best chance in life and I'm proud to say that after a great deal of hard work they've all managed to achieve every one:

1. Learn to speak
2. Learn to use a toilet
3. Learn to eat with a knife and fork
4. Learn to read and write
5. Be happy

To some of you this might seem like a very basic list of goals, while to others it might seem like an impossible one. Only you can decide what's right for your child and how much progress they might make, but it's definitely worth having some sort of idea in mind to help you chart their journey.

Your secret weapon in the fight for change

By its very nature, your child's autistic brain wiring will make it seem as if they don't actually *want* to learn new things a lot of the time. This isn't true of course, but what *is* true is that they'll have a deep, almost obsessive interest in some very specific things to the exclusion of pretty much everything else, and this can make learning new skills incredibly hard.

Dinosaurs, space, LEGO and trains are all very common fascinations for autistic children and they'll be quite happy to repeat the same behaviours over and over again as long as they involve whatever their specific interest is at the time. If you want them to progress, you'll have to entice them out of these rigid routines or they'll get stuck.

Now, when my boys were young I was told the best way to do this was to take their special interests away, because apparently this would 'make them' become interested in something else. It was the 'he's got to learn' mentality and just so you know, *this doesn't work with autistic children* so save yourself (and your child) a lot of heartache and use a different approach. Since Christopher's LEGO and Dominic's trains were the only things that gave them any peace of mind I thought it sounded downright cruel to take them away and flatly refused to do it, much to the disgust of my family and all the specialists. Instead I used their interests to build a relationship with them and help them learn, and thankfully this is the very advice given to new autism parents today.

So as I said, in the ongoing battle to widen your child's life experiences you're sometimes going to have to push them outside their comfort zone, and yes it's going to seem like you're in the middle of a war at times, but their special interests can act as a ready-made secret weapon to make the struggle a whole lot easier. You're going to have to be inventive here but with a bit of creative thinking you'll soon find ways to incorporate them into the learning process. If you can get to the point where your child's love for their special interest is stronger than their fear of completing the new task, their motivation will change and you'll start to get things done.

For example if your child is obsessed with trains but can't cope with noisy, crowded environments, start by showing them footage of steam railways and build up to taking them for a day out on a steam train. Once you've mastered that you can repeat the process using more modern trains and with luck you'll eventually reach the point where they can tolerate catching a train in the middle of rush hour. To your child this might seem like having fun, which it is, but it's also a great way to teach them new life skills. It won't all be plain sailing of course – there'll be plenty of setbacks, I'm sure – but doing things this way, with your child's special interest at the centre of it all, will definitely make the learning process a whole lot easier.

If the worst happens and something causes them to go into meltdown, their brains and bodies will be experiencing all the intense emotions associated with anxiety, panic and sheer terror and although it might seem as if it's all over nothing to you, to them these fears are very real. Their fight or flight instincts will be raging through their systems at an unbearable level, and whether the trigger of their anxiety is something other people think of as completely harmless or whether they're in real, immediate physical danger, the feelings they're experiencing will be just as intense.

Telling them 'It's okay, there's nothing to worry about' is the natural thing to do but in this case it's not going to help you much. Often it will actually make things worse, because if they're looking to you for reassurance and expecting you to sort the situation out, it can be very scary for them to hear that you don't think there's a problem. They'll feel like they're on their own and have to sort things out themselves which of course they don't know how to yet, so it's highly likely they'll start to panic and things will become even worse.

If you can, reassure your child that no matter what's upset them, you'll handle it together, and always, always validate their feelings. Acknowledge that they're upset even if you don't understand why. Do your absolute best to stay as calm as possible otherwise your reactions will convince them something really *is* wrong, because they won't realise your stress is being caused by their behaviour.

Where was this book when I needed it?

When Dominic was three I decided to take a huge leap of faith and encourage him to mix with other children outside the family. The aim was to get him ready for school when he was old enough and after a lot of searching I managed to find a small, friendly nursery run by a lady whose son had autism. I signed him up there a few days a week and needless to say, things didn't go well. They didn't go well *at all*.

Every morning I'd physically fight for up to an hour to get him dressed while he did his very best to remove every item of clothing as quickly as I'd put it on. This happened with all his clothes except his padded dinosaur costume, so he eventually wore it non-stop for a year because at the time, how he dressed was the least of my concerns.

I'd carry him kicking, screaming, biting and clawing from the car to the nursery door, stuck under one arm to protect my face, and by the time we got inside he'd be completely hysterical. The staff eventually had to clear an entire room and cover it in padding so they could sit there in a safe environment with him while he had his huge daily meltdown. They were amazing and promised me that shortly after I left he'd calm down and come with them to start his day, but I'd go home every morning feeling physically sick with stress and guilt that I'd left him there against his will.

Every day I'd phone to see if he'd settled down and the answer was always the same: he'd carried on screaming, head-butting the walls and throwing his bottle of milk across the room for about half an hour, then he'd quietened down and carried on as if nothing had happened. This went on for three whole *months* and it was one of the toughest things I've ever done, but I knew he was safe there and apart from this terribly upsetting transition period in the mornings he was coping with things in his own way, so I persevered. I also knew that if I stopped sending him now, I wouldn't have a *chance* of getting him into school, so I gritted my teeth, hoped for the best and carried on. More than once I was accused of being cruel and heartless by my family but my reasoning on this one was very clear: I was playing the long game *for* him this time because he wasn't able to do it himself just yet.

Then, quite suddenly, something changed.

One morning I got him ready as usual and braced myself for another round of utter chaos as I moved him from the car to the nursery door but instead of going rigid, screaming and attacking me, he jumped calmly out of his car seat and walked inside. Resisting the temptation to phone the local church and report a miracle, I spoke to the nursery staff and asked what on earth had happened that might have caused such a dramatic change in him. Dominic had started nursery in the winter, and it turned out the weather had brightened enough the previous day for them to take him to the park for the first time. Apparently he'd loved it.

I'd known all along he had no idea why I was taking him to nursery, but I hadn't realised that until this particular day he'd thought it was some kind of punishment. Now he understood he was there to have fun, he relaxed and although we still had some difficult mornings, the padded room was never needed again.

Naturally I was wracked with guilt once again over my appalling failures as a parent: Why hadn't I realised how he felt? What could I have done to make him understand sooner? The truth is, back then there was nothing I could have done. I had no way of communicating with him and I knew next to nothing about autism; I was completely out of my depth and had simply done what I felt in my heart was right for him, with as much kindness, patience and love as possible.

Nowadays I'd make full use of his special interests and would use weighted blankets, sensory fidgets, visual timetables and a whole host of other ideas to help him manage the transition from home to nursery, but back then I had no idea they even existed and I was faced with a very stark choice: somehow get him into the education system in time to start primary school at five or leave him to his own devices and face almost certain failure when the time came. With hindsight this whole process was a huge turning point for him, so in fact what I did was definitely for the best, but at the time that didn't stop me feeling like a monster.

But what about 'functioning' labels?

If you're new to the world of autism, you may not have heard of functioning labels, but if you're not, I'll guarantee you've come across them somewhere along the line. It's perfectly natural for humans to want to categorise things – as I've said before, life would be chaos without some structure – so because autism is a *spectrum* condition, it tends to be imagined as a straight line, with 'high functioning' people at one end, 'low functioning' people at the other, and everyone else sitting somewhere in between.

'High functioning' people are thought of as those who can speak, live independently, get regular employment, have relationships and contribute something specific to society. 'Low functioning' people on the other hand are seen as those who can't or won't speak, can't look after themselves, can't form relationships with other people or hold down a job and are sadly often thought of as a general drain on society's resources. So, let's be honest here: reading that, no-one's going to want their child diagnosed as 'low functioning', are they?

Just for the record, when he was young Dominic was diagnosed as 'the most profoundly autistic child I've ever seen' by various different specialists. I was advised that he was, and always would be, extremely low functioning: that he'd never speak, never feed or dress himself, never attend school and never interact with other people. I was told he'd never live independently and that it would be best to make plans to put him into full time care.

But never is a long time, isn't it? And fortunately, neither Dominic nor I believed a word of it.

He's twenty-one now and has lived away from home for the last three years. During that time he's only set fire to the microwave once, which isn't the worst thing a newly independent young man has ever done to a kitchen appliance in my opinion. He's just left Cardiff University with an LLB degree in Law and Politics, has a lovely circle of friends and is engaged to a beautiful young woman who genuinely adores him, which is more than can be said for many neurotypical men of twenty-one, let alone 'low functioning' autistic ones like him.

That being said, I can completely understand why the specialists diagnosed him that way at the time, so I'm not saying the diagnosis was wrong, just that it was open to the possibility of change, however unlikely it seemed. He really did show every one of the Triad of Impairments at such a profound level that they couldn't really have concluded anything else. They knew a lot more than I did about autism, there's no denying that, but what they didn't know about was Dominic. That was where I came in.

No-one will ever know the amount of sheer hard work we've done together over the years to get Dominic from where he was to where he is today, and he'll continue to work at making sense of the world in his own unique way for the rest of his life, but he's never let his difficulties stop him from pushing forward and achieving great things, and knowing him as I do, I can safely say he never will. Interestingly, only a few years ago someone accused me of making up the fact that Dominic had autism, because I was supposedly looking for attention. There was a time it would have been so unthinkable for anyone to suggest something like this that I couldn't help but let out a snigger. Laughing in her face didn't go down too well as you can imagine, but honestly, I wasn't sure whether to be insulted or delighted by her rudeness.

The spectrum at war

Something that always makes me unhappy is how divided and resentful the autism community can be when it comes to functioning labels. I've seen people with 'high functioning' children who are horrified at the very idea of their child being associated with 'those poor low-functioning children' as if they're a completely different species. I've also seen parents of 'low functioning' children become consumed by the most appalling venom and hatred towards people whose children are more able to cope, believing that 'they don't understand what suffering is all about because they'll never know what *real* autism is'. These same people cry out for society to accept their children's differences, when in reality they have no intention of even accepting each other's.

How can it be any other way though, if the autism spectrum is being neatly laid out in front of them as a straight line with two opposing ends? Division is bound to happen, along with feelings of competitiveness between parents about where each of their 'high functioning' children is said to be sitting on that imaginary line, and feelings of despair and hopelessness from those who feel their children have been written off as 'low functioning' and will never achieve anything worthwhile as a result.

The ironic thing here is that the autism spectrum couldn't be any *less* like a straight line if it tried. I've given this a lot of thought and the most accurate way I can describe it is as a brightly coloured, ever-changing kaleidoscope. Although every kaleidoscope works using the same basic mechanism, each one produces an endless variety of different shapes, patterns and colour combinations which is what makes them all so unique and fascinating. In the same way, while people on the autism spectrum might show similar behaviour traits because they have a similarity in brain wiring, each individual autistic person will develop their own unique personality, perspectives and ideas. Autistic people don't experience life in a straight line any more than neurotypical people do; their sensitivity grows and shifts, expands and contracts depending on the tiniest of details and the smallest of changes.

Autism affects every part of who a person is: their mind, their body and their spirit, so being autistic is just that: a way of *being*. In the same way that being human isn't an experience that ever stays the same, neither does being autistic. Human thoughts, feelings and emotions move, flow and change from moment to moment and although they process them differently, autistic people still feel the same things all humans do, so always, always assume they have the potential to make progress, even if it seems impossible from one moment to the next.

HD Humans

So as it turns out being autistic is, funnily enough, a lot like being human, only it's more like being human in high definition. Over the years I've heard autistic people describe themselves as everything from aliens to mutants as they struggle to identify with a world that's often too bright, too loud and too overwhelming for them to process. I think I'll coin a new, more inclusive phrase right here though: High Definition humans. Living in HD isn't always easy and that's an understatement, but at the same time there's no way you'd want to miss out on the sheer awe-inspiring beauty of it all. Experiencing life at this level of intensity can be painful, there's no getting away from that, but it can be exhilarating and ground-breaking too.

Think of it this way: imagine someone dragging their nails across a chalk board while you're listening to your favourite song. It's not that you can't listen to the song anymore, so you're not incapable of listening to it, it's just a lot harder if the environment is overwhelming you and your senses are competing with too much information from another source. If they suddenly stop making such an awful racket, it becomes much easier to enjoy the music again. Being autistic and having difficulty processing your environment can be very much like this, only when the noise stops, you can experience the music at far more intense level to most people. As a result, autistic people who can cope really well with, and even excel at, a particular task in one environment can find themselves totally overwhelmed by that same task in another, so does that make them high functioning or low functioning? Does it mean they're *unable* to learn or do they simply find it *difficult* to learn in certain situations? The answer depends on so many different factors in so many different environments that it's impossible to say without over-simplifying everything, but when it comes to education it's inevitable this kind of categorisation will happen.

Structuring a diagnosis

When it comes to diagnosis there has to be some kind of structure otherwise nothing would get done at all, so it's understandable that the idea of being able to place an autistic person in an exact position between two fixed points is a popular one, and in some cases it's invaluable: if they're perceived as being in a specific place, they can be given a specific level of help and expected to do specific things. Once that place has been established, it's easier to measure how much progress they're making and whether they still need the same amount of help as they did to begin with.

There's nothing wrong with the thinking behind this, which is to provide some kind of framework to support autistic people and help them navigate life's challenges. The reality of how being autistic affects each individual is something that can never be completely structured or regulated though, any more than you can predict the pattern a kaleidoscope will make the next time you shake it, but since it would be impossible to help people without classifying at least part of what they're dealing with, this is the system that's currently in place.

The important thing to remember here is that although this kind of classification is very helpful within the education system, it can't sum up who your child is or what they're capable of, any more than a neurotypical child's exam results can show whether they're a kind, generous or inspirational person, or a child's chronological age can accurately predict how mature they'll be from one year to the next.

All children, whether they're autistic or not, have to go through the education system in some form or another. The main focus of any childhood diagnosis is to get them the support they need educationally and give them the best chance of achieving what they want to in life. The diagnostic process isn't perfect as anyone who's been through it will tell you, but having some idea of where the health professionals think your child is currently placed on the spectrum is a starting point to help both you and your child's support team work out the best plan of action. They can only diagnose your child based on what they see of course, and sometimes the same child who's a whirlwind of uncontrollable activity at home will sit beautifully still at their assessment and complete the specialist's tasks without a murmur, while others who behave passively in their own environment suddenly transform into spitting, snarling monsters intent on destroying the entire consulting room. I've experienced both scenarios and it's equally frustrating either way.

The autism spectrum is full of vibrant individuals, all experiencing the world in their own unique way which is what makes it so fascinating, but expecting health professionals to make any kind of useful diagnosis based on each person's ever-shifting kaleidoscope of symptoms is naïve to say the least.

That doesn't mean *you* can't approach it that way though, and that's where the pushy parenting comes in. Teachers and care givers have an enormous effect on children, there's no denying that, but at the end of the day, as a parent *you* are the most important influence on your growing child, and you *can* treat your child as the amazing individual they are. Parenting really is the most important job in the world, and whether you passively accept your child will never make progress just because their 'label' suggests it, or you gently push the boundaries with them and find out just how much they can *really* achieve, will make all the difference to how they mature.

Progress and achievement can only happen when you work consistently at something and when it comes to autistic people, the amount of work involved in learning new skills can vary hugely from one subject to another. It can take them years to learn to tie a shoelace, but seconds to solve a complex mathematical problem other people find impossible. The term 'low functioning' seems to imply they're hardly functioning at all, which isn't true; they're just functioning in different ways to neurotypical people. Functioning labels can be misleading then, because they're referring to *how someone can function in society*, not as a human being, but they're a necessary part of getting your child the help and support they need. My advice is to accept them for what they are and never, ever let them stop you believing in your child's own unique potential.

It's vitally important to remember that achieving their potential is about so much more than gaining academic or financial success. There are countless ways to live a fulfilling life, and endless possibilities to be explored and enjoyed along the way, so above all else, always encourage your child to be happy and fulfilled in their own exceptional way.

But everyone in my family does the things my child does

Now this statement I can definitely believe! I've covered this in more depth in the 'Playing the Generation Game' chapter, but let's just say that if 'everyone in your family' behaves in the same quirky ways as your child, it's a pretty strong indication that he or she is indeed on the autism spectrum.

A Day at the Circus

July 2000

- 7am: Preparing children for school run and notice Child 3 (age 14 months) is missing.
- Ask Child 1 (age 8) where his brother was last seen. Child 1 informs me that 'he's playing with the cat.' We do not own a cat.
- Child 1 elaborates: 'The cat outside by the cars...'
- Panic blindly as realisation strikes that somehow back gate has been left open and Child 3 has escaped onto main road.
- Spend next twenty minutes racing up and down street in bedroom slippers with Children 1 and 2 (age 4) in tow, desperately trying to locate Child 3.
- Child 3 is discovered 150 yards away crouched in a neighbour's front garden. He is still 'playing with the cat' which is doing its best to escape his unwanted attention.
- Return all three children to safety of house while neighbours look on in horror.
- Continue with school run. #JustAnotherEscapeAttempt
- 3pm: Collect Child 1 from school to find him in a state of high anxiety, demanding to know where we can buy a live lamb.
- Child 1 has learned about the Passover, and informs me that by tonight we must slaughter the unfortunate lamb, smearing its blood on our front doorpost to save him being killed by the spirit of the Lord.
- Reassure Child 1 this won't be necessary since, unlike the Egyptians, we haven't actually enslaved any Israelites. He remains unconvinced and argues for the lamb's slaughter, stating 'It's alright for you; you're not the first born son, I am!'
- 8pm: Locate lamb chop in fridge. Carefully mark doorpost with its blood to avoid total meltdown from Child 1. Hope against hope no neighbours are watching this time. Happy to report that our lamb chop sacrifice was clearly accepted, as Child 1 survived the night intact. #WeAreTheNeighboursFromHell

'What we see...

...depends mainly on what we look for.'

Chapter Five

Grieving What Isn't Lost

'Letting go sounded like such an easy thing to do...
but actually involved a lot of pain.'

Kathy Shuker

Over the years I've met many families living with autism and helped them deal with all kinds of challenges from eating disorders to potty training, sleep disturbances to suicide and pretty much everything else in-between, but something no-one has ever come to see me about (at least not at first) are the feelings of bereavement they're experiencing since discovering their child has autism. You might be wondering why, and the simple answer is this: Guilt.
It's really not all that surprising when you think about it. Who on earth wants to admit to anyone, least of all themselves, that they wish their child wasn't made the way they are? Is anyone going to feel good about secretly wishing their child would just *stop* being autistic for a change, because it's making life so incredibly hard for everyone? Feeling frustrated with your child, feeling anger towards them and even feeling that you don't actually *like* them at times can quickly convince you that you're a terrible parent, so it's no surprise that most people don't want to discuss these uncomfortable reactions to begin with.
When they do eventually start to talk about them, they'll look totally guilt-ridden and quietly ask me: *'Does this mean I don't love my own child?'* They're clearly horrified at the very idea of such a thing, and horrified with themselves for asking the question in the first place, because let's face it; as parents, we're not 'supposed' to feel like that, are we?
All first-time expectant parents watch the 'new baby' adverts and imagine how lovely it will be when their own child arrives: the smiles, the cuddles, the moments of overpowering joy. In reality of course, although these things certainly can happen, they tend to be somewhat overshadowed by the sheer grinding exhaustion of it all. Having a baby can make anyone feel frazzled, tearful, resentful and overwhelmed, and while most new parents are certain they're the only ones who've ever felt these things, the truth is that *every* parent feels them from time to time. Since autism parenting is so much more intense, you're bound to feel like

this more often, especially if you have no idea why your child is behaving this way. In good news, feeling like this has nothing to do with not loving your child. In fact, it's a pretty good indication of the exact opposite! It actually shows that you *do* love your child and that you're deeply concerned about the way autism is affecting their life. Bad parents don't worry about that kind of thing, and trust me they certainly don't spend time beating themselves up over how they feel towards their own children.

What is bereavement?

We're all aware there are some pretty appalling things happening in the world every day, and one of the worst is, without doubt, the utter devastation caused to any loving parent by the death of their child.

As I mentioned in Chapter One, the desire to produce, nurture and protect children of our own is potent, instinctive, biological stuff. We're dropped into a pool of emotions so deep that we could never have predicted how we'd feel before we actually became parents ourselves. To have the focus of these overwhelming feelings of love, care and attention ripped away, leaving you with nothing but an achingly empty space where your child once belonged is unbearably painful to imagine, let alone experience. Personally, I'm thankful every single day that all I can do is imagine the horror of this situation, and can honestly say that any parents who've suffered this kind of loss and somehow carried on despite being utterly broken are, from my point of view, absolute heroes.

Having an autistic child is nothing like this horrendous experience of course, so where do these feelings of bereavement in autism parents come from? Our children aren't dead or missing, so what is there to grieve? They're still here with us, and they're very much alive, so is it possible to grieve for something that isn't lost, and more importantly should we feel guilty for doing so? If we grieve, does it mean we're disappointed in our children or we don't like them? I think the best way to understand what's going on here is to first get a clear idea of what bereavement is, and how the grieving process actually works.

The cancellation of expectations

Bereavement is a powerful, natural process we all go through when we lose something we think is valuable, and there's no getting away from the fact that it hurts. A lot. As hard as it is to go through, the process is designed this way so that we'll slow down and reassess what the future holds without this valuable 'something' being part of it; dealing with the loss at our own pace and somehow managing to survive it without being destroyed by it ourselves.

I'm using the term 'something' here because grieving doesn't just happen when you lose a person, it can happen when you lose an object, an opportunity or an idea too. In very simple terms, the grieving process is triggered when something important that you expect to happen doesn't happen after all. Some forms of grief will naturally be a lot more painful than others, but in essence the process is the same: *bereavement is caused by the cancellation of expectations*.

There's no right or wrong way to grieve and no-one can tell you how to do it or how long it should take; it's a deeply personal experience that everyone handles in their own way. What I can describe to you though, are the various different aspects of the grieving process: some of the general steps along the winding road to recovery that have their roots in the same basic emotional responses.

The five stages of grief are loosely categorised as follows:

Stage 1: Shock/Denial/Searching

Stage 2: Anger/Guilt/Regret

Stage 3: Bargaining

Stage 4: Depression

Stage 5: Acceptance

This doesn't mean that when you grieve you can neatly classify how you're feeling on a particular day then work out how far you've travelled through the process; not at all. You'll often find yourself bouncing from one feeling to another, or being overwhelmed as several of them hit you at once, and that's all perfectly normal, even though it feels anything but normal at the time.

So what's the difference between grieving for the loss of a child and grieving because your child has autism? Well, there are certainly differences but there are also many similarities too.

Coping with the death of a child

During the shock/denial/searching stage of grief you may well have some or all of the following thoughts:

- I don't believe this has happened.
- I *refuse* to believe it
- This *cannot* have happened

- I can't handle this!
- If I ignore it, it won't be real
- There must have been a mistake
- If I don't eat or drink/don't talk about it, it won't have happened
- I'm going to *prove* this hasn't happened

Remember that logic has nothing to do with this process. This train of thought is all about self-preservation as your mind struggles to protect you from the pain it fears is about to destroy you if you accept the situation as being your new reality.

During the anger/guilt/regret stage you might start thinking this way:

- Why me? This isn't fair!
- I don't deserve this
- This must be somebody's fault (even if it isn't)
- What about people who abuse their children?
- I hate them! (this is your anger response being directed outwards)
- What did I do wrong? Could I have prevented this? Am I being punished? Do I somehow deserve this? I must be a terrible person (this is your anger response being directed inwards)
- If only…

Logically you already know none of this is going to help, but again, logic has nothing to do with grieving. This is all about your mind protecting you, and at this stage it feels safer experiencing these kinds of emotions than the ones it's trying so hard to help you avoid.

During the bargaining stage things make even less logical sense, and you may find you're:

- Telling yourself that if you run a thousand miles for charity or plant a hundred trees, it might somehow bring your child back
- Acting out imaginary scenarios where your child is still alive, to 'convince' yourself and the world that they're still here
- If you're religious, pleading with your God to take your life instead of your child's

Your mind is practising avoidance at all costs by now, and you might begin to wonder if you're losing your grip on reality. Don't worry, you're not; it's just another part of the process. Your mind is still convinced the pain will completely destroy you if it allows you to feel it, so it does whatever it can think of to delay things, whether its methods make any rational sense or not.

Next comes possibly the hardest stage of all: depression. It's worth remembering that not all depressed people look or behave in a conventionally depressed way, so you may experience some or even all of these symptoms:

- Being hyperactive and unable to sleep
- Burying yourself in work or hobbies
- Trying to make yourself feel better using alcohol, drugs, parties or sex
- Exhaustion and listlessness
- Chronic insomnia despite feeling constantly tired
- Memory loss and mental fogginess
- Tearfulness, emotional outbursts and asking 'What's the point?'
- Suicidal thoughts

There's no denying this is a horrible experience for anyone to go through, yet within it are the first seeds of hope for a brighter future. Once your mind has run out of ways to avoid feeling the pain, it will finally give in and allow you to experience it, so although you're not ready to accept it yet, you are at least starting to acknowledge it's there, and trust me, that's a big step in the right direction.

The final stage, one of acceptance, doesn't happen after a set period of time, nor does it happen all at once. It's a very gradual progression, gently reminding you bit by bit that life goes on even if it will never be the same again. How you reach this stage is entirely personal, but you'll probably experience some or all of the following:

- Realising that sometimes things happen that you simply can't control
- Knowing you don't have to understand the reason *why* something happened in order to accept it
- Having less intense and less frequent feelings of sadness
- Recognising that with every birthday, Christmas and missed milestone you experience the process will be repeated, and although it will be tough, these times can make you feel poignant rather than devastated
- Beginning to look for any positives that might come out of this loss: perhaps it's made you less afraid and you'll branch out in new directions or maybe you'll share your story to support others

However and whenever you get to this stage, just remember that you'll never get *over* this tragedy, only *through* it, and most importantly remember this: *how long you grieve has nothing to do with how much you care.* You will always care – *always* – and whether you become stuck in a constant cycle of grief or manage to pull yourself through it and move forward with your life is something only you can decide.

Grieving when your child has autism

Okay, having written that sub-heading I can almost hear the outraged cries from certain groups of people: 'Autism is a gift! Being an autism parent is a blessing! Autistic children are amazing! How *dare* she suggest there's anything to grieve for if your child has autism?' Firstly let me reassure you that I'm 100% in agreement with you on the gift/blessing/amazing stuff, otherwise I'd have gone under years ago, but let me also assure you that I absolutely *do* dare to suggest there are things to grieve for when you're living through this experience.
Anyone who's *too* offended by this idea and is thinking of starting an argument with me over it at some point is welcome to re-read the 'Warning – May Cause Offence' section at the start of the book and follow the helpful advice I've given there.

WAITS

To those brave souls who are still reading, I say this: Never, *ever* let anyone shame you into pretending to feel something that you don't, or pretending *not* to feel something that you do. Seriously. All emotions, whether they're considered positive, negative or somewhere in-between, are there for a reason: to act as a personal guidance system and send you an alert to let you know, loud and clear, whether something is or isn't working for you.
Your mind's number one priority is to move you away from pain (physical, emotional, psychological or spiritual) and towards pleasure, by making the good things feel good and the bad things feel bad (all fairly straightforward stuff as you can see) so if it's telling you something's hurting, the worst thing you can do is pretend not to hear it.

Listening to yourself

The healthy response to feeling sad, angry, frustrated, jealous or afraid is to take a moment and work out why you're feeling that way, then take positive steps to sort it out. Now I'm certain I can hear all the autism parents laughing out loud and saying 'Oh, sure, during my child's meltdown I've got all the time in the world to do a bit of psychoanalysis on myself. I don't even get to pee alone anymore!' Believe me, I get it, I really do, but if I hadn't discovered how to do just that, the job of raising four children on the spectrum, largely single-handed, would have defeated me. No question about it. So how *did* I manage it? I'll explain later on in the book, and give you the tools to do the same thing, I promise.

Meanwhile, back to the inner workings of your mind. It's important to remember that your mind is always on your side, even if it doesn't feel that way to you sometimes, and that it has no idea that you're just too ridiculously busy to pay attention to it at any given moment. Obviously you can't drop everything and instantly sort through your feelings, find an answer and resolve it, but if you ignore it long enough and don't find the time to do it later, it assumes you haven't heard its repeated signals and does the only thing it can think of: it turns up the volume. A great piece of advice I absolutely swear by when times are tough is this: *Always listen when your mind whispers; don't wait for it to shout*. Because I can promise you one thing: shout it will, and loudly. Symptoms that your mind is 'shouting' include insomnia, changes in appetite, frequent bouts of physical illness, anxiety, depression and all manner of other delights.

PTSD or OTSD?

The human mind isn't designed to be under high levels of stress for indefinitely long periods of time. It's designed to react to stress instantly using its survival instincts, and to either fight whatever's threatening its safety or run away from it, by employing the *fight or flight* response; so what happens if you can't fight what's making you stressed and you can't run away from it either? What if you're trapped in an endless cycle of sleep-deprivation and dealing with meltdowns? What if your day to day life is more like navigating a war zone than raising a family? What if your family doesn't seem to need a mother, it needs a ringmaster instead? Oh, hang on, that's my family...

As I'm sure you've guessed by now, if you don't somehow learn to cope, it's really not going to end well for anyone, least of all you and your family. As difficult as it might be to snatch a little time to help yourself manage the stresses and strains that go with autism parenting (for difficult, read 'near-impossible') it's absolutely vital, and is actually one of the greatest, most loving things you can do for both yourself and your child. 'You can't look after your child if you don't look after yourself' may sound like a bit of a cliché, but believe me, in this case it's absolutely true, so you need to make it a priority at all costs if you're going to make it through this experience in one piece.

I once saw a study that described how the brain scans of autism parents matched those of war veterans returning home with PTSD (post-traumatic stress disorder). PTSD happens when your brain has experienced events that are so shocking it's been unable to process them in the usual way, so it remains on high alert long after the actual danger has passed.

People suffering from PTSD are constantly waiting for the next disaster to strike, and if it doesn't they can become very anxious, believing it's only a matter of time before they'll need to employ their fight or flight response again at a moment's notice. They can appear very jittery and tend to over-react hugely to the tiniest stresses and strains of everyday life; some can even develop paranoia, imagining all kinds of catastrophes are actually happening, even when they're not. Again this is simply their mind trying to protect them from what it thinks of as being an immediate threat, albeit in a rather extreme way. No matter how illogical it seems or how much damage it's causing, their mind will keep on instinctively reacting like this until they get the help they need to recover and put their ordeal back into perspective.

If you're an autism parent I'm sure you can identify with this description of traumatised military personnel returning from a war zone. We too spend the majority of our time on high alert, overflowing with adrenaline and constantly ready for anything, but there's one big difference between PTSD and autism parenting: it's not *post*-autism parenting, because we haven't survived it and lived to tell the tale; we're *surviving* it, right now. What's more, not only are we living this high-speed, full-volume lifestyle twenty four hours a day, seven days a week, but as far as we can tell, we'll be living it for the rest of our lives, and that's a whole different level of stress for our minds to come to terms with. Rather than PTSD, it's more like OTSD (Ongoing Traumatic Stress Disorder) and yes, I did just make that up, so it's not an official term but personally I think it's a pretty accurate description of the way autism parenting can affect you!

Grieving as a way of life

That subheading sounds a bit dramatic, doesn't it? Don't worry; I'm not suggesting autism parents should spend their time moping around in a constant state of devastation and sorrow (although to be honest I have met a few who do just that). What I'm talking about here is the continual on-going process of grief we somehow have to learn to deal with when we watch our children struggle so, so hard to overcome obstacles we hadn't even realised existed. Remember what I said about bereavement being the cancellation of expectations? Well, while there's *everything* wrong with pushing your child to achieve things *you* believe are important at the expense of their happiness, there's nothing wrong at all with having some reasonable expectations about their life and assuming they'll achieve them with relative ease.

From the moment your child is born, it's fairly safe to assume the following will happen:

- My child will be comforted by my cuddles
- My child will be able to express love for me
- My child will enjoy my company
- My child will make eye contact with me
- My child and I will have a close, easily maintained bond

As children get older, our expectations for them naturally increase. Here are just a few examples of what parents tend to expect in the area of education:

- My child will attend school
- My child will learn to read, write and count
- My child will be able to dress themselves after P.E.
- My child will eat school dinners or a packed lunch
- My child will make friends
- My child will be invited to birthday parties
- My child will achieve a reasonable standard of academic education
- My child will have the option to attend college and university

I'm not talking about forcing your child to conform and do exactly the same thing as everyone else here, I'm just highlighting a few of the familiar milestones many people understandably take for granted when they have a new baby.

Watching your child desperately want to be part of these things and not being able to work out how to do it is incredibly tough. I've cried many, many tears over my children's frustration as to why they couldn't master skills that other children their age found so easy, but I've cried many more over the cruelty and ridicule they've suffered as a result.

As your child grows, it's also perfectly reasonable to expect some or all of the following to happen:

- My child will be valued by society
- My child will be independent
- My child will experience what the world has to offer
- My child will enjoy new adventures and learn about other cultures
- My child will have the opportunities I never had
- My child will be self-sufficient after I'm gone

Again, it's not about forcing your child to do things that make them uncomfortable, it's about assuming they'll be able to choose a life that makes them happy, whatever form that life might take. None of us know the life-choices our children are going to make, but as parents it's natural to wish for them to have the *opportunity to choose*, and to experience as much happiness as possible in the process.

We may or may not have the following expectations for our children - I most certainly do:

- My child will fall in love
- My child will have a family of their own
- My child will know the joy of having happy, healthy children
- My child will be a good parent
- My child will be there with me when I'm old

Obviously we all have different hopes and dreams for our children so this isn't an exhaustive list by any means, but I think most expectant parents would agree that these are some of the things they hope their child will be able to experience if they choose to.

Working through the process

Just as your child will never grow out of their autism, the feelings of bereavement you'll experience about the struggles it brings will never truly end. I do appreciate this sentence sounds terribly harsh and upsetting, but understanding what I mean by it will ultimately save you from a great deal of pain. I promise.

Shock/Denial/Searching/ Guilt

Once you've come to terms with the initial feelings of shock and denial, you'll almost certainly begin to search for answers as to why your child is autistic, and the 'guilt' stage will begin in earnest. Blaming yourself is a pretty standard place to start: 'Have I done something wrong? Did I cause this? Could I have done more to prevent it? Can I make it stop?' and so on.

At this point, the world in general (and the 'Google experts' in particular) will happily provide you with a whole host of extra reasons why you should blame yourself. They 'know exactly why your child is autistic', because they read about it on Google. Sigh. Anything from your age (too old or too young) to your choice of diet (too strict or too relaxed) or even your use of technology will be held up as 'proof' that your child's autism was entirely preventable and is, in fact, all your fault.

Just for the record: it isn't.

How do I know this? Firstly because it's nobody's *fault* that a child is born autistic since fault doesn't even come into the equation, and secondly because autism is absolutely, categorically not caused by anything you have or haven't done.

The way your child's autism is expressed can most certainly be *affected by* the things they experience, and I for one am immensely grateful for that particular fact, but the *cause* of autism is a different matter altogether.

No matter what *anyone* tells you, you can take it from me that you haven't done anything wrong, you're not being punished and your child is neither defective, evil or in need of more discipline. Feel free to read that sentence back to yourself as many times as it takes for you to believe it.

Sadly I've heard all these 'reasons' repeated to new autism parents more times than I can remember. Usually described, quite wrongly, as 'facts' and presented by close family members, healthcare professionals and other hugely influential people, they can be very persuasive when you're scared, exhausted and desperate for answers. That still doesn't make them true.

At this point you may be wondering how I can make such bold statements when I've never even met you. That's the point: I don't need to have met you, nor do I need to know anything about you, your child or your lifestyle to be able to tell you, without a shadow of a doubt, that your child is not autistic because you made some kind of mistake. Trust me, I really do know about this stuff because like I said before, I'm a giant nerd and I've done a ridiculous amount of research about it. The fact that it's not your fault doesn't mean you won't feel plenty of guilt though. I certainly did, especially when my boys were young, although to be fair I didn't have a handy book like this one to turn to for reassurance!

When Dominic was just approaching five years old he had one of his regular assessments with the paediatrician. I usually spent these sessions trying (and failing) to coax him out from underneath a chair while he kicked, punched and screamed at the poor woman if she came anywhere near him. This particular time I was incredibly excited because he'd recently had the biggest breakthrough of his life and actually started to talk. He was responding to instructions and being so much more cooperative that he really was like a different child to the one she'd seen at our last appointment.

She'd brought a set of tests disguised as games that he completed very easily within a couple of minutes and I was beaming - I genuinely couldn't keep the smile off my face. She told me, rather apologetically, that she hadn't brought any harder tests with her because she just hadn't expected him to have made so much progress. I can still remember the feeling of sheer exhilaration bubbling in my chest. I wanted to shout and punch the air and dance and celebrate and...and then she asked him a question.

It was a pretty straightforward one, so I obviously wasn't worried about his answer. 'Dominic, are you a boy or a girl?' she asked. Without hesitation, he answered 'Girl' and gave her the most charming smile. I felt like I'd been hit in the gut with a bucket of ice. My face fell and seeing my confusion, she explained she'd deliberately asked the question that way round, putting 'girl' at the end instead of 'boy' to see what he would do. Since he had absolutely no idea what she was talking about, he simply echoed back the last word of the sentence and smiled politely to show that yes, he could play this 'talking' game just as well as all the other games she'd presented him with.

Seeing the tears spring into my eyes, she was wonderfully reassuring and told me there was nothing to worry about and everything to celebrate because he was doing amazingly well and had made enormous progress since his last assessment.

So did I celebrate? Nope. I came out of there and sobbed all the way home. How could I have missed this? How could he be almost five years old and not even know if he was a boy or a girl? I thought he was doing so well. I'd just taken it for granted that he knew. I'd spent my time focussing on whether he could build a sodding archway out of coloured blocks and all this time he was unaware of something as simple as his own gender. What kind of parent was I? Clearly an absolutely dreadful one.

I beat myself up like this for weeks, simply because at the time I didn't understand enough about autism to realise his development wouldn't be the same as other children's. The fact that he'd leapt ahead in certain areas was no guarantee he'd progressed in others but back then I had no idea this was to be expected from a child on the spectrum. As it happened this progress came in its own time, but back then all I could do was destroy myself with guilt for failing to realise something so fundamental about him.

Anger/ Regret/Bargaining

Now after a while, when feeling guilty doesn't provide you with any useful answers, you'll probably find yourself doing some classic bargaining as well. Asking the 'What if I just did this...?' and 'What if I hadn't done that...?' kind of questions won't help, but they're a perfectly natural part of the process, so they're nothing to worry about. One of the most common 'What if?' questions I've heard is 'What if we just ignore it? Do you think he might grow out of it?' Nope. Not going to happen.

As hard as it sounds, realising this fact is a hugely positive step forward, but it can be a very painful one too, because that realisation is pretty terrifying when all you want is a happy, content child but for some reason you have the exact opposite and you have no idea why.

As time passes, your frustration at not being able to 'solve the problem' of your child being autistic will grow and you're going to feel plenty of anger about it, so be prepared. Feeling angry with yourself or your child is okay, resenting everybody else who isn't dealing with what you're going through is also fine. Hating the very *sound* of the word 'autism' is totally acceptable and being so furious with the entire Universe that you just want to explode into a million pieces at the absolute and utter injustice of it all is perfectly all right too. There's nothing wrong with feeling angry; nothing at all. The important thing is what you do about it.

People will tell you that autism is a blessing. They'll tell you that you're lucky: that only special people are chosen to be parents of special children. They'll say that they admire you, that you're a hero, and that they wish *they'd* been given the chance to experience an extraordinary life like yours.

Having times when you want to kill these people is completely understandable. Just don't actually do it.

To be fair, the vast majority of people who say this kind of thing to you will genuinely have the best of intentions. Partly it's because they're not really sure *what* to say and they're trying to be positive and encouraging, and partly it's because they just don't have the first idea about the reality of parenting an autistic child: they're doing their best but they just don't get it, which clearly isn't their fault at all, so it's always a good idea to be kind and patient when you're dealing with this sort of situation.

Other people will say these same things to you in a sickly-sweet voice with the sole intention of patronising and disempowering you. It's absolutely fine to kill anyone who does this.

I'm joking of course, but believe me, having homicidal thoughts isn't uncommon when you're living with autism. Continual stress and prolonged sleep-deprivation can do funny things to your brain, but the chances are that you're not actually going to turn into a violent maniac, especially if you're reading this book, because fortunately for you, I have some rather excellent strategies you can use to stay sane, even in the face of seemingly overwhelming odds.

Depression

So what happens when it starts to dawn on you that this autism thing might just be forever? When you've followed all the well-meaning advice and done everything you can think of to help your child but they're still unable to cope with even the simplest aspects of day to day life; what then?

Well, this is when you'll face what's undoubtedly the hardest part of the process, and one that as I've already mentioned, can manifest in all sorts of unpleasant ways.

First of all, if your child is still young and you're feeling very low, it's a good idea to speak to your GP or Health Visitor and ask them to assess you for PND (post-natal depression). Never underestimate how serious PND can be, and whatever happens, don't put off asking for help because you think you 'should be able to cope'. Having any baby is an enormous physical and emotional wrench whether they have autism or not, so as a new parent you're bound to feel overwhelmed and out of control at times even if everything is going well, but if you're feeling this way *all* the time and you're seriously struggling to see the light at the end of the tunnel, please do speak to someone. No-one will think you're being silly or making a fuss about nothing. Your healthcare team is there to support you because they know from experience just how hard this stage of parenthood can be, and they'll be only too pleased to help you if they can.

Depression itself, post-natal or otherwise, can be a terrifying thing to deal with, but it doesn't have to defeat you. As with all mental health issues, people can be affected by depression on many levels: you could be mildly depressed for only a short time or you could suffer from chronic, long-term depression that leaves you feeling utterly suicidal. However it affects you, don't keep it to yourself. Let someone know how you're feeling and take the appropriate steps towards getting yourself well again. If you can't find the motivation to do it for yourself, *please* do it for your child, because as we all know, if you're running on empty you'll soon have nothing left to give and your child will be the first one to suffer as a result.

I know there are lots of people who hesitate when it comes to letting a health professional know they're feeling depressed because they don't want to be given anti-depressants and 'labelled' as being mentally ill, but they're far from the only option available nowadays. Health food shops stock lots of natural remedies designed to help calm your nerves or lift your mood, and even a good quality multi-vitamin can make a huge difference to how you feel. If you're under a lot of stress (which is kind of a given if you're an autism parent) then you'll need plenty of B vitamins to get you through the day and a decent dose of vitamins C and D can also work wonders. Looking after yourself may seem impossible at the moment, but it's absolutely vital if you want to stay the course and survive this parenting thing in the long term.

You could try a course of St. John's Wort and 5HTP which can help boost and regulate serotonin and dopamine levels in a similar way to prescription drugs. Many people swear by the Bach Flower Remedy range, especially Rescue Remedy (I use this regularly myself) and although not everyone believes they work, complimentary treatments such as aromatherapy, homeopathy, cranial osteopathy and reflexology have helped thousands of people get through times of crisis in their lives, and yes, I'm one of them. Not everyone responds to all these holistic medicines, so my advice would be to see which ones (if any) suit you and do what feels right. Make sure you speak to your GP before taking any specific supplements like St. John's Wort though as some natural remedies can interact badly with prescribed drugs.

If things are really serious though, and you're having intrusive thoughts about hurting yourself or your child, *please don't wait*, visit your GP and sort things out as soon as possible. There's nothing wrong with taking anti-depressants if they're going to improve the quality of your life and your child's life. You won't be hurting anyone, and without them there's every chance you might do just that. If anyone disagrees with you looking for help, ask them to walk in your shoes for six months and see if they still feel the same way. They can't of course, because even if they lived your life they still wouldn't be living inside your mind. No-one lives there except you and no-one regulates your emotions except you either, which makes it *no-one's business but yours* whether or not you take a course of medication to help you cope.

One thing I'll guarantee is that if you *are* depressed and feel like you'd be some kind of failure if you took medication, when you *do* start taking it you'll soon stop feeling like that, because depression is an absolute bugger for sitting on your shoulder and whispering things like 'You're not good enough', 'What's the point in taking medicine? It won't help, you'll still be useless', 'it's way too much effort to visit the doctor; you don't have the time' and 'medication will turn you into a zombie so you won't be able to look after your child anymore.' The reason it says these things is very simple: it's fighting for its own survival. If you get help and stop being depressed, *you win and the depression loses*. It's not going to allow that without a fight, and believe me it can put up a pretty nasty, vindictive one, so be prepared. Take my advice and don't listen to it any more. Listen instead to the quiet voice saying 'You can do this, just hang on, things will get better somehow…' How do I know you can still hear that little voice of hope? Because you're reading this book and you've got this far, so a part of you, however battered and bruised it might be, is still hanging on and looking for answers.

There's no shame whatsoever in realising you can't cope and taking steps to get better, so the important thing to remember here is that if you're struggling, it's okay to ask for help and it's also okay to help yourself. If some people find your approach to getting well again a bit strange, so what? If you're an autism parent then your whole *life* is going to seem a bit strange to them anyway! You don't owe negative people an explanation, and you most certainly *do* owe it to yourself and to your child to stay healthy. In the end, if something is working and you're feeling better, that's all that really matters.

One thing I'd certainly recommend using are the therapeutic suggestions I make in this book. No surprises there then. There's no question whatsoever that I would have gone stark raving mad many years ago without them, so I can safely say that they work, and they work really well too. Not every suggestion will be right for every single person, that's just not realistic, but the support I'm offering has been meticulously researched and designed to help as many different types of people as possible so it's definitely worth giving it a go.

If you think it sounds like rubbish and decide not to use it, I can promise you it *definitely* won't work, so even if you're sceptical it's got to be worth a shot. If it doesn't work then you're no worse off than when you started, but if it does, it might just transform your life in the same ways it's transformed mine: I'm calmer, more enthusiastic, more proactive and more refreshed (even if I do only manage to grab a few hours of sleep every night). I'm also able to calm myself down in an instant wherever I am and whatever I'm doing, and that alone has changed the course of my life and my children's lives more than anything else.

You can find out all about my unique approach to not losing your mind in the midst of madness in the very honestly titled 'There Is No Magic Wand' chapter. In the meantime, here are some ideas to help you get through this stage and move you on to the next one.

Acceptance

I remember quite clearly the moment I realised that if I didn't accept Christopher's autism I was going to have a breakdown. At the time of course I had no idea he was autistic because I didn't even know what autism was, but I knew something was going on, and I knew the structured approach to parenting him I'd planned so carefully before he arrived just wasn't working.

He was just approaching two and I'd spent his entire life living by the 'This is What Good Mothers Do' rule book; unsurprisingly, he was having none of it.

Every morning I would drag him out of bed (literally drag him – nothing was ever done without serious physical resistance on his part and boy was he strong!) and start the exhausting process of getting him washed, brushed and into clothes. Screaming, biting, kicking, punching, writhing and sobbing would follow as I did my best to reassure him that it was all going to be wonderful because we were going to the park.

Following constant advice from my family that 'all children love the park' and 'you *must* take him outside for some fresh air every day' I'd bravely soldier on despite his objections and do my very best to interest him in the swings, climbing frames and see saws while he threw himself on the ground and roared or launched himself at me and beat me as hard as he could with his hands, feet and forehead. Another of his favourite strategies for ending a visit to the park, the shops or even a friend's house (yes, I still had friends who were prepared to entertain us in their homes in those days) was to dry heave until he was violently sick. He ate next to nothing but always managed to produce a huge amount of vomit nonetheless. Both of us being covered in sick would usually signal the end of the day's outdoor adventures at which point I would take him home, suffer the absolute *hysteria* of bathing him and sit him in front of the TV where he'd watch a Winnie the Pooh video on repeat wearing nothing but a nappy.

On this particular morning I was sitting with him watching his videos when something just snapped. By the way, when I say 'watching' his videos I actually mean rewinding them over and over and *over* again so he could watch the same sixty seconds of the story until (this being before the days of DVD's) the tape literally wore away and all that was left was a snowy outline of the characters moving through some kind of black and grey blizzard.

'Christopher,' I said brightly 'shall we go to the park today?' Although he showed no obvious signs of having heard me and kept his gaze fixed firmly on the screen, he instantly stiffened and his eyes became as dark as coal. He gripped his bottle (which he still had despite the family's best efforts to get me to remove it) and ground his teeth into the teat. Hard. And then it hit me that today would be the same as every other day since he arrived: a soul destroying battle of wills that ended in devastating defeat for me and massive disapproval from everyone else. Every. Single. Time.

At this stage I'd have taken *anything at all* over the nightmares we were going through on a daily basis, but I'd been so brainwashed by all the good advice from well-meaning friends, family, Health Visitors and GP's that the fact we could do things differently and I could follow my own instincts about how to bring him up hadn't actually occurred to me yet. I know it sounds ridiculous now, but this was in the early 1990's when autism was virtually unheard of, and it's hard – it's *beyond* hard – to stand up to all these people who are supposed to know better than you, when they're telling you to just stick it out, that he's being stubborn, that he'll get used to it in time etc. etc. especially if your child is behaving in such an extreme way (and for 'extreme' read 'naughty' according to literally every person I met at the time). I was even told by a Health Visitor that he'd never find employment when he left school because he could only do things in his own way (yes, she could apparently tell this about him when he'd just turned three) and no vulnerable first-time mother wants to hear that said about her only child.

So, as usual, I psyched myself up for the oncoming battle, but just as I made the decision to get started, something in my mind said, quite clearly, 'NO' and instead of getting up, I sat where I was and started to cry. Christopher was oblivious to crying at the time, which I found strange back then, but this time it was a blessing, because once the tears had started I genuinely couldn't stop them. I cried and cried until my cries turned into great wracking sobs, then I began to howl; wailing and keening as wave after wave of grief forced its way from the depths of my exhausted soul and out through my mouth.

I'd heard the expression 'being beside yourself with grief' before but this was the first (and so far, thankfully, the only) time I'd actually experienced it. For want of a better description, I had a kind of out-of-body experience where I found myself standing behind my body and watching this drained and devastated woman breaking into pieces in front of me. Somehow, looking at all this pain from the outside made everything become clear, and a voice in my head said 'You have a choice. You can do things at his pace, or you can go under.' Just that, nothing more, but it was as if a light had suddenly come on in the midst of seemingly endless darkness and slowly I began to feel calmer.

Now, I appreciate how that sounds - being outside my body, hearing voices – and no-one is more aware than I am that it makes me seem like a bit of a fruitcake, but that's how it happened and telling you it happened any other way would be a lie, so I'll leave you to make your own mind up about what was really going on that day. Whatever it was though, it was most certainly the turning point for me, the moment I became not just a parent but an autism parent. Again, I didn't know I was an autism parent at the time, but I knew something momentous had happened and I knew exactly what I had to do: I had to change and start doing what felt right for both me and my son.

Up until that point, I'd bought into the idea that *Christopher* was the one who had to change, so he could get used to the way *I* did things. I really believed what everyone was telling me: if he wouldn't cooperate then he was just being naughty and stubborn, and with enough reinforcement and repetition, he'd eventually learn to do things my way. Despite two solid years of the most positive reinforcement I could think of, all I'd managed to do was make him (and myself) utterly miserable, so this was the moment I stopped following other people's advice and started doing things that worked for Christopher, whether I understood why they worked or not. I let him take the lead as much as possible that day and it really was a revelation.

He spent the entire day in his nappy, never once complaining of feeling cold and incredibly *not* instantly dying of exposure as I'd been absolutely *promised* he would if I didn't get him fully dressed every day. Instead of battling to get him to eat his food 'in a civilised way' (i.e. all on one plate while sitting at the dinner table) I made him several different bowls of his favourite foods, lined them up like he usually did and let him eat them separately while sitting in his high chair. He happily ate the whole lot while watching TV and sharing mouthfuls with his imaginatively named toy cat, 'Cat'.

Instead of running behind him and tidying everything away as I'd always done in the past, I let him spread his toys out wherever he wanted, and left them there all day, where they did no harm whatsoever (who knew?) and helped stabilise his mood no end. Back then I had no idea why leaving things exactly where he'd put them would have this effect, but I could see the difference it was making to him so I did it anyway.

Everything was going splendidly until Pat came home. He took one look at the state of the house and exploded with fury. This was followed a few days later by a pretty similar reaction from my mother and various other relatives who felt that I was suddenly letting things slide because I just couldn't be bothered any more. In fact the opposite was true: it was taking everything I'd got not to tidy up and stick to the routines I'd been clinging to all this time because they were the only things that made me feel I had a little bit of control over my whirlwind of a life, but I'd realised I was doing them at the expense of Christopher's happiness so they'd been put on hold until he could cope. What I was allowing him to do now was create an environment where he felt like he was in control and although it made no sense to me, it clearly made perfect sense to him.

'What if someone comes over?' people would ask with a look of absolute disgust. 'They'll think you're a slob.' 'Don't worry,' I'd say 'I'll tell them what I'm doing and they'll understand.' How wrong I was.

Despite my best efforts to explain my thinking to other people, no-one understood at all and Christopher and I became more and more isolated as a result. Friends turned their backs on us and the family spent so much time criticising my parenting and housekeeping skills that eventually it became a trial to spend time with them at all. Pat and I were arguing more and more frequently and I might well have given up on the idea entirely if it hadn't been for the progress I suddenly started to make in my relationship with my son. Instead of focussing on changing him into who he 'should' be, I started to accept him for who he was, and the more I allowed him to be himself, the more I got to know and understand him.

He had no spoken language yet, but I found that once I'd stopped wasting my energy worrying about what everyone else thought of me, I was able to understand a lot of what he was trying to tell me without the need for words. His behaviours certainly seemed very strange to me back then, but they were definitely consistent, and most of the time (mainly through guesswork and a lot of trial and error) I realised what he wanted and was able to work *with* him instead of against him all the time. I stopped focussing on age appropriate goals and decided to work on taking one simple step forward at a time. Naturally I was warned I was spoiling him; that he'd grow up into the most appalling human being imaginable and that I was making his 'naughtiness' worse by reinforcing his behaviour. Wouldn't this be a lovely story if I told you that from then on he made amazing progress and we never had any setbacks? It would, I'm sure, but it would also be a lie. When I say we focussed on one small step forward at a time, it could be something as seemingly unimportant as moving his Duplo bricks to a different part of the room without him having a meltdown. Even doing something as simple as this took weeks and weeks of consistent effort, and for every two steps we'd take forward, we'd always take at least one step back. Little by little though, Christopher started to relax and open up to me. He smiled more, and most importantly of all he began to cope more easily with the outside world. It seemed as if having his home exactly as he wanted it provided him with a soft place to fall – somewhere he felt safe and accepted – and this gave him the confidence to explore other environments.

He'd still become very easily overwhelmed, but as long as 'Cat' was with him, he'd hold his emotions in check for longer and longer periods of time when we were out. He even managed a couple of mornings a week at a playgroup by the time he was three. Some of the other children occasionally bullied and ridiculed him because of his lack of speech, while the mothers gave me the usual disapproving death stares when he had meltdowns or clung to me, but for us it was a great step in the right direction and a big leap towards his eventual independence.

I remember one particular time at playgroup when all the children were asked to sit in a group on a big mat, while 'the Mummies', as we were collectively known, sat round the edges. Christopher was instantly anxious and started to stiffen in his 'I'm about to have a massive meltdown' way, so I sat down in the middle of the mat with him and we linked little fingers. Linking little fingers was something we'd worked on for months at playgroup. We'd gone from him desperately clinging to my legs to full hand-holding, then down to just our fingers touching and eventually I'd reduced things to this tiny physical connection between us, in the hope that the next stage would be independent play.

One of the women got up and came over especially to tell me that I was 'going to have trouble with that one when he's older...' a sentiment that was clearly shared by the rest of the mothers, who sat tutting and clucking with concern at my apparent inability to parent my child. I was used to this kind of public humiliation by now, so I smiled sweetly and resisted the temptation to trip her up as she returned to her seat.

Interestingly, several years later I met the same woman at the GP's surgery, where her little boy was causing absolute mayhem while Christopher sat patiently waiting for his turn with the doctor. Credit where it's due, she came over to me and said 'What on earth have you done to him? He's so beautifully behaved, not like my son. Tell me your secret.' Taking this at face value, I explained how I'd let Christopher learn in his own way, at his own pace, and that although I knew it all seemed a bit odd when he was at playgroup, it had worked perfectly because he wasn't actually naughty at all, he was just overwhelmed. 'Well, bloody good for you!' she said. 'We all thought you were mad, but you've had the last laugh.' I blushed and managed a rather pathetic 'Oh...err...thanks.' At the time it was such a rare thing to get any positive feedback from another parent that I was genuinely lost for words, but it's a moment I'll remember for the rest of my life nonetheless.

Riding the dragon of bereavement

So those are the stages of bereavement, but understanding and having a name for them doesn't mean they won't hurt you, because they will. Bereavement is awful: it twists and turns like an angry dragon, throwing you around and turning your world upside down when you least expect it, so you'll need all your strength just to get through the day sometimes. As I've said though, it's a process, so as impossible as it might seem, your mind is putting you through these feelings for your own good. It's encouraging you to find answers and move forward, to learn and grow, and once you start accepting your child's autism, even though the other parts of the process will sometimes gang up on you and attack all at once, you'll soon find you're doing just that.

I can't tell you exactly *why* your child is autistic and I can't tell you exactly how they'll progress, but I can tell you that if you put your mind to it, you can begin to enjoy a life filled with wonder and magic along with all the hard work, and I can also tell you that it's absolutely worth the extra effort. It's not going to be what you were expecting, but when it comes to wonder and magic, surely it's a case of the more unexpected, the better.

Since your brain's most important function is to move you away from pain and towards pleasure, the best way to ride the dragon of bereavement is to find something that makes you happy and focus on it at least once a day. Now, I appreciate that finding something to be happy about isn't always easy (understatement) but it's a lot easier if you use a bit of creative thinking.

I'm sure you've heard of something called 'developing an attitude of gratitude' but if not, it's basically a way of looking at the difficult things in your life in a different way and turning them into positives. For example, rather than being upset that you have a sink full of dirty dishes, you could choose to be grateful because it means your family has food to eat. In the same way, instead of despairing when you look at the never-ending pile of washing in your basket (believe me, I know *all* about that one...) you could be grateful that your family has clothes to wear. You get the idea, I'm sure.

When it comes to being an autism parent however, finding the positives can be a whole lot trickier.

How do you find the positives when your child will only cooperate if he's seen every traffic light in town turn from red to green in a particular order first? Well, think about it this way: at least he's getting plenty of exercise and fresh air, and who knows? Maybe he'll develop an interest in town planning when he's older, or become an electrician if you encourage him to find out how traffic lights actually work. The possibilities are endless when you think outside the box.

Let's say your child is utterly obsessed with anything to do with dogs. Depending on how they do academically, they could become a vet, a volunteer at a dog shelter or anything else in between. Chris Packham, the famous naturalist and TV presenter who was recently diagnosed with Asperger's, channelled his early passion for animals into his work and has a hugely successful and rewarding career as a result.

And what about Christopher, the Duplo and LEGO obsessed child who was 'never going to find employment when he left school'? He now holds a First Class Master's degree in Architectural Engineering from Leeds University and has a fantastic job in the City of London. With love, patience and a whole lot of hard work it really can be done, and he's living proof.

Keep your face to the light & the shadows will fall behind you

Having this approach to your challenges can really help get you through the tough times, so when you're feeling cheerful, write your ideas down, and when you feel like giving up, which you inevitably will at times, read them back to yourself and remember that there's always, always hope if you look for it hard enough.
Better still, find something that's just for you and make the time to enjoy it. Easier said than done, I realise, but take a tip from your child's ability to hyper-focus on just one thing at a time and forget the housework and everything else for a few minutes while you do whatever it is that makes you smile.
For example, while it's fair to say that I'm not the world's best cook, when Christopher turned one I decided to make him a cake, and discovered quite unexpectedly that I had a talent for sugar craft. I worked tirelessly on a Teddy Bear's Picnic cake for him, decorating miniscule apples with streaks of red and green food colouring and making marzipan ducks the size of my thumbnail. I was so tired while I was working on it that I felt like my eyes were going to burn through their sockets, but I absolutely loved it, and when it was finished I became quite upset because I didn't have an escape from the trauma of my everyday life to focus on any more. I realised just how much I needed something different to occupy my mind and decided to start making cakes for friends and family as well. I'd hidden Christopher's cake in the wardrobe to stop him destroying it before his party but that wasn't going to work in the long term, so over the next few years I gradually cleared the box room with a view to using it for my cake decorating. I deliberately made it the most boring room in the house: it was very plain with nothing in it except a desk and a chest of drawers. There were no TV's, children's toys or videos, in fact nothing that could possibly interest Christopher or indeed Dominic, who'd arrived by now and was a very inquisitive toddler. I then left the door open for several weeks until both boys had realised this fact. One day I shut the door and didn't lock it, which caused a huge amount of renewed interest in what might be behind it. When they'd thoroughly investigated the closed door and discovered it wasn't worth bothering to open after all because the room was still just as boring, I locked it.
Obviously most parents would simply tell their children not to go in. Parents of children on the autism spectrum are now convulsed with laughter at the very idea

of where that instruction would lead.

So began my time as a cake decorator. Having a new project to work on was guaranteed to lift my spirits, taking my mind off things and helping me forget situations that can only truthfully be described as nightmarish. Psychologically, this is a massively important thing for anyone to do. Having something you can look forward to while you endure having your hair pulled out at the roots, being bitten, punched, scratched, kicked and spat on is beyond price. Watching your home, clothing and treasured possessions being systematically destroyed day after day, coupled with a severe lack of sleep, is enough to loosen anyone's grip on their sanity, so having something that's yours, something that can't be ruined or taken from you is a real lifesaver.

The cakes I produced were truly beautiful if I do say so myself, and were often described as works of art. Unbelievably fragile, complex and intricate, they were designed, baked, decorated, photographed, boxed and transported to their destinations in utter secrecy. The security levels surrounding their journey from oven to table would have put the Pentagon to shame. If the boys had had so much as an inkling of what was going on at this stage, it would have been the end of the whole project, without a doubt.

Once the photos were developed (this was before the invention of digital photography) the best ones would be carefully secured in a good quality album which was immediately hidden and taken out only when the boys were at nursery and school. I can honestly say that the album was the only thing that survived those years intact, remaining free from teeth marks, dribble, felt tip pen, paint splatters or worse and not having been ripped, screwed up, shredded or (in Christopher's case) eaten, which was no mean feat. It remained one of my most treasured possessions until I took it apart many years later to scan the photos into a digital album. There are a few examples on the next page...

As time went on, I turned my hobby into a business and made dozens of cakes for all kinds of occasions including birthdays, weddings, retirements and homecomings. Each picture remains to this day a powerful reminder, whispering to me across the years of those tiny oases of calm I managed to create, right in the middle of all that anarchy.

So, finding something that moves your focus away from pain and towards pleasure will help you no end. It doesn't have to be anything creative like cake making, it could be starting a collection of paperweights or planting flower seeds and watching them grow. Anything that makes you feel better will work, and you'll know if it's working because your emotions will tell you, loud and clear. If doing something for yourself is causing you so much stress that it's actually making you feel *worse*, change tack and do something different. It doesn't matter what it is and it doesn't matter whether it makes sense to anyone else, just find that little 'something' and give yourself permission to enjoy it.

Emotional archaeology and fortune telling

Here you are then, accepting your life is now very different from the one you'd imagined. How do you keep the momentum going when a day trip with your child is an endless nightmare of stress, they have no idea when it's their birthday or who Father Christmas is, or they drink washing up liquid as if it's orange squash? Even the most positive-thinking parent on the planet is going to struggle to stay optimistic at times if this sort of thing is happening on a daily basis.

The good news is that to stay positive you don't have to be happy and cheerful all the time; not at all. You don't have to like what's happening and the even better news is that you don't have to accept these situations forever; you just have to accept this is how your child is behaving *now* and set about changing their behaviour for the better in the same way all good parents do.

Remember your child is always learning, growing and changing, just like all children, and who they are at three years old is going to be very different to who they are at twelve or sixteen. As long as you're planting the right kind of seeds when they're small, you'll see them blossom as they get older.

The easiest way to defeat yourself when you're living this kind of life is to practice something I call 'emotional archaeology and fortune telling'. Here's an example of this kind of thinking:

'My child is seven years old and he can't even dress himself. He's never been any good at this kind of thing. He can't even tie his shoelaces. It took him years to learn how to brush his teeth. He'll never live independently when he's older. What will happen to him when I die? This is unbearable!'

Thinking like this about what your child can't do yet really isn't helpful because what he's 'never been any good at' isn't going to tell you what he might be good at in the future, it's only going to tell you what he's struggled with so far. Predicting such a bleak future for him when he's still so young isn't going to help you either, because let's face it, no seven year old is ready to live independently, so how he's going to develop between now and twenty one is something you can't possibly know at this stage.

While it's easy to let your thoughts run away with you like this, it's much more productive to tell yourself something along these lines instead:

'My child is seven years old and so far he can't dress himself. I'm going to focus on one thing he's finding difficult (doing up buttons/tying shoelaces/putting on gloves etc.) and when he's mastered that, we'll move on to the next thing, then the next.

He might not get to grips with dressing himself at the same age other children do, but he'll still make progress in his own way, and if he never learns to tie his shoelaces, so what? We'll buy him slip-ons.'

Setting achievable goals like this is a great way to keep an eye on how much progress your child is making, and again, if there are any small achievements, write them down and read your list back to yourself when you feel like giving up.

Everything you experience in your life, not just as a parent but as a human being, starts with the way you speak to yourself, so although you might be thinking this positive self-talk doesn't make a lot of difference, I can promise you that it really does. It's absolutely transformed my life and the lives of my children too, so it's definitely worth considering.

The easiest way to stop digging around in the past for things that make you feel bad or looking to an unpredictable future for answers to your current problem is to focus your attention on what's happening right now. I'm not saying this is an easy thing to do and it will take a bit of practice to get a hold on your thoughts, but if you do it often enough it'll become automatic and eventually you'll find you've become one of those annoyingly positive, proactive people like me!

When things are tough, which they often will be, take a deep breath and bring your attention back to what's happening right now, in this moment. What can you do to change it for the better? If you can think of something, do it. If not, then 'there's nothing I can do about this right now so I'll just have to get through it' is a perfectly reasonable response. You'll be surprised how much calmer it will make you feel. Remember, stress and frustration mean your brain is looking for answers and sometimes there just aren't any immediate answers to be found - some things take time - so don't be afraid to remind yourself of that every now and again.

Bubbles in the air

I often describe raising my children as being a bit like flying a jumbo jet: when you fly long-haul, the aircraft will automatically drift slightly off course along the flight path from one country to the next. Rather than waiting until they're flying too far in the wrong direction then taking big, sharp turns to correct the route, pilots will constantly make subtle movements to compensate for the drift, and eventually you'll reach the right destination in what seems like a straight line from A to B but is actually anything but.

The secret to parenting autistic children is to use the same strategy: play the long game, stay on top of things and if you notice something's drifting a bit, make small movements to correct it rather than waiting until it's become a big problem. In the same way, if something is *already* a big problem, don't try to wrench your child into a different behaviour pattern too quickly, just keep making those small corrective movements, one at a time until you get them from where they are to where they need to be. Break everything down into the smallest steps you can think of and make absolutely sure your child has mastered each one before moving on to the next.

For me, the way to make those small movements most effective has been to imagine each of my children is surrounded by a delicate bubble. My goal is to get through the bubble and reach them without breaking it. If I push too hard or do anything too suddenly, the bubble will burst and any connection I've made with them will vanish; they'll withdraw back into themselves and we'll have to start the process all over again. If I'm gentle though, and infinitely patient, I can break down every one of the small adjustments I want them to make into tinier and tinier steps until my instructions can pass right through the bubble and reach them, leaving it intact. Autistic people need to process new information at their own pace, so sometimes this process seems like it's taking forever. At other times they'll surprise you and pick things up straight away, but the process is always the same: keep the bubbles in the air by being calm, patient and consistent and praising every bit of progress they make, no matter how small.

Crying, shouting and screaming with the sheer frustration of going through this procedure time and time again are all perfectly acceptable and are certainly things I've done many times over the years. The important thing is to save those reactions until your child is out of the way and you can release your feelings without making them think they're disappointing you or doing something wrong. In my experience there's no naughtiness in autistic children when it comes to learning, no pretending they can't do something just to be difficult or because they can't be bothered, just a genuine need to be taught in a unique way.

Oh, and never be afraid to get creative with this approach. If they're fascinated by trains and you want to teach them about colours, ask them to identify which train is red and which is blue. If you're working on maths skills, ask them to sort their trains into colour groups and count how many are in each one. If they love dinosaurs and you're learning relative sizes, line their dinosaurs up in size order and ask who's the biggest and who's the smallest. Forget about how your child 'should' learn and set about making a tailor-made strategy just for them.

Your child will need your support to learn the basics most children automatically pick up at school, so get involved and be hands-on when it comes to their education. Whatever you do though, don't suddenly behave as if you've become a teacher unless you're home-schooling them. If your child is attending school, they're going to find it pretty overwhelming, so they need you to be their parent first. They need 'home' to be distinctly different from 'school' - somewhere they can chill out and be themselves - so make your teaching as subtle, unstructured and enjoyable as you possibly can, and remember to write down every little bit of progress they make because it really will save your sanity when things start to get on top of you. I've done this with all four of my children and it really does work wonders. Have a look in the 'Further Reading' chapter for a book called The Asperkid's Game Plan – it's an excellent resource for turning special interests into learning opportunities.

Positive thinking in the real world

Between the ages of three and four Dominic always wore a dinosaur costume, complete with padded belly, paws and large sculpted headpiece.
When I say he always wore it, I mean he literally wore this one outfit for a year and nothing else. Ever. He wore it to the park, to nursery, to the cinema and in bed every night. For a whole year.
At the time I didn't understand why he'd only co-operate with me or interact with other children if he was dressed as a dinosaur so I just accepted there had to be a reason for it and let him carry on. I won't even bother to describe the number of death stares this particular behaviour quirk earned me – this was almost twenty years ago when children dressed in costume for costume parties and nothing else, certainly not for a trip to the supermarket or a day at nursery school...

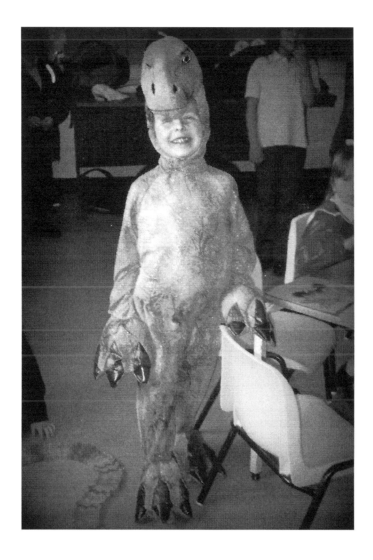

It wasn't until many years later that I realised how the tightness of the costume and the thickly-padded headpiece were soothing his sensory overload problems and helping him stay calm. All I knew back then was how hugely important it was to him and that he wouldn't be parted from it.

It got pretty dirty as you can imagine, so I developed a ninja-style method of cleaning it while he was asleep: I'd peel it off him, wash it, tumble-dry it and slip it back on before he woke up. This worked perfectly for months until one unforgettable evening when he woke up just as I'd turned the washing machine on. Oh dear.

He came racing down the stairs to see his dinosaur sloshing round and round in the soapy water and let out an earth shattering scream. There was nothing I could do but wait for the cycle to end, so for the next forty-five minutes he roared, head butted the washing machine and ripped out his toenails in utter despair. It was both terrifying and heart-breaking to watch and all I could do was try my best to calm him down, which did precisely nothing at all to help as you can imagine. My hands ended up black and blue from using them as a barrier between the washing machine door and his forehead, and despite my best efforts to stop him, we were both covered in blood because of the damage he'd done to his toes.

I thought about stopping the wash mid-cycle but that would've left us with a costume full of detergent which he'd instantly have thrown an allergic reaction to, so there was nothing for it but to wait. The second it was finished I whipped his costume out and he climbed straight back into it while it was still soaking wet. Then something amazing happened.

As I'd expected, his meltdown gradually subsided into quiet sobs but as he sat on the floor he suddenly looked very puzzled; then he started to shiver. Obviously he was dripping wet and freezing cold so you might expect this reaction from him, but Dominic didn't feel the cold and would happily run into the garden naked in deep snow if he was given half a chance without his body registering any signs of being uncomfortable. Not only that, but as the shivering continued, he lifted both his arms towards me and said 'Towa, mummum' (I need a towel, Mummy).

It's difficult to put into words the absolute elation I felt in that moment. He'd just registered a change in body temperature and made the connection that if he was wet and cold he'd need a towel to get dry. What's more, he'd formulated that thought *into a sentence* (he had no spoken language at the time) and used his body language to reach out towards me because he realised I was the one who could find him what he wanted. In that moment of desperation, his brain had responded to what he needed and come up with a solution we could *both* understand. We were communicating!

I wrapped him in the biggest, warmest towel I could find and sat there grinning wildly for hours, telling myself he was clearly a genius and it was only a matter of time before he took another step in the right direction.

As I mentioned before, earlier this year he graduated from Cardiff University with a degree in Law and Politics and he now works full time in central London. It's been a long road to say the least, but with courage, determination and lots of hard work, he's achieved something quite spectacular and I really couldn't be prouder.

You Might Have More Than One Autistic Child If…

1. You can simultaneously create so many different meals at such high speed that if you ever competed on Ready, Steady, Cook, the other contestants wouldn't stand a chance.
2. Your uncanny ability to locate lost keys, phones, lunchboxes etc. would put a sniffer dog to shame.
3. You could give CSI a run for their money by identifying whose shirt is whose purely by observing their unique patterns of staining.
4. Your night-time routine could decisively settle all debates on whether human beings can exist without sleep: they can.
5. After doing a day's worth of washing, you've collected enough 'treasure' (a.k.a. 'crap') from your children's pockets to fill a small skip.
6. You understand the vital importance of cutting sandwiches into triangles, squares or rectangles and of NEVER offering the wrong shape to the wrong child.
7. You have to make the instantaneous mental note 'Does this one like hugs?' before showing any physical affection, to avoid inflicting severe trauma on an unsuspecting child.
8. You have to resist a powerful urge to phone the local church and report a miracle if there are no odd socks left after the washing is sorted.
9. You only own plain white crockery to avoid the small variety of food your children will actually eat being served on the 'wrong' coloured/patterned plates, thus spoiling the flavour and making it inedible.
10. By the end of each day, the state of your house reminds you that if all else fails, you can always start your own family demolition business.

I'M SORRY BUT IT LOOKS LIKE YOUR CHILD HAS CAUGHT A SERIOUS CASE OF AUTISM

162

Chapter Six

Kill or Cure

'More children will be diagnosed with autism this year
than with AIDS, diabetes & cancer combined.'

Someone Unenlightened

Is this statement true? Many people are certain it is, while many more are just as certain it's an outright lie. Since the ways in which people are diagnosed are constantly changing and I therefore have no idea what the statistics will be at the time you're reading this, I can't actually give you a definitive answer on that one I'm afraid.

What I can do, however, is share with you my thoughts about this statement, because those are *always* the same. Every time I see this written down or hear someone blindly reciting it, the first thing I ask myself is this: 'Is it really very *helpful* to put autism in that sentence?'

ASD: Autism Spectrum Disease?

For me, whether the statistics are correct or not isn't the real issue here. The real issue is that by repeating this statement, so many people are unintentionally comparing autism to diseases like AIDS and cancer, both of which not only cause unspeakable distress to those who suffer from them, but also have the sole purpose of ending those same people's lives in the most gruesome ways.

Even diabetes, although nowadays nowhere near as terrifying a diagnosis as AIDS or cancer, is still a devastating and potentially lethal condition imposing a lifetime of restrictions and inconvenience on people affected by it, while offering them nothing constructive in return.

Don't get me wrong, human beings are amazing and their ability to find the positives in difficult situations is incredible, so of course if a person is suffering from any serious disease and they're determined not to let it beat them, they're going to find all kinds of benefits that have come about as a result of dealing with it (strength of character, new relationships, fortitude, valuing your health, living life to the full, inspiring others to overcome adversity etc.) and all power to them for being so optimistic.

The achievements made by people diagnosed with serious diseases like these can be incredibly positive and beneficial, but the important thing to remember is that the benefits they experience don't actually originate from the disease itself, but from their own choices in how they handle its effects.

This is where autism is so fundamentally different, because autism *does* bring its own benefits: unique, amazing and often life-changing ones that are all part and parcel of the condition.

It's still about perspective of course, and a trait that one person feels is an advantage could easily be interpreted as a disadvantage by someone else, but autism isn't a destructive force that invades the body, so to me, the fundamental difference between autism and an *actual* disease is clear: autism isn't trying to kill you, and if left undiagnosed and untreated, it's still possible for autistic people to live a long, healthy life.

Looking at things like Ebola, Rabies, Malaria, Meningitis, Tuberculosis and all the other indescribably dreadful diseases that continue to swirl around the world, they certainly have a few things in common:

1. Unless they're treated, they cause devastating damage (and often death) to anyone affected by them.

2. No-one in their right mind wants to suffer from them.

3. Society is wholeheartedly in agreement that they should be contained, their causes should be discovered and a *cure* should be found which is then made available to anyone who needs it, as quickly as possible.

4. No-one with any sense wants their children to suffer from them. Ever.

As I mentioned previously, describing a person using the name of a disease first, as in 'a cancerous person' rather than 'a person with cancer' is never okay (actually it's quite shocking when you see it written down like that, isn't it?) yet calling someone a 'person with autism' rather than an 'autistic person' is something many people on the spectrum dislike. They feel it implies that they're carrying their autism around with them in a suitcase as something separate from themselves rather than it being the fundamental spark that defines them as individuals.

I'm sure you've realised by now that personally I don't consider autism to be a disease, and if what I'd written here was the whole story then surely no-one would have any reason to disagree with me. Many intelligent, rational people do still believe autism *is* a disease though, and what's more, a disease that needs to be wiped out as quickly as possible, so why do they continue to see it like this? Part of the reason may lie in something as simple as terminology.

Back to basics

The first recorded use of the term 'disease' can be found way back in the late 14th century and means 'discomfort and inconvenience'. This derives from the Old French word 'desaise' meaning 'lack, want, discomfort, distress, trouble, misfortune' and so on. It's a word which, when you study it, quite literally translates to 'without any ease'. Naturally I *have* studied it because as you've no doubt realised, I'm a total grammar nerd as well as being a general nerd about everything (big surprise).

As you can see, this definition is pretty much open to interpretation when it comes to autism. Do autistic people experience discomfort, inconvenience and distress? Absolutely. Are autistic people's lives full of ease? Well, no, not as a general rule! So, it's easy to see why people reading this would identify autism as a disease, but are those effects coming from the autism *itself* or from the autistic person's reactions to the world around them? Does autism *cause* physical pain and distress or does an autistic person *experience* pain and distress when their environment is too bright, too loud or too overwhelming? Conversely, if autism *causes* them to be unable to tolerate the kind of environmental conditions that most non-autistic people can handle with ease, therefore making their lives more difficult, does that make it an illness?

These are interesting questions, and if you stop to think about it, the fact that we're able to wonder these things *at all* highlights a major difference between autism and diseases like Ebola or Meningitis, both of which leave absolutely no room for doubt whatsoever.

Modern-day dictionary definitions of the word 'disease' are also pretty vague and cover any conditions considered to be 'abnormal' that are caused by inflammation, infection, environmental factors or genetic defects.

Autism is certainly viewed as being abnormal by many people and the arguments over its causes continue to rage on and on. Diseases are also described as having a specific group of identifiable signs and symptoms, and again, autism most certainly has its own set of those.

Personally, I wince whenever I hear autism described as a disease but I think the majority of people aren't describing it like this for any other reason than because they've never really stopped to think about it all that much. In fairness, if they're not affected by it, why would they? I certainly didn't. In fact, if anyone had described it to me as a disease when I was a child, I have no doubt whatsoever that I'd have accepted it as being just that and looked on the parents of autistic children with the usual mixture of pity and admiration I generally saved for anyone dealing with a child suffering from cancer.

There are exceptions to this rule of course: people who definitely know better but *still* choose to use the term in a derogatory way. Generally though, people talk about it like this because they don't know very much about what autism is and what it isn't. I genuinely hope my books will go some way towards changing that situation.

Should autism be cured?

Having established that I don't consider autism to be a disease, the question of whether I think people should be looking for a cure seems a bit irrelevant. It appears to be a simple enough 'yes' or 'no' type question needing the same kind of answer, but as usual the answer is anything but straightforward.

People – especially autistic people – love to think in absolutes. Feeling like you know the answers to some of life's questions *for certain* is very comforting, and there are some things you definitely *do* need to be certain about: 'gravity makes things fall' is a good one, as is 'fire is hot' and 'humans need air to breathe'. Other than these type of indisputable facts, I've found that Life – in all its gloriously random unpredictability – is never truly black and white, especially when it comes to something as complex as autism.

Just to be clear about this: I don't believe for one second that autism *itself* should be cured, and furthermore I don't actually believe that it *can* be. I do believe however that autism should be thoroughly researched and understood, and that as a result, autistic people should be supported, encouraged and celebrated as the infinitely diverse human beings they are, with the focus put firmly on reducing the difficulties they deal with as a result of the condition. The thing is, no matter how much I believe that this *should* happen, I'm not naïve enough to think that it *will* happen, or that research like this would ever be properly funded if the desire to find a cure was completely removed from the equation.

The truth is that research into providing a 'cure' is going to continue whether I want it to or not, and to use up my energy worrying about what might happen as a result, isn't something that will make anyone's life any easier, especially my children's, so it's not something I'm willing to do.

I know people who spend their whole lives consumed by fear over a future where autism could be detected using a prenatal blood test, believing without question that this will lead to the persecution and ultimate destruction of all autistic people. Clearly, feeling like you know the answers to *some* of life's questions *for certain* is anything but comforting. The reality of the situation however is far less dramatic. There are some people walking this earth who believe all autistic people should be annihilated. For what it's worth, there are also autistic people walking the same earth who believe being autistic means you're part of the next step in human evolution and that anyone who's *not* autistic should therefore be annihilated instead. It sounds outrageous, but these people really are out there. I know, because I have to deal with them (although I avoid doing so whenever possible nowadays). People like this, you'll be unsurprised to hear, are very much in the minority, and no matter what's said or done, their opinions won't change. If you meet someone like this, my advice would be to follow my lead and unashamedly head in the opposite direction. Remember, you don't have to attend every argument you're invited to, especially those that are impossible to win.

These scaremongers will try to terrify you into believing their particular point of view, and those on both sides of the argument are just as passionate about their extreme beliefs. I imagine putting them in a room together would be something like dropping a large chunk of sodium into a bucket of cold water: fascinating to watch but only from a safe distance. Yes, that was a little bit of chemistry humour there, just in case anyone had briefly forgotten what a total nerd I am.

Personally, I prefer to walk a more moderate (and therefore more optimistic) path. Please don't mistake this for ignorance or naivety on my part, because it's actually anything but. I *choose* to focus on the positives in every situation, no matter how tough, not through a desire to close my eyes to the more difficult issues, but as a result of many, many wasted years of focussing on the negatives. With experience I've gained a lot of insight into the most productive ways to focus my energy, and as a result I've learned that in certain situations, acceptance, flexibility and going with the flow is nothing to do with being lazy and everything to do with being wise.

The road to finding a 'cure' will be a long one, I'm sure, and with proper research it's possible that many of the difficulties experienced by autistic people will become better understood along the way. Make no mistake; being autistic isn't all sunshine and roses. Living with autism is beyond tough, and it's far more likely that the reason most people are looking for a cure is because they want to reduce the distress it causes, not because they want to destroy anyone.

The crucial point here is that many people are trying to cure autism without really understanding what it is, and looking at it as a foreign entity (like a disease) isn't going to help, because autism doesn't really work like that. If you approach autism as a disease and try to eradicate it from a person, you'll fail. If you approach it as a way of being, and accept it, you're on the right track towards successfully handling it. Autism itself doesn't need to be eradicated; autistic people need to be shown that it's okay to be as they are, that everyone is different and that thinking and behaving differently isn't necessarily a bad thing. They can then be taught self-acceptance and all kinds of new strategies to reduce the anxieties that are a natural part of life on the spectrum.

I'm not pretending it's easy being autistic or living with someone who has the condition – it can be frightening, overpowering and utterly exhausting. Looking for the positives among the large number of obvious negatives can be hard to say the least, but sometimes even the smallest change in the way you look at autism can make all the difference.

So, practicing what I preach and focussing on the positives here, I have great faith that increased understanding will give us fresh opportunities to help relieve some of the inevitable distress that autism brings with it. All kinds of new approaches for intervention and support, from behavioural to social and even medical, are likely to be developed as a result of this kind of research and anything that improves the lives of people living with autism is okay by me.

The more facts that are proven by science, the more tolerant and accepting the general population are going to become towards autism. It's true that science is still working on things that many of us have known for a very long time, but knowing something happens and proving *why* and *how* it happens in a way that's accepted as a fact by people with no experience of the condition are two very different things.

During my time as an autism parent the official guidelines on what causes autism have changed beyond recognition, leading to far greater acceptance and understanding of the way autism affects both children and adults. Whether you're pro or anti-cure, the fact remains that this wouldn't have happened without billions being invested into researching its origins with a view to curing the condition.

Ultimately, for me, the answer lies not in wiping the condition out but in accepting it as a natural part of being human, then putting everything you've got into understanding it and alleviating the pain, trauma and heartache it involves.

Looking for a cure isn't ideal then, but a lot of good still comes from the search for it and hey, with any luck, one day scientists will be able to prove beyond doubt that autism isn't a disease after all. Until then, my advice would be to recognise this fact for yourself and get on with the business of integrating autism into your life rather than trying to get rid of it.

Quack, quack!

Sadly there's a much darker side to the search for a cure as well, and one that completely sickens me at times. 'Quack' cures and those who sell them have popped up throughout history when people are confused, afraid and desperate to stop the pain they or their loved ones are going through.

As long as people continue to be uneducated about what autism *really* is, then parents, families and even autistic people themselves will be easy targets for anyone who offers them a 'miracle cure' to magically stop their anguish.

It's easy to judge people who turn to alternative treatments to deal with autism, but can you really blame them for being convinced of even the most unlikely ideas when they're in such a hugely vulnerable state? Sometimes, hope may be all people have left to keep them going; I know that was the case for me for many years, but not only do many of these so-called 'cures' not work, but in some cases they actually cause a great deal of harm.

Some of the most disturbing 'cures' I've heard of include using chemicals to strip metal from autistic people's blood, making them drink industrial strength bleach (yes, really – look up Miracle Mineral Solution), exorcism (I simply have no words to describe the horror of this particular process), and even chemical castration. Unfortunately I'm not making any of these treatments up. There are *so* many more, but focussing on them for too long is incredibly upsetting for me so I'll leave you to do your own research on this particular subject, I think.

Suffice to say that children (and adults) all over the world are being subjected to unimaginable torture in a quest to rid them of their autism.

When you read about these kinds of abusive practices there's a danger of thinking that *every* form of complementary medicine must be totally useless or even harmful for autistic people, but that's certainly not what I've found myself. Like many autism parents, I've given lots of different treatments a try over the years to see whether they could improve the quality of my children's lives, and I've discovered two interesting things as a result: Firstly that there *are* unconventional treatments out there that can and do help, and that secondly what works for one person won't necessarily work for another. The treatments I've found the most successful are those which are suitable for *everyone* whether they're on the spectrum or not (i.e. *not* exorcism!) because, unsurprisingly, autistic people have a lot of the same needs as everybody else, so meeting those needs can help them handle autism's challenges more successfully.

Should autistic people be changed?

As with any condition that causes adverse effects, there'll always be a small minority of people who believe it's morally wrong to intervene in any way. Their opinion is that if a baby is born with impaired hearing, mobility or sight, it should remain impaired, because that's how the individual was designed. They believe curing blindness or deafness is wrong because it's implying there's something bad about not being able to see or hear, which they think of as an insult to blind and deaf people. I'm sure it won't come as a big surprise to you that I don't agree with these people in the slightest.

By the same token there are some people (although not many, obviously) who believe that using any form of support to encourage autistic people to make progress is wrong, because by doing this you're not completely accepting them as they are; unsurprisingly, I don't agree with these people either.

Often they believe being born this way is some kind of test or that some divine being has decreed it as part of His (or Her) unfathomably mysterious master plan. This usually involves the idea of family and friends, or sometimes even the world at large, needing to learn the lessons that an autistic person has come to teach them.

With the development of modern scientific techniques, I would argue that perhaps *the relief of distress through intervention* is just as likely to be part of that same plan. I can also assure you absolutely and categorically that many people – myself included - wouldn't have learned anywhere *near* as much from my children as we have as a result of them being able to communicate well and live independently. Obviously not all autistic people will be able to do those things, but giving them the chance to progress and achieve their own goals is *so* important, whatever those goals might be.

Autistic people are *not* passive martyrs sent here to teach us virtues like patience and humility by remaining in a state of dependent suffering; they're living, breathing, developing human beings with an incredible amount to contribute, who have as much right to be encouraged and educated as every other person on the planet. Change is a natural part of the process of being human and to deny autistic people the opportunity to experience it goes against everything I believe in.

So, until we know the details of this supposed 'plan' for sure (which we clearly never will) perhaps it's best to remember that life is short, and to simply do whatever we can to make the world a happier, healthier place for everyone, using *all* the tools we have available.

It's easy to laugh at religious or ethical beliefs if they're very far removed from your own, but for some people this is a genuine dilemma. As much as they must surely hate seeing their children or grandchildren suffering, their conscience simply won't allow them to address the challenges and work towards overcoming them in an effective way, so please don't be too hard on them if you meet someone like this.

Another reason for refusing to intervene can come from a mistaken belief that disabled people are entitled to be treated as 'special' because they're somehow *better* than able bodied people. Personally I've found that the vast majority of autism parents have no interest in receiving special treatment at the expense of anyone else, but there are those who expect their children to be accommodated *exactly* as they are by the world's general population, whether or not it's practical or even safe.

Other people's rights or feelings become irrelevant to them and anyone who disagrees with their ideas is usually labelled as 'ignorant', 'prejudiced', 'privileged' or 'ableist' (which is definitely not my favourite expression). To deny anyone access to whatever help might be available, leaving them in a state of permanent dependence just to prove that they're 'special' and that their autism is being 'fully accepted' because you think this makes them (or indeed you) somehow superior to other people isn't something I'll ever agree with or understand.

To me, accepting autism doesn't mean giving up or giving in to it, it means recognising that it's there and acting accordingly. Once you find out what it is, you can put your energy into handling it properly by reducing the negative impact it brings while celebrating and encouraging all the positives too. Teaching autistic people to value themselves but not to think of themselves as being entitled to better treatment than anyone else definitely seems like the best course of action to me. Isn't that what it means to truly embrace the diversity of *every* human being, and what all decent parents want to do for their child whether they have autism or not?

Choices, choices...

At the other end of the scale there are those who believe all autistic children are so utterly worthless they should automatically be aborted before they even draw breath. I'll always remember the first time I read about the idea of a prenatal test being offered to pregnant women so they could choose whether or not to keep their autistic child. It suddenly struck me how parents of children with Down's syndrome must feel, and it genuinely made my blood run cold just to think of it. Now it's fair to say that my children and I agree on most things. None of them smoke, take drugs or commit crimes, nor would they tolerate bullying without stepping in to help. There are all kinds of social, moral and ethical issues that never need to be argued over in our family simply because we all feel exactly the same way about them. The highly sensitive subject of abortion, however, isn't one of them.

More than one of my children can accurately be described as being about as 'pro-life' as it's possible to be. They believe 100% in every child having the absolute right to be born, whether its parents want it to be or not. Their view is that no matter what the circumstances are, there's always, *always* a way for every person on this planet to experience a decent quality of life and that everyone should be given the chance to live, right from the point of conception.

This attitude makes me immensely proud of both their faith in the goodness of human nature and of their ability to relate to countless numbers of potential human beings, the vast majority of whom they'll never meet. I totally support them in this view even though it's one I no longer share.

As a child, the very idea of deliberately terminating a pregnancy revolted me. When I was born in 1966, abortion was still against the law and wasn't legalised until the passing of the Abortion Act in 1967. As a result, the world I grew up in was saturated in shame and guilt – both religious and social – about *anything* related to what was seen as the wilful murder of an unborn child, no matter how extreme the situation was.

When I became a parent myself, I fully expected to still feel the same way, but what I've realised over the years is that there will never be a 'one size fits all' solution to an issue as complex and important as this one. We can't possibly predict all the different scenarios that might lead to a woman deciding on an abortion, so personally I believe that when a woman finds herself in this kind of situation, she should have as many options and choices available to her as possible, including the option to terminate her pregnancy.

My personal choices

I remember when I was pregnant with Christopher everyone asked me 'Do you want a boy or a girl?' and instead of the standard reply of 'Oh, I don't mind as long as it's healthy...' I was adamant I wanted a boy. In fact, I *only* wanted boys, no matter how many children I had in the future. Having grown up in a house full of women, I'd made my mind up long ago that boys were definitely the answer and would be far more fun to bring up than girls (yes, that would be the sound of Life laughing up its sleeve at me yet again).

When I did indeed produce a fine, healthy son, everyone was thrilled, and in truth no-one was more delighted than I was.

Three years later I was expecting again, and this time I found that everyone's attitudes seemed to have changed for some reason. 'Oh, I bet you're hoping for a girl this time...' was generally the first thing anyone said to me.

By then my own perspective was very different and I'd realised that babies, rather than being little objects you could choose to dress up in one set of colours or another, were in fact living, breathing individuals whose gender, while shaping a large part of who they were, wasn't actually all that important to me as a mother. This time I was more interested in *who my baby was* rather than the body he or she would be born into, so my answer was 'Well, if I had the choice I'd rather have another boy, but the most important thing is that the baby's healthy' and I meant it.

This didn't seem to go down all that well with a lot of people, as if there were some weird gender conspiracy going on behind the scenes whereby I *had* to want a girl otherwise there was something wrong with me. Still, when Dominic was born people congratulated me and seemed to be happy enough, and personally I was over the moon to have another son.

Over the next few years the boys both suffered horribly as a result of their autism and it's safe to say that it was more like living in a war zone than a family home most of the time, yet I adored them both and was fascinated by how incredibly different they were from each other. As Dominic approached three I was gripped by an overwhelming desire to have a third son and having thought long and hard about the pros and cons, I made up my mind to go for it and was soon expecting my third child.

This time something very interesting happened: As you'll already know, I was now carrying Aidan, but at the time no-one was aware of this, and for some reason he was much smaller than both his brothers had been, pretty much all the way through the pregnancy. 'Oh, this time it's *definitely* a girl then!' I was told, time and time again, along with 'Wow! You must *really* want a girl to have *another* baby!' and 'Won't it be lovely to have a little girl this time?' as if the outcome was already decided.

As with the other two pregnancies, I didn't want to know the baby's gender in advance, so I never asked at any of the scans, but fate intervened on that one, which is when things took a rather nasty turn.

Pat is very tall (6ft 5 with size 13 feet) and I'm 5ft 8, so it's not surprising that our babies were very large. In Dominic's case though, he was *too* large; so large in fact that I was unable to give birth to him naturally and had to have a caesarean three weeks before his due date so that we'd both survive. I very nearly didn't, which is another story altogether, but as I said before, when Dom was born he was the skinniest baby I'd ever seen, yet he was enormous and weighed almost ten pounds.

To be on the safe side, with my third pregnancy my consultant decided I should have a late scan to decide whether or not I could have a natural delivery this time. Babies can sometimes be 'shy' when you have an ultrasound and keep their legs crossed so you can't work out their gender. Aidan was definitely *not* one of those babies. The instant the first image appeared on the screen both the sonographer and I were in no doubt whatsoever that he was a boy. I remember she was quite upset and said 'I'm so sorry – I know you didn't want to know.' 'That's okay' I said 'clearly *he* wanted us to know, didn't he?'

I drove home feeling on top of the world that I'd soon have three beautiful sons, but pretty soon a thought started to nag away at me: 'Should I tell people before he's born? They're all going to be so disappointed, and I don't think I'll handle that too well when I've just given birth...'

Testing the water

I decided to mention it to one or two people to start with and see how it went. The first person I told was very excited that I'd found out the baby's gender and couldn't wait to hear what it was. With a huge smile, I told her that I was having another boy, and that's when her face fell. We were in a public place and she said *way* too loudly 'Oh, NO! Don't you wish you'd had an abortion?' She might as well have slapped me in the face. I was completely stunned she thought it was okay to say something like that to a very heavily pregnant woman, but she wasn't finished yet. 'Look' she said 'I have to ask you this: why on earth would you want to have another boy when you've already got those two?' By now I was fighting back tears so I mumbled 'I love my boys', made my excuses and left. I have to admit I was extremely upset by what had happened, but I didn't fully understand it yet, so being an optimistic person, a couple of days later I told someone else. 'Oh my God, I'm SO sorry!' she wailed – I mean she really did *wail*, like it was the end of the world or something – 'Don't you wish you'd had an abortion while you still had the time? What on earth are you going to do now?'

What are you supposed to say to that when you're almost nine months pregnant?

'Errr…have another son?' was all I managed at the time.

The third person I told was the last. She was a child care professional so I expected a better response from her. Once again I smiled and said 'It's a boy!' 'Oh, no! That's terrible!' she said 'Don't you wish you'd had an abortion now rather than having another one of *those* children?'

And that was when it hit me; less like a slap in the face this time and more like a punch in the gut: it wasn't that people didn't want me to have any more boys, it was that they didn't want me to have any more *autistic* boys. Back then no-one had a clue autistic girls even existed, so here was the answer to why they were all so desperate for me to have a girl: they thought she wouldn't be like her brothers – they thought she would be 'normal'.

I finally understood that when they looked at my boys they saw something defective and unlovable, something that should have been rejected and destroyed. It's no exaggeration to say that when I realised what people *really* thought of my beautiful little family, what they talked about in whispers behind my back and what they *truly* considered was the best way to deal with my sons, it simply broke my heart.

The beloved youngest son

With just over two weeks to go before Aidan's due date, I spent much of my time crying bitterly about their heartlessness whenever I could snatch a moment to myself. When I told Pat what had happened he just couldn't understand why I was so upset. His response was the same every time I mentioned it: 'Why do you care so much what other people think? Just ignore them.' While I could see his point, the truth was that I *did* care what people thought. I cared desperately. Not for myself, but for my boys. I cared that people would judge them and reject them; they were already dealing with so much and I wondered how they were ever going to succeed in a world full of people who secretly wished they didn't exist at all.

Aidan was born right on time and to me he was gorgeous: blonde haired, blue eyed and a perfect miniature of his father and brothers. I remember looking over at his tiny, perfectly round head as he slept in his cot on our first night in hospital and feeling such a rush of happiness that had I not been hooked up to several drips and full of endless stitches I might well have got up and danced for joy. As it was I settled for punching the air and letting out a quiet 'Yes!' so as not to wake the other women on the ward.

I called him Aidan (meaning 'the small, fiery one') because firstly he was so much smaller than his brothers and secondly he didn't stop kicking, punching, wriggling and twisting from the moment he first grew arms and legs. By now I knew Pat and I wouldn't have any more children together so I gave Aidan the middle name Benjamin, meaning 'the beloved youngest son' because, quite simply, he was, is and always will be just that.

The reaction to Aidan's arrival was...well...muted to say the least. Several people actually avoided eye contact with me when they saw me holding him; some even crossed the street.

Aidan himself was far more like Christopher than Dominic as a baby and screamed piteously for hours on end. Unlike my other two boys I was completely unable to comfort him, and cuddling him - or even touching him at all - actually made him *more* upset for some reason which I didn't as yet understand.

I've felt isolated many times since Christopher was born, but I think the months after I had Aidan were when I felt most completely alone. My marriage to Pat was collapsing under the strain of living with such intense levels of autism day after day, and those few people I considered I could still speak to about my boys had all reacted incredibly badly to the news of Aidan's arrival. There was no internet support network like there is today; no links to other families across the world who loved their autistic children as much as I loved mine, just day after day filled with endless isolation and new ways to experience rejection from people who clearly thought I'd lost my mind.

Why I had four of 'those' children

I was aware by the time Dominic was born that any more children I had would also be autistic, and I've been asked many times why, knowing this, I still went on to have four. Yes, I know, it's shocking isn't it? People still, *to this day*, think it's okay to ask me why on earth I wanted four of *those* children. I've even been told that I *shouldn't* have had four. That always goes down about as well as you'd expect.

In my opinion *every* mother's reasons for the number of children she has are entirely her own and I don't believe women should have to justify their choices on this subject, whether autism is a factor or not. Human beings are driven by hugely powerful forces when it comes to reproduction and whether someone decides to have one child, lots of children or none at all, the reasons for their decision are deeply personal, and not something any of us have the right to judge when we know nothing about their circumstances. Since it's such a relevant question here though, I'm happy to explain it to you in my own case.

The answer is actually a very simple one: It turns out I absolutely *love* autistic people. I've never had a child without autism, and although I'm certain that in many ways it's a lot easier to parent neurotypical children, ever since Christopher was born I've never really felt it was a *better* option, only a different one. That doesn't mean parenting autistic children is easy – far from it - but the truth is I find autistic people endlessly fascinating and inspiring. To say it's hard work would be a massive understatement, but there's so much more to parenting any child than just the work involved, and autism really does take the rewards of parenting to a whole new dimension.

All good parents rediscover the world through the eyes of their children; autism parents get the opportunity to explore its wonders on a level they never even knew existed. The way autistic people make sense of the world gives me hope for a better future for the whole of humanity, and when I meet them it's like a spark is ignited inside me. It's hard to put into words, but somehow they bring me to life, and unsurprisingly no one does that more powerfully than my own children. Is it any wonder I wanted more than one?

You see, I didn't have more children in the hope that the next one might not be autistic, so I could somehow make up for the 'defective' ones I'd already got, I had them for the same reason most women do: because I loved the ones I had very deeply and I wanted more children who were a little bit like them, only different. If one of my children *hadn't* been autistic, would I have loved them any less? Not a chance.

As long as autism is seen as a disease or something to be wiped out, there'll always be people who'll judge me for my choices and that's something I've got used to over the years. It saddens me, of course, but I can honestly say that no-one who's actually *met* any of my children still feels my choices were in any way wrong, and that says it all really, doesn't it?

Ultimately, even with all the thousands of words I have at my disposal I'll never be able to express how much I adore all four of my children, so if I'd been given the option to abort one (or all) of them because a blood test had shown they were autistic, would I have done it? No prizes for guessing that the answer to that one is 'No', but what if I'd been told all the negatives about autism and none of the positives when I was expecting Christopher and I knew nothing about autistic people? What then?

As it happens, I would still have gone ahead with the pregnancy, because in my case abortion isn't something I could ever bring myself to do, but as I've already said, I still believe it should be an option that's available to other women, just not for the sole reason that their child is autistic.

Should autistic children be aborted?

I've got the benefit of over twenty five years of autism parenting behind me now so it's not surprising to hear that I disagree with the idea of ending a pregnancy because your baby is autistic, but suppose you're new to the condition and you know nothing about it except all the scare stories you read in the papers and see online? Surely they'd give you pause for thought, and rightly so in my opinion. Becoming a parent is a serious business. You're never the same once you have a child, and your life will change forever in ways you can't possibly imagine before it happens. Not everyone is cut out to be a parent as we all know from the horrific reports we see on the news about children being tortured and murdered by their own mothers and fathers. Making the decision to have a child is one of the biggest, most overwhelming things you'll ever do, and that's nothing to do with autism, it's something that applies to *all* decent parents, whatever their circumstances. Becoming an autism parent is really, really tough, and anyone who tells you differently is either lying or doesn't actually know what they're talking about.

What if I ever had to choose?

I'm writing this book in 2017 and as yet there's no pre-natal test that can tell you whether or not your child is autistic. If it ever came to making this choice though, there'd be no point running away from the reality of the situation, so the most important thing would be to make sure you were very well informed before you made any decisions at all.

If you find yourself in this situation one day, my advice would be to research as much as you can about what living with autism is really like. Not just the wonderful, inspiring stuff but the difficult, scary stuff too. Really get a sense of what being an autism parent might mean, in the same way you would research being a parent if your child didn't have autism. Nowadays there are parenting magazines about raising autistic children (something I could definitely have done with when my boys were small) and all kinds of free online support right at your fingertips, so do your homework and find out what autism is all about. Only you can decide whether or not to end your pregnancy and you really do owe it to yourself (and to your unborn child) to make an informed choice rather than acting out of fear or from a lack of understanding.

One vital thing to remember when it comes to autism is that there *is* no clear-cut reality where everything is either one thing or the other, so a blood test can only tell you that you're carrying a person who'll potentially struggle with life at some level or another. What form those struggles will take isn't something that can ever be foreseen.

There can never be a blood test that will predict how autism is going to develop once your child has been born because they'll also be shaped by their environment. Your child's brain can, and will, change, develop and grow according to what he or she experiences, and no blood test can predict that for you.

There is some good news though: if your pre-natal test shows that your child *is* autistic, they can get all the help and support they need right from the very start (and so can you) and believe me that will make a whole world of difference to how much progress you both make.

Having an autistic child is hugely rewarding and it's also very hard work. It's like having any child then always having to go the extra mile. It's about letting go of your ideas about what it's like to bring up 'a child' and instead becoming flexible enough to nurture and support an individual. If that's something you're prepared to do, I'd definitely suggest you go for it, and once you do, you'll find reserves of strength and resilience within yourself that you never even dreamed of. What you really need in this situation though is lots of information and practical help, and with those in place from Day One, anything is possible.

The Parable of Good or Bad

An ancient Chinese proverb tells of a poor farmer who had only one elderly horse to help him in his fields. One day, the horse slipped its rope and ran off into the hills. The other villagers were horrified and told the old man how sorry they were to hear about his terrible luck. Much to their surprise the farmer didn't seem upset about it and simply said "Bad luck? Good luck? Who knows?" The villagers went away shaking their heads, because they *knew* this was a terrible thing to have happened.

A week later, the horse returned, bringing with it a herd of beautiful young horses from the hills and this time the villagers congratulated the farmer on this wonderful piece of good luck. Once again, his reply was, "Good luck? Bad luck? Who knows?" The villagers shook their heads again and said 'What's wrong with him? *Of course* this is a piece of good luck!'

Some time later, the farmer's son was trying to tame one of the wild horses, and it threw him from its back. He broke his leg so badly that it was questionable whether he would ever walk unaided again. Now the villagers *knew* that this was bad luck, and were even more confused when the farmer's only reaction was: "Bad luck? Good luck? Who knows?" By now, the villagers were sure that the old man was losing his mind. "Why can't he see what terrible luck this is?" they asked each other, and once again went away shaking their heads.

A few months later, the country was plunged into a violent war, and soon the army marched into the village. Every able-bodied young man they found there was forced to join up and fight, but when they saw the farmer's son with his badly broken leg, he was allowed to stay at home with his father. The question is, was that good luck or bad luck?

Who knows?

Some things that appear to be dreadful could turn out to be a blessing in disguise, while others might seem wonderful on the surface but could in fact be a terrible trial.

The wisest thing to do is to go with the flow and look for the positives, even if sometimes they're very well hidden indeed.

Helen always took one or two
suggestions along to the IEP meeting...

Chapter Seven

String Theory:
Untangling the SEN System

'If you've met one person with autism,
you've met one person with autism.'

Dr. Stephen Shore

I'm guessing most people reading this have heard the expression 'How long is a piece of string?' For anyone who hasn't, it's something people say in response to an unanswerable question, such as 'How long does it take to become a great painter?' or 'What shape is a cloud?'

The reason these questions are unanswerable is because their answers rely on so many different factors that it's impossible to predict them. It's the same with a piece of string: to know how long a piece of string is, you'd have to…well…you'd have to already know how long it is to start with, otherwise you'd just be guessing, wouldn't you?

People ask me all the time 'What is autism?' or 'What's it like to be autistic?' and ultimately, even with everything that's known about the condition, the only 100% accurate answer here would still have to be 'How long is a piece of string?'

The challenge with autism is that no matter how much you identify about its physical, emotional, psychological or spiritual origins, even down to the microscopic level of someone's DNA itself, you still won't be able to fully understand what it actually *is*. Why? Because autism is there right from conception, building and shaping each individual on every possible level, and not only that, but it affects every individual in a huge variety of different ways. As a result, no two people will have the same experience of being autistic, and no two people will *be* the same just because they're both autistic. Just like being human. We can analyse, investigate and categorise what it means to be human and with luck we can get closer and closer to understanding some of the different aspects of what makes us who we are, but that's really not the same thing as being able to fully explain every human being on the planet. Explaining autism is a lot like that. Just to make the condition even *more* difficult to understand, the way autism affects each individual will also change depending on their environment, their emotional state and an endless number of other factors, so at certain times it can overwhelm them and at others they can be largely unaffected by it, even though to the outside world there seems to be no logical reason for these differences in behaviour since nothing in their environment appears to have changed.

These *super*-helpful facts about autism lead directly to three things: firstly, parenting autistic children is beyond confusing (understatement), secondly, diagnosing someone with autism is notoriously difficult, and thirdly, unless some revolutionary miracle occurs, then providing an education system which meets every autistic person's needs is always going to be impossible.

Yes, I said it: the diagnostic procedure is complicated and when it comes to autism, the special educational needs (SEN) system isn't perfect. I'm sure that doesn't come as much of a surprise to anyone who's been involved with either one or both of them, whether they're a parent, teacher or health professional and since these things can be incredibly frustrating for everyone, it's understandable that tensions run very high when the SEN system is being discussed. It's easy to blame the education system for failing to meet the needs of your child, but the reality is that with the best will in the world, there's never going to be a 'one size fits all' solution here, which is where your ability to work through the inevitable glitches and tangles of the system without going under is going to make all the difference.

Imagine for a moment we're not discussing autism but we're discussing diabetes instead. Supporting children with diabetes requires extra training for staff covering how best to meet their needs on a day to day basis, during school trips and when they're taking exams. Making sure they have the right equipment to test their blood sugar and administer their insulin as well as giving them access to regular snacks and drinks will be vitally important in keeping them safe and healthy, and although each child will need an Individual Healthcare Plan (IHP) to cover the variations in dosage, who to contact in an emergency etc. the basics are pretty much the same. This really isn't the case with autism at all.

I've had more than my fair share of moments when frustration at the SEN system has got the better of me, but the increase in support offered to autistic children since my boys were small has been beyond anything I could have imagined back then. When I was born in 1966 the SEN system as we know it today didn't even exist and it wasn't until the publication of the Warnock Report in the late 1970's that the term 'special educational needs' was even introduced. Without it my children's lives would have been totally different, so I've always been grateful for the opportunities it's given them, despite the system itself being far from ideal. Personally, I've had a mixed experience when it comes to my children's education.

I've seen first-hand the unforgivable damage that can be done by ill-informed and insensitive teachers: emotional and psychological damage that haunts my children to this day. I've also met some of the most patient, dedicated and compassionate people I could hope for; people who keep persevering against seemingly impossible odds to draw out the best in autistic children, simply because they believe that everyone has potential no matter how hard it might be to uncover. I can tell you about *my* children's experiences, but what will *your* child's experience of the SEN system be like? Again, the only honest answer to that question is 'How long is a piece of string?' which I realise isn't a great deal of help. Fortunately I've learned some very useful coping strategies along the way which I'm happy to share with you, so even if you're tearing your hair out over their education at the moment, don't despair because there's always hope.

Could do better

Christopher was born in 1991, when the word 'autism' was very rarely heard in mainstream education and was generally reserved for children who attended special schools. Thinking back to the way he was treated by some of his teachers, it's not unreasonable to describe their behaviour towards him as 'shocking'. Despite being in speech therapy since the age of three, no-one (well, no-one other than me of course) seemed to recognise that his speech delay was only a very small percentage of what he was trying to cope with. By this point I'd had his hearing tested several times because I was certain he couldn't hear properly, and had researched everything from iron deficiency to childhood schizophrenia in the hopes of discovering the answer to his unusual behaviour. Naturally I'd looked into autism as a possible reason and to me it seemed to fit him perfectly, but whenever I mentioned it to a health professional they'd instantly dismiss it, and they seemed so certain he couldn't have it that eventually I started to doubt myself. Remember things were all very new to me at this point, so although I was determined to do something positive and proactive about his difficulties, it had got to the point where I was starting to believe that perhaps we'd never find any real answers as to what was causing them.

Since he had no diagnosis, Christopher was expected to just get on with it and manage, which of course he couldn't, and when I tried to explain that he needed some extra support, I was told that whatever he was going through was my fault. Oh, and also that he was everything from spoilt, humourless and oversensitive to stubborn and unemployable. One health professional told me he couldn't speak because I spoke too much and never gave him a chance to get a word in edgeways, then on her next visit (having presumably forgotten her previous advice) she told me he couldn't speak because I didn't speak to him enough. As unbelievable as this might sound to today's generation, this kind of thing happened so often, in so many different environments, that by the time Dominic came along a few years later I deliberately avoided taking him to have developmental assessments with any health professionals unless they really were essential.

I'd already been labelled as one of *those* parents and had been in the middle of more arguments than I care to remember, none of which seemed to be getting me (and more importantly Christopher) anywhere except onto the 'Avoid at All Costs' list. Constantly raising my stress levels by dealing with people who had no idea about autism was beginning to cause Christopher a lot of stress as well, and to start the process all over again with my second son, while still desperately trying to help my first, just didn't seem worth it.

As it happened, Dominic was so vastly different to his brother and I knew so little about autism at this point that I often wondered whether he had it at all. His developmental delays didn't seem *too* bad to me and were certainly similar to his brother's at the same age. Although Christopher was still struggling, he'd made a lot of progress, so if by some miracle we'd had a half decent day, I'd do my best to convince myself that perhaps my sons were just late starters and would eventually catch up with the other children without any outside intervention being necessary. Although this was the unanimous opinion of every other member of my family, in my heart I always knew it wasn't true, but it's incredible what you'll believe when you're desperate.

There came a point of course where I couldn't deny it to myself any longer. When he was eighteen months old I decided to take Dominic to a mother and baby class that focussed on music and movement, and to say things went badly would be a bit of an understatement. We sat in a circle on the floor and I looked on in horror as babies of at least a year younger than Dominic joined in and copied their mothers' clapping, smiling and hand movements, things that were completely beyond him at the time. While the other eighteen month olds happily sang along with the familiar nursery rhymes, Dominic ran round and round the circle without showing the slightest understanding of why we were there, before breaking into a side room, stealing the group leader's sandwiches and squashing them between the keys of her piano. We were politely asked not to come back.

By the time we got home I felt numb with shock. It had suddenly dawned on me that until now I'd only been comparing Dominic's progress to his brother's, who had some serious issues of his own of course, and now, having seen him next to these happy, cooperative children who had no developmental delays at all, I finally understood just how much he'd fallen behind. I realised he needed much more help than I could give him on my own and reluctantly made the decision to get him assessed.

Bracing myself for what was to come, I took Dominic to have his two year check. Sure enough it was every bit as grim as I'd imagined, and to this day it remains the only meeting I've ever attended where I was reduced to standing up and shouting at a health professional from across a desk. I could quite easily write a whole chapter on how badly this particular woman handled the situation, but suffice to say that her insistence that he 'could quite easily draw an elephant if only I would stop saying that he couldn't' when he wasn't even able to pick up a pencil, and that she'd seen 'lots and lots of children whose only problem was the way their mothers spoiled them' didn't go down very well with me at all.

She told me very loudly to 'shut up and stop making excuses for him' (yes, that's exactly what she said to me) which I duly did, whilst almost biting my tongue in half with the effort, as I watched her fail time and time again to get him to pay her any attention or complete the age appropriate tasks she was certain he was just too stubborn (or too badly parented) to try.

About half way through the meeting she seemed to change her mind about him when she offered him a book to look at which opened from the bottom upwards. Having never seen a book that opened this way, he turned it on its side and opened it the normal way instead. She watched him bend his head *way* too far over to one side to look at the pictures (he has hypermobility) and said contemptuously 'Look at him – just look at him – he doesn't even know what a book is.'

This woman then became the first (but certainly not the last) person to tell me that the best thing I could do now was give up on my son. She told me with utter certainty that he would never progress, never speak, never feed himself, never use a toilet, never attend school; never do *anything* really except stay as he was or get progressively worse. There was no way at all he could be educated in her opinion, so it was best to accept that now and start making the appropriate plans, because, you know, she was the expert here, so that was that.

Funnily enough I disagreed and began to explain how far his brother had come since he was Dominic's age, despite all the dire predictions that he too was beyond help. This was the point at which she stood up and raised her voice just that little bit too much to inform me that Dominic was a different person to his brother, so there was no point in making comparisons, and that I was so far in denial about the fact he would never progress that there was also no point in talking to me about him anymore. Cue one rather unpleasant shouting match.

I won't lie to you: at the time I could've cheerfully strangled her. The mixture of desperation, exhaustion and sheer bloody terror I was experiencing on a daily basis by this stage, with two young undiagnosed autistic boys to care for, had transformed me into a dangerously unstable woman whose only concern was finding out what on earth was going on and how best she could help her sons. No-one seemed to have any answers other than 'boys develop more slowly than girls' or 'well, he's just a bit backward, isn't he?' and yet, being the annoyingly determined parent that I am, I still refused to give up on either of them.

By the time I left the meeting it had been agreed (somewhat *loudly*, I might add) that Dominic would be sent for speech therapy at the local hospital. I believe the words 'He's *my* son, so how about you do your job, leave me to do mine and we'll both see what happens next, shall we?' might have crossed my lips rather forcefully at one point. Not my best contribution to parent/health professional relations, and not something I'm particularly proud of, but it seemed to get the job done nonetheless. Clearly we disagreed about whether or not there was any point in her recommending this course of action for him, but she very reluctantly did so, and a few months later Dominic and I found ourselves attending our first session of speech therapy. Needless to say, to start with things didn't go well for us. At all.

Communication chaos

The first session began with the senior speech therapist gently rounding all the children up and sitting them at a long table. 'This way' she said brightly while guiding them along with her hands. Yes, you read that correctly: she used her *hands.* Twelve little boys allowed themselves to be manoeuvred into position, while one (no prizes for guessing *which* one of course) felt her hand resting on his back, jumped like a startled rabbit and bolted straight out the door. I found him some time later hiding under the sink in the ladies' toilets. After slowly enticing him back and explaining that no, she must *never* physically touch him, I was encouraged to leave Dominic with the rest of the children and join the other parents in a side room for some tea and biscuits.

As the weeks went by, things didn't really improve for us but we carried on attending because, well, at least they hadn't thrown us out yet. A lot of children in the group already seemed to understand basic Makaton sign language when they got there and those who didn't had picked it up by the third or fourth week. All except Dominic of course, who spent his time wedged under a table, hissing and scratching like a cat. Despite some genuinely heroic efforts on the part of the therapists, the only hand signals they ever got from him were his fingers shooting like lightning towards their eyes as he tried to gouge them from their sockets. If they managed to get him out from under the table, he'd sit and smash his head into the nearest hard surface, rip his arms open with his nails and rock backwards and forwards screaming until he could disappear underneath it again. I know, because I've seen the training videos they made with Dominic in them. It's safe to say that at this stage things weren't looking too promising for him education-wise. Once again I was told there was no hope of any progress being made and believe me I can totally understand why the specialists thought that way. I'd explain over and over again that Dominic was completely different at home and ask if perhaps something might be upsetting him during the sessions, but so little was known about autism and sensory processing disorder in those days that no-one understood how the combination of being under the harsh glare of the fluorescent lighting, feeling trapped in a room filled with noisy children and unfamiliar adults, and having no idea whatsoever why he was there might be causing him to go into meltdown.

I was advised many times to apply for a place at a local special school with a view to putting him into a care home when he was older and at this stage I did start to think it might be the best thing for him. I knew how he could behave in his own environment, but if this was the result of putting him into an unfamiliar one then perhaps it really was the only option open to us. It certainly didn't look like he'd cope in mainstream school, or indeed that the mainstream education system would be able to cope with him.

The majority of parents in the group did put their children into special schools without questioning the idea at all, but what held me back was how strongly I disagreed with all the other 'expert' advice I was being given on how to handle his developmental difficulties.

Dominic was a huge fan of Thomas the Tank Engine and would happily watch episode after episode and play with his Thomas toys for hours. We had die cast models of every train in the series (most of whom I can still name to this day) and I'd sort them into colour and size order and use them to explain things like red, blue, green, bigger and smaller to him. He never showed the slightest interest in what I was doing or saying but still I had a gut feeling he was getting something out of it so I persevered. One of the best things about the characters on TV was how overly simplified their faces were. 'James is happy today' or 'Thomas is angry' were represented by a very simple smiling or frowning face, and again I used the opportunity this gave me to teach him something about facial expressions.

The 'experts' were horrified, and told me I was encouraging his obsession which would delay his progress even further. Their advice was to take everything to do with Thomas away from him and *force* him to play with something else, which I should only give him if he made eye contact with me and asked for whatever it was using words. While the other parents followed these instructions to the letter, I thought it was downright cruel to do things like that to a non-verbal three year old and flatly refused. As you can imagine there was much tutting and shaking of heads at my rebellious ways, but this was nothing new to me so I stood my ground.

I had nothing against special schools, I just wanted to give Dominic the opportunity to go to mainstream if he possibly could, with the view that if it got too much for him there was always another option available. Thankfully the advice given to parents today is vastly different and much more in line with my way of parenting, but at the time I was very much a lone voice, lost in an overwhelming chorus of disapproval.

As it happened, when Dominic was four, everything began to change when he had a bit of a revelation after starting a course of cranial osteopathy. I'll talk about it in more detail in the next chapter, but suffice to say it was a definite turning point and the first step on a very different path to the one that had been predicted for him. It also proved that all my input (and that of the speech therapists) had indeed been working after all, as it turned out he'd taken everything we'd taught him on board but simply hadn't been able to let us know about it before.

Today so much more is understood about the way autistic people's brains work and how being non-verbal doesn't mean someone can't understand what's being said, so my advice if your child doesn't seem to be responding to you is this: if it's not upsetting them, grab every opportunity you can to teach them as much as possible about anything and everything, because you just never know what's going in and how much it might be helping them develop.

Believe me, I know it's hard and it can often seem like a thankless task, but there are lots of stories nowadays of autistic people who've learned to communicate later in life using electronic devices and have explained to their families and carers that yes, they did understand what was being said to them (and *about* them) when they were younger, so always, *always* assume that's the case. If it isn't, you've lost nothing, but if it is, then imagine how much good you're doing by engaging with them like this.

No matter how much support your child gets educationally, you will always be their greatest teacher, so find their special interest and use it to bond with them and encourage them to learn whenever you can. Again, don't turn yourself into a teacher because that's not your role unless you're home educating (and even then you can't be a teacher all the time) just find little opportunities to help them develop whenever you can while still being the same parent they know and love.

Managing in mainstream

I've spoken to many, many autism parents over the years who'd never even dream of sending their child to a mainstream school because they've heard too many horror stories about autistic children being bullied and don't want to expose their child to anything they can't handle. It's completely understandable because none of us want our children to suffer, but my advice is to think very carefully before dismissing mainstream as an option without at least trying it out first. I appreciate in some cases it simply won't be possible, but if it is, I'd urge you to be brave and give it a go, because although some of the lessons your child will learn there might be painful, that doesn't necessarily mean they're not useful ones too.

Nowadays many mainstream schools have specially designed units for children who need extra support and if your child attends one of these, they're still going to experience being in a mainstream environment which will help prepare them for life in the adult world far better than keeping them separate from neurotypical children. All four of my children have experienced bullying at one point or another during their school years and it's horribly upsetting, but we dealt with it together and came out the other side stronger and wiser as a result.

The sad truth is that children get bullied whether they have autism or not, and adults get bullied too unless they live in total isolation. There are random encounters with bullies like the aggressive customer behind them in the supermarket queue who intimidates them because they're taking too long to pay, and the red-faced, fist-shaking tyrant who screams obscenities at them in the grip of road rage. Harder to handle are the oppressive boss and disapproving supervisor who seem to delight in undermining their confidence, or the jealous work colleagues who exclude them from the clique. Trickiest of all are the 'friends' (or sometimes even family members) who pretend to be on their side while taking advantage of their trusting nature.

Everyone has to deal with bullies at some point in their lives and whether we like it or not, it's in the classroom and especially the playground that these battles are first fought, and the lessons we learn, however hard, are valuable ones nonetheless.

In our family we treat each other with love, patience and respect; we don't cheat or lie or steal from each other and we never put people down through jealousy or resentment because that's just not how we're made. Learning that people *can* behave in these ways, and more importantly how to handle them if they do, was something my children learned at school. They also learned how to make good friends and that (just as in the adult world) the vast majority of people are decent, trustworthy and kind. There's no denying there are some nasty people in the world though and I've always believed it's better for our children to get used to dealing with them when the stakes are lower and we're still largely in control of their safety and peace of mind than to suddenly expect them to learn about it when they're adults.

If your child is in danger, get them out, but first do everything you can to prevent that from happening. Stand up. Speak up. Use the free support that's out there. Get a second opinion. *You are all that stands between your child and the rest of the world.* Teach them by example how to be assertive and persistent, determined and focussed. Children learn from what you do, not from what you say, so show them how you can help resolve their problems if they tell you about them, and eventually they'll learn how to solve those same problems for themselves.

In the end of course, it comes down to what suits your child best. Each child is an individual and yours may do better being home educated, attending a smaller school, a special school, a unit or even going to a large, noisy comprehensive. However, my advice would always be to give them the best chance to function in the outside world as an adult by getting them used to the rough and tumble of life in mainstream to begin with, and if they're coping, not to give up and pull them out without a fight if things get tough.

Being actively patient

It's safe to say that with four children on the spectrum who've all attended mainstream schools, I've had a lot of first-hand experience of the SEN system.

Much of it has been hard and frustrating, while some has been genuinely rewarding and uplifting, but the important thing is that we've survived (and continue to survive) it and each of my children are thriving in their own way. Without question, the most frustrating thing has been watching my children struggle and fall behind during the seemingly endless wait for appointments and assessments. Unfortunately the mainstream school system is set up in such a way that your child has to experience difficulties before they can be given help, or even considered for it. As a parent this can be beyond hard because none of us want to see our children suffering like this – it goes against every parenting instinct we've got. We want the problem solved *now* because we're the ones living with the psychological and emotional trauma they're going through as a result – the damaged self-esteem, the anxiety, the desperation - it's hard, there's no getting away from that. Still, the reality is that if your child goes to mainstream school, to start with they'll be given the same opportunities to learn in the same way as all the other children in their class (unless you've managed to get a diagnosis while they're at nursery school so always push for this if it's an option).

In an ideal world, once it becomes clear they're not keeping up and need to be taught differently to their classmates, the SEN team will get involved with a view to offering extra support in the classroom, and if you're lucky, at break times too. I'm very much aware that the world is far from ideal of course, so never be afraid to start the ball rolling yourself on the extra help front because as a parent you're bound to be the first one to notice when things aren't going to plan. Always make an appointment to see your child's class teacher and start the conversation as soon as you're concerned. Trust me, if you don't, you're going to regret it later on. Obviously I can't predict the kind of teachers you're going to meet but in my experience they generally fall into one of two categories: the nightmare teachers who refuse to listen, think your child is spoilt or naughty and treat you with contempt (the ones I've reported to the Local Education Authority and Board of Governors) and the dream teachers who take on board what you're saying, work *with* you and really do have your child's best interests at heart (the ones I've sent baskets of muffins to as a 'thank you' for transforming my children's lives). Believe me they're all out there somewhere, but in the decades I've been dealing with the education system I've seen a definite decline in the number of nightmare teachers, so with luck you'll meet some decent, hardworking people who are there because they genuinely want to make a difference.

Either way, how you build your relationships with these people will have a profound effect on your child's life, way beyond their years in school, so always do your best to be cooperative and respectful, because although there are still a few teachers out there who really don't deserve your respect (I know, I've met them) your child *does* deserve the best possible chance of a good education, and the way to achieve that is by having the most productive relationship with all the school's staff that you possibly can.

When you're living in a constant state of uncertainty and frustration, it's easy to let your feelings build up to the point where they boil over, and very often it can be your child's teachers who become the target of your rage. I've lost count of the number of times I've sat outside classrooms waiting to see my children's SEN teachers and overheard parents screaming abuse at them in front of their own children. Yes, I understand why they feel that way, but no, I don't agree with it because, apart from anything else, they're teaching their children to problem-solve using aggression and trust me, autistic people need to learn the *opposite* of that approach if they're ever going to become successful members of society.

So what's the answer then? Well, firstly it's important to realise that teachers are people too, and they can get just as frustrated by the system as we do. Having to work within a very strict framework of rules and regulations that restrict most of them far more than they'd like, can be very tough, so if your child's teacher tells you something can't be done immediately, there'll usually be a good reason why. Ask what it is. Don't assume they're just being awkward and obstructing you, because that will lead to resentment and turn them (in your mind) into the enemy, then no one wins. Find out how their set procedures work and what, if anything, can be done to speed them up.

Remember, the big decisions about your child's education will be made much further up the line by people who deal with hundreds and hundreds of SEN cases every week. To get the best support for your child, their teachers will need to produce solid evidence that's been gathered over time to convince people *who've never met them* that they really do need extra help, otherwise their application will just be thrown out. It's mind-bogglingly annoying, I know, but that's the way the system works at the moment so until it changes, it's best to find a way to be patient and work *with* it rather than *against* it if you can.

This, of course, is easier said than done, because one thing that's certain about the SEN system is that it is, in fact, *always* changing. Just when you think you've got to grips with how things work, another piece of legislation will be passed and there'll be a whole new set of rules and acronyms to learn. It's a good thing of course because that's what we want it to do: change and adapt and improve so it can meet our children's needs better, but it does mean the whole thing gets even more complicated the longer you're dealing with it.

Luckily there are some fantastic organisations out there who can help guide you through the twists and turns of the SEN maze and I've listed them for you in the 'Post-Diagnosis Survival Pack' chapter so do check them out if you're struggling because they really can be incredibly useful.

The other vital strategy you'll need to adopt if you're going to survive the system without losing your mind is one of being 'actively patient' – in other words, getting busy changing what you can while you're dealing with the things you can't. I'll explain: you can't make the wheels of the SEN system turn any faster than they do; you can't make a nasty, vindictive person into a warm and helpful one; you can't rearrange the world so your child never gets upset or feels afraid, but what you *can* do is work on your reaction *to* those things, because that you can *always* change and that really can make all the difference.

There's no question that it's easy to fall into despair and focus on the negatives when things are impossibly hard like this. Feeling resentful, jealous, angry and overwhelmed are all perfectly reasonable responses to the ongoing strain of living with autism, so if you're feeling that way, don't worry, it doesn't mean you're a bad person, it just means you're human. The important thing is not to get *stuck* in those feelings and let them become your identity. I've seen it time and time again with autism parents: as the relentless trauma gradually grinds them down, they turn away from positivity and optimism and towards bitterness and spite, and it breaks my heart every time. Our children need us to fight for them, there's no doubt about that, but the fight doesn't have to make us negative and miserable because that's the last thing our children need us to be.

Instead, be proactive: work out what it is your child's struggling with, research the best ways to help them catch up and go in and suggest some strategies to their teachers. A lot. In other words, be *that* parent: be informed, be consistent, be *persistent* and whatever you do, don't be put off if you start getting the 'Oh no, not *her* again' look when you turn up with yet another helpful idea. This isn't about making a nuisance of yourself or not caring about other people's feelings, it's simply about putting your child's welfare above your own sense of embarrassment and doing what you can to give them the best chance of success while you're waiting for the formal assessment process to be completed. By the way, if the office staff don't start avoiding eye contact with you when you turn up for appointments then you're really not putting in enough effort! British readers will understand just how excruciating this can be, as it goes against all our social conditioning to voice our opinions, let alone our concerns, for fear of being thought of as a 'complainer' (gasp) but desperate times call for desperate measures, people, and if your child needs your support, you'll just have to let your voice be heard, even if no one wants to hear it, and even if it shakes.

What can I suggest?

There are countless books and articles around today offering ways to support autistic children in the classroom and while a lot of mainstream schools are working hard to incorporate them, many are less aware of the options available, so don't be shy when it comes to giving them information.
Social media sites like Facebook, Twitter and Pinterest can provide you with some truly ingenious ideas if you search for something like 'sensory friendly classroom' so have a look around and you won't be short of inspiration. Since sensory overload is one of the biggest challenges for children on the spectrum, and classrooms can be noisy, smelly, overcrowded places, autistic children can really struggle to process this jumble of incoming information, so much so that learning becomes impossible. The good news is that with some appropriate changes, any classroom can be made more sensory-friendly and this can benefit everyone, whether they're on the spectrum or not.
I've included details of where to find more information about this in the 'Further Reading' section, but for now, here's a very basic list of suggestions that could make all the difference to your child's day to day experiences including plenty of sensory-friendly ones:

- Find out whether their school has a designated quiet area that pupils can use to cool down and if not, suggest they create one that includes soft beanbags, weighted blankets and a variety of handheld 'fidgets' (small tactile objects that are stretchy/squeezable/light up/make soothing sounds etc.)
- Ask whether it's possible for your child to use a 'privacy screen' – a desk partition system that works a bit like blinkers on a horse and blocks out sensory input while they're trying to concentrate

- Make sure your child has enough personal space around them when they're working and if not, come up with a way to provide it without isolating them from the other children
- Suggest they introduce a 'sensory station' into the classroom that contains ear defenders, non-intrusive fidgets, weighted lap trays etc. so your child can learn to self-regulate and choose appropriate items to use when they're needed without always having to leave the classroom and go to the quiet area
- Have a look round the classroom and if it's full of brightly coloured clutter or displays that flutter in the breeze, work with their teacher to come up with ideas to reduce the visual noise a bit while still showcasing the children's work
- Check the lighting and see if it's possible for it to be reduced at all if it's overly harsh
- If the flooring is hard and produces lots of loud echoes, ask about having properly secured mats fitted that can help reduce the noise levels
- Ask whether they'd consider introducing visual timetables and countdown timers, as these can make a huge difference to your child's peace of mind throughout the day
- Experiment with different ways of sitting, including using an exercise ball or a resistance band placed across the legs of their desk
- Ask whether the staff have had any specific autism training and if they haven't, offer to contact a suitable local organisation and sort out a talk for them
- Instead of a 'Show and Tell' day, ask if they can arrange a 'Special Interests' day so your child can talk to the class about something they love – it's a great way to get them to open up socially
- Offer some suggestions for creating a 'quiet zone' where children could play games or do colouring at break times if they prefer being less physically active
- Put forward the idea of a 'real life learning' class where children can be taught things like cooking, cleaning, caring for animals etc. to help prepare them for independent living

- Suggest the idea of a 'buddy system' both in the classroom and the playground, giving a more confident child the responsibility of 'looking after' your child and helping them feel included

There really are so many more ideas you can use, and the more these strategies are integrated into the classroom, the more the other children will come to accept them as simply another way of learning. If they're properly explained and your child's autism is understood as something that makes them different but not less, you'll find most children will be very understanding and supportive even if they're new to the condition.

Where will I find the energy?

That's a very good question! No-one understands better than I do what it's like to be absolutely, utterly and permanently exhausted yet still be expected to push on through and deal with the never ending demands of day to day life with autism. Do I really think you've got enough spare energy to do everything I'm suggesting here? If you're anything like me years ago, then probably not. You've most likely read book after book in the hope of finding one that contains some real, practical suggestions you can use to improve your life, only to finish each one and think 'Nope. That was another very interesting read but it doesn't actually help me much.' Obviously I don't want this book to be one of those, so I've included a whole chapter on the strategies I've used to help myself and my children across the years and most importantly how I've managed to boost both my physical and mental energy levels so I'm able to go the extra mile and get things done.

I'm guessing this will be of interest to you because if there's an autism parent anywhere on the planet who doesn't need a bit of an energy boost then I've yet to meet them! I've called the chapter 'There Is No Magic Wand' because, well, it's true: there's no magical answer to the struggles we face as autism parents, but there are techniques you can learn that will let you take them in your stride and help you find your way through life, and even through the tangled strings of the SEN system with more courage, patience and good humour than you ever thought possible. I know, because I've invested years in perfecting them.

More on that later, but for now, on with the story...

A Day at the Circus

January 2001

- 6:30am: School run in full swing.
- Place Child 3 (age 20 months) on chair in front room. Rush to kitchen to grab packed lunches. Tell Child 2 (age 5) 'watch your brother – he's going to fall.'
- Loud scream is heard from front room. Child 3 is on floor.
- Ask Child 2 'Why didn't you watch him? I told you he was going to fall!' Child 2 replies proudly 'I did: I watched him and he fell.' #TotallyMyOwnFault
- 8am: Today is bin collection day. Child 1 (age 9) offers to help take recycling boxes outside, including large cardboard box he's taped closed by himself.
- Finish putting rubbish out and discover Child 2 is missing.
- Frantic search for Child 2 begins until I notice Child 1's smirking face.
- Ask Child 1 if he knows the whereabouts of his brother and am told he is 'with the recycling'.
- Check recycling. No sign of Child 2. Sudden realisation dawns.
- Rip open cardboard box to discover Child 2 grinning inside. Remove him just as recycling lorry appears at top of street. #NoSenseOfDanger
- 9am: Complete school run. Drink chamomile tea to soothe nerves.
- 11:30am: Torrential downpour all morning. Shows no sign of stopping, so decide to brave the weather and visit shops.
- Open front door to find Child 2 standing on doorstep, shaking and looking like drowned rat.
- Bring Child 2 inside and wrap him in towel. Discover he left school by himself at 9:10am, crossed main road, walked home alone and has been on doorstep ever since. Didn't ring bell because last time he escaped from school he got into trouble when I opened the door.
- Phone school to complain that another successful escape has occurred.
- Explain to Child 2 that he could have been killed on the road. Child 2's response: 'But did I die? No, I didn't.' Said with an air of 'the Defence rests'. #StillNoSenseOfDanger

Chapter Eight

Meetings and Partings

'If nothing ever changed, there'd be no butterflies.'
Anon

When Aidan was three months old things reached the point of no return in our marriage and Pat and I decided to separate. It goes without saying this was an incredibly hard decision to make, but looking back I can honestly say it was the right one for all of us. Pat and I get on so much better as friends than we ever did as husband and wife, and he's an amazing dad to the boys now he doesn't have to deal with the overwhelming pressures of day to day life in an autism household. At the time of course, things were beyond hard. I had a new baby who never stopped screaming but totally refused to be held, a three year old in the grip of profound autism and a newly-diagnosed autistic seven year old whose anxiety levels were right off the chart. I also had a ruptured caesarean scar, an aggravated hernia and absolutely no idea what was going to happen next. These were some of the darkest days I've ever experienced as a parent and they very nearly broke me, but as always the darkest hour is before the dawn, and better times were on their way, even if I didn't realise it yet.

Aidan had been delivered by emergency caesarean because thanks to being completely hyperactive in the womb (he has ADHD so nothing's ever changed!) he'd managed to twist his umbilical cord once round his neck and twice round his shoulder. He'd also succeeded in wriggling himself into a position where he was presenting face first rather than head first and was so battered when he eventually arrived that he was described by one of the midwives as looking like he'd gone ten rounds with Frank Bruno. It was a pretty accurate description if I'm honest.

As a result, he had something called cranial compression which, unbeknown to me, was giving him a massive headache, hence the non-stop screaming. Someone suggested we try cranial osteopathy which they said might help Dominic's autism too. I'd never heard of it before and although I couldn't imagine how it might help with autism, I was willing to try anything at the time so I booked them a double appointment with a chap who practiced something called the Sutherland method. Somewhat predictably, our first meeting didn't go too well.

Aidan spent the entire appointment screeching at the top of his lungs, while

Dominic pressed himself against the back wall underneath the treatment couch and kicked, spat and clawed at the poor man whenever he came within arm's reach. We'd already ventured out to several parent and toddler groups and been politely asked never to return, so I fully expected the same response from him. Instead, having braved the flailing arms and legs and managed to place his hands on Dominic's head for a few brief minutes, the osteopath told me (over Aidan's screams) that he worked at a clinic in London for severely autistic children and how Dominic was the most profoundly autistic child he'd ever treated.

Working miracles

I'd heard this several times from specialists already as you know, so I wasn't really surprised, but I genuinely didn't expect what came next: 'What I can't understand' he said 'is how on earth he's functioning so well.' So well? Dominic was four years old, had no speech, was wearing a fully padded dinosaur costume and had just tried to murder him. Believe me, no-one had *ever* said he was doing well before. He went on to explain how Dominic's brain wiring was so profoundly affected by his autism that he shouldn't be able to walk, eat or do pretty much anything at all really. 'Whatever you're doing, keep doing it' he said 'You're working miracles.' Yes, you read that right. Someone thought I was working miracles. I can honestly say I didn't see that one coming at all.

It was decided he'd see the boys once a week and I have to say the improvement in Aidan was immediate. He stopped being rigid (he was a carbon copy of Christopher at the same age: stiff as a board with his hands and feet screwed up into tiny claws) and his screaming reduced dramatically overnight. By the time his next appointment was due he'd be getting very stiff again and screaming most of the time, but once he'd had the treatment he'd relax again and occasionally even sleep.

As usual, Dominic was another matter. For the first couple of appointments we went through the same routine of screaming, snarling and biting the poor man's hands, but on the third visit something changed. Instead of hiding under the couch, Dominic allowed the long-suffering osteopath to gently hold and manipulate his head for around twenty minutes. All of a sudden he said 'Oh my God, he's letting me in! I can feel his speech centres opening.' I had no idea what he was talking about and it sounded a bit odd to me at the time, so I smiled, nodded politely and just kept focussing on how grateful I was that Dominic wasn't trying to kill him again.

And then, right there in that little treatment room, without any warning at all, our lives transformed. Forever.

It was a miserable, blustery day; Dominic was facing a small window and Aidan was screaming the place down as usual, when suddenly I heard a little voice say 'It raining.' I honestly thought I'd imagined it until the osteopath said 'Did he just speak? Did he say "it's raining"?' I went as cold as ice. Dominic didn't speak. Dominic *couldn't* speak, everyone knew that, and as much as I'd hoped he might, deep down I suppose, having been told it was impossible so many times, I'd never really believed it would happen.

While I was struggling to answer him, the same little voice said 'My baby crying.' I looked at the osteopath who was standing there with tears streaming down his face while he held Dominic's head, and promptly burst into tears myself. By now Dominic was the only person in the room who wasn't weeping; instead he looked totally unconcerned about his new found ability and carried on chatting away to himself in short sentences as if he'd been doing it all his life.

So began a series of weekly visits to the osteopath for all three of the boys and the changes in them were remarkable each time. Within weeks I found Dominic bouncing on the bed singing a perfect rendition of 'Five Little Monkeys' which he'd been taught when he was eighteen months old and had never shown the slightest sign of understanding before now. It was as if when it came to communication, he'd been on permanent 'receive' and something had suddenly allowed him to get the words back out as well. Obviously his language was way behind where it should have been and he still had some serious behavioural challenges to work through, but for the first time in years I had real, tangible evidence that he was making progress.

I've put details of how to find an osteopath who practices the Sutherland method in the 'Survival Pack' section in case you'd like to give it a go yourself. I have to say I've been treated myself with it many times since and I find it superb, but when Isabelle was born she had quite a few sessions and it made no difference to her at all as far as I could tell, despite being literally life-changing for her brothers, so it's important to remember it doesn't work for everyone.

Going it alone

For the next two and a half years I brought the boys up by myself and to be honest, time passed in a bit of a blur. If something wasn't reported on Cartoon Network or the Disney Channel it's safe to say I knew nothing about it as there was no time to read a paper or catch the news on TV, and the internet was still a mystery to me back then. If World War Three had broken out during those years I'd definitely have been the last to know.

Looking after three young autistic boys without any support was more than just a full time job, it was a feat of superhuman endurance. I had no friends left by now and no family anywhere nearby, so as we settled into our new routine, I turned into what can only be described as a desperately lonely yet powerfully unstoppable machine. Surviving on a mixture of adrenaline, sleep deprivation, vitamin supplements and positive thinking, I'd get up at 5am when all three boys would finally be asleep for an hour, grab a quick shower and start preparing for another day of kicking, punching, biting mayhem.

You may be wondering at this point why I didn't just give up, and how on earth I managed to stay positive each morning in the face of such overwhelming chaos. This is something I've been asked countless times over the years and apart from the obvious answer of 'I didn't give up because I didn't have the option to' there was something else that made all the difference to my life and to the boys' lives as well; something that seemingly happened quite by chance.

Mind over matter

When I was five months pregnant with Aidan I was busy dragging his brothers round the supermarket when I spotted a parenting magazine with the rather bold headline 'Have the Birth of Your Dreams!' Since both my previous births had been absolute nightmares I decided it might be worth a look and grabbed myself a copy while simultaneously wrestling a jar of pasta sauce out of Dominic's hand, much to his disgust as he was doing his best to launch it over the side of the trolley and watch it explode on the floor, thus meeting the same fate as last week's unfortunate jar.

When I read the article later on, it explained there was a course running in London that could teach you how to enjoy a healthy, happy pregnancy and a safe, comfortable delivery. I was sceptical to say the least, but also intrigued, so I thought I'd give it a go and some weeks later I arrived for a weekend of training in self-hypnosis. I'd assumed the course would be full of pregnant ladies like me, but I was actually surrounded by a whole variety of men and women from different professional backgrounds, all looking for ways to enhance their lives by training their minds to think in a more positive, proactive way.

This was my first inkling that maybe I could change more than just my experience of pregnancy using the methods being taught here, and sure enough by the end of an intensive weekend covering everything from applied psychology to practical demonstrations, I was well and truly sold on the idea that I'd just been given access to a place inside me where I could create real, lasting improvements not just for myself but for my boys too.

Learning self-hypnosis was a genuinely life-changing experience for me, and I worked on improving everything from my self-confidence to the quality of my sleep (that one came in *very* handy as you can imagine), but to help the boys I needed to learn how to apply the techniques to other people too, so after Aidan was born I arranged for Pat to have the boys once a month while I completed a diploma course and over the course of a year and a half, became a fully qualified hypnotherapist and self-hypnosis teacher in my own right.

During that time I met some of the most wonderful people I know and because these particular meetings took place without the boys climbing all over me, for once I had the chance to be myself, not just the frazzled 'autism mum' who never got to finish a sentence. It was bliss! A group of us have stuck together and remained good friends ever since, supporting and encouraging each other from those early days of training when we had no idea how anything worked, right through to setting up and running our own successful practices.

I then went on to train in more complex psychological strategies and qualified five years later with a first class post-graduate diploma in psychotherapy (proof that my brain hadn't been turned to mush by lack of sleep after all). I gradually developed my own combination of treatments not just for the boys but also for the many hundreds of clients I've treated over the years, and that, in a nutshell, is how I became a therapist specialising in the treatment of families living with autism.

I'll go into more detail about all this in the chapter called 'There Is No Magic Wand', but suffice to say I wouldn't have invested so many years of my life in learning and using these techniques if they didn't produce some very impressive results. As you might have guessed from the chapter title, they're not a miraculous cure-all and things were still incredibly tough, but using them definitely gave me an advantage, and I have no doubt at all that without them the boys and I wouldn't have achieved half as much as we have.

Dressing for success

One distinct benefit of training my mind to think positively was that I never missed an opportunity to help the boys develop, even if the way I achieved it seemed a bit bizarre to other people. A case in point was their love of dressing up which, rather than tailing off as it did with other children, actually seemed to increase as they got older. I realised by making use of this fascination, not only could I build a bond with them but I could also teach them some vital life skills at the same time. Nowadays, using children's special interests to connect with and educate them is a recognised strategy for autism parents, but it's safe to say that when I was applying this theory in the 1990's, I was considered both overindulgent and certifiably insane in pretty much equal measures. Fortunately for me, the children's club the boys attended at the local YMCA had a themed fancy dress competition once a week, so I had plenty of opportunity to put my ideas into practice.

I'd never actually learned to use a sewing machine, so this wasn't an easy thing to achieve and although I can embroider a mean cross stitch, and even sew the occasional escaped button back onto a school shirt, sadly that's where my skills as a seamstress grind to a shuddering halt. Still, considering the huge challenges I overcame on a day-to-day basis, this didn't seem like too much of a drawback to me and I quickly became a bit of an expert at sticking and stapling, as well as the creative use of Velcro, papier-mâché, upholstery foam, double sided tape and safety pins.

During these years the distinctive smell of Copydex often clung to me for days like an exotic perfume, and thanks to the amount of time they spent immersed in soggy tissue paper, my fingers would generally be stained a variety of interesting colours, doing nothing to dispel the rumours that I was to be avoided at all costs since I was clearly some kind of escaped lunatic.

As a result of my terrible dressmaking skills, most of the boys' costumes only lasted the day, before unceremoniously disintegrating like Cinderella's ball gown at midnight. Undeterred, I'd collect the remaining scraps of material together and recycle them into yet more of my unique, if slightly precarious, home-made creations.

Money was very tight with so many things being regularly broken or lost, so I'd turn up at the fabric wholesalers with my now customary 'autism parent look' of split lips, bruised arms, ripped clothes and food-smeared hair, to rummage through the offcut bins like an abused bag lady. No-one ever said a word; they didn't have to: their looks of silent pity and disapproval said it all.

One of my all-time 'best buys' was a £5 offcut of burgundy satin I turned into a robe for Christopher when he dressed as Mickey Mouse from The Sorcerer's Apprentice, recycling it later into both Aladdin's waistcoat and Pinocchio's dungarees. Eighteen years on and it's still going strong: it recently became part of the German football strip for his New Year's Eve costume party. Definitely money well spent.

From these random scraps of fabric would appear (after several hours of frantic sticking, pinning and painting) a procession of the most unlikely characters you can imagine. Some people applauded my efforts; most gave me looks that would blister paint and avoided me with renewed vigour, tutting loudly and rolling their eyes to the heavens at the very idea of a mother making such an effort when 'Obviously the children don't appreciate it anyway'. Needless to say, this wasn't an opinion I shared. I remember people asking me more than once 'But why do you bother?' My reply of 'Because it makes the boys so happy and it teaches them that nothing's impossible' fell largely on deaf ears and often led to ridicule and sometimes even open hostility.

Some mothers went so far as to request that my boys be banned from future competitions, as I was 'clearly a professional costumier' and therefore had an unfair advantage. I remember receiving a phone call from a woman who asked me to make her daughter a costume for an upcoming school play because she'd heard I was a professional dressmaker. Strangely, my explanation that in fact I couldn't even sew and I made the boys' costumes from scraps of material and double-sided tape seemed to do nothing to improve my reputation as a mad woman.

Still, since my social life was at absolute zero (bear in mind this was before I discovered the internet, so when I say I was isolated, I do mean *completely*) I decided whatever I did couldn't actually result in me losing any friends since I didn't have any, so I carried on, and actually I felt more sorry for the children of those judgmental parents than I ever did for myself.

Those who mind don't matter...

Naturally, with Christopher's mind working in such a unique way, the costume ideas he came up with were...well...*interesting* to say the least. The first week's theme was Harry Potter and he decided he wanted to go as Hedwig the owl (helpfully informing me of this the night before the event) and went along the next morning looking rather magnificent thanks to some artfully applied face paint, lots of feathers and a pair of yellow washing-up gloves for feet. He was delighted, but of course not everyone shared his enthusiasm and he came home crushed by the cruel teasing he'd suffered at the hands of some of the other boys. Resisting the urge to both sit down and weep at the injustice of it all and to drive back to the club and strangle the offending children without delay, I took a breath and decided to use it as an opportunity to teach Christopher a life lesson instead, which I must say has served him extremely well ever since.

'They kept following me around laughing at me and saying I looked silly.' he said, with a heart-breaking look of confusion and sadness in his eyes. Without missing a beat, I nodded and said 'Hmmm. And these boys didn't have any costumes on, did they Christopher?' The look of astonishment he gave me would have been comical in any other situation. 'But...but...how did you know?' he spluttered.

As we're all aware, the moment you find out not everyone in the world is on your side and that people can be jealous, small minded and cruel is always a tough one for any child, but for children with autism this can be a really difficult thing to grasp, and often takes a long time to be fully understood. The reasons for this are varied and complex, but put simply, autistic people aren't generally interested in competing: they don't feel the need to put others down to feel better about themselves because to their logical way of thinking, that just doesn't make any sense. Personally I would agree with them on that, but trust me, I've met enough bitter, petty, envious people in my time to know that whether these reactions make logical sense or not, there are plenty of them about.

Understanding the concepts of jealousy and spite requires a very elaborate thought process which includes being able to view the world from another person's perspective, something autistic people will inevitably struggle with. I'm not implying they're unable to empathise with others (in fact the opposite is usually true) just that it's a difficult thing for them to get to grips with.

Although I did my best to explain that maybe these boys felt embarrassed that they hadn't dressed up, so they'd tried to make him feel embarrassed too and that people like them were best ignored, Christopher was unconvinced. His main objection to this reasoning was that doing something like that to someone else was 'just mean' and since they'd just been taught at school to treat other people the way they'd like to be treated, he was doubtful anyone would even consider doing such an unkind thing.

Realising that for now I'd gone about as far as I could with this explanation, I decided to go for the 'if you're going to be weird, be confident about it' idea instead, and this one definitely hit the mark.

'You know what I would have said to those boys?' I asked him 'I'd have said "Hey, I'm dressed as a four foot *owl* for goodness' sake, I'm meant to be funny!" then I would have flapped my wings and squawked and had as much fun as I could, without worrying about whether they were going to join in or not.' And this, I'm pleased to say, has been his attitude to life's inevitable critics ever since.

The next theme was 'Down on the Farm' and he wanted to be a crow. Out came the rubber-glove-feet again and combined with some carefully crafted bin bags and a black balaclava, he transformed yet again into a giant bird, only this time he spent most of the day chasing hordes of giggling children round the club: flapping, squawking and *socialising* with more people than I'd ever dreamed possible. He came home positively glowing with pleasure, and on that day the sentiment behind this message was received loud and clear: "Be who you are and say what you feel, because those who mind don't matter, and those who matter don't mind."

A 'Wild West' theme came next and naturally for this one he decided he should be a cactus, because hey, what else would you be? For the 'Halloween' theme he was a broomstick (obviously) and carried Dominic on his shoulders dressed as a black cat. Various other costumes followed, and all were created using crepe paper, corrugated card and a very unlikely mix of general household objects. Who knew, for example, that a gravy boat covered in gold lamé could make such a perfect Aladdin's lamp, or that a feather duster coated in bubble wrap and brown paper would be the ideal caveman's club? We live and learn.

Of course I'd love to say all the negativity then magically stopped and Christopher's unusual ideas were accepted and applauded by all the other children, but I'm sure you won't be surprised to hear that wasn't the case. Having given up on shaming him into dressing 'normally' on fancy dress days, the bullies decided to take a more subtle approach, listening to his ideas and telling him, week after week, 'You can't make that into a costume, it's impossible'. Over and over again he got this unhelpful feedback and every time his answer was the same: 'Yeah? Well you haven't met my mum.'

When I heard this, my first thought was 'How can I help him change that statement to "You don't know what *I* can do."?' so from then on, if he dreamed up any unusual costumes, I'd ask him to explain them to me using both drawings and words, then I'd set about doing my best to create exactly what he'd designed. Watching the wonder on his face as he saw his ideas spring to life in 3D was a real joy, and the procession of roller-blading robots (for 'Space' week), mud-spattered cave men (for 'Time Travel' week) and giant three-eyed monsters (for 'Aliens' week) that followed were truly a sight to behold. Naturally with each costume I produced, I became more and more unpopular with most of the other parents, and often the feeling of disapproval as we walked into the room was so strong you could almost taste it. Bear in mind, not only did I keep producing these costumes in spite of the many eye-rolling and tutting marathons they were creating, but my children, who'd so far appeared to be enjoying the club as much as everybody else, would more often than not transform into screaming, head banging tyrants the moment they set eyes on me, demanding that everything was done exactly as they expected it to be or God help us all.

A little ray of light

Clearly I could understand the other parents' point of view about this all too predictable daily routine. They had no idea the boys had been holding it together with increasing difficulty all day, only to collapse with relief when I appeared and they realised they could come home and be themselves again without having to follow all the mysterious unwritten social rules that were causing them so much anxiety. To see me appearing to pander to this behaviour, and reward rather than punish it, must have been very hard to understand. If anyone had asked me I'd have been only too happy to explain, but as you can imagine, most people had their own ideas about why my children behaved this way and just wanted to get as far away as possible from what they believed to be a thoroughly incompetent mother and some of the most spoilt, ungrateful offspring they'd ever seen.
I remember walking across the car park one evening surrounded by the usual chaos of ear-piercing screams and children who were suddenly so floppy you'd swear their bones had just disintegrated: Car seat with screeching baby on one arm, boneless toddler trying to gouge my eyes out with his finger nails under the other and behind us a limp, frazzled eight year old refusing to walk to the car because the vending machine had sold out of his favourite snack – all pretty standard stuff for me at the time. I headed for the disabled bay, which was yet another source of general disapproval among the parents because clearly my sons all had working arms and legs so they couldn't *possibly* be disabled, when one of

the other mums approached me.

Bracing myself to explain yet again that if my car wasn't within easy dragging distance of the entrance there was a good chance Dominic would break free and bolt straight into oncoming traffic, which is why we had a disabled parking permit, I was genuinely taken aback by what she had to say.

'I've been meaning to tell you this for ages' she said 'I think you're bloody amazing and you put the rest of us to shame.' I remember turning a brilliant shade of red and spluttering something incoherent about how that really wasn't the case, but she was insistent. 'No,' she said 'I mean it. We don't put in half the effort you do. Not just with the costumes (which are amazing, by the way) but with everything you do for your kids. I've watched you and you never shut them up with fizzy drinks or ignore them to chat with the other mums like most of us do, you're just totally focussed on them all the time. I think you're brilliant.' And off she went with her two beautifully behaved daughters in tow, leaving me only slightly less shocked than if she'd just announced I'd been elected Prime Minister.

Afterwards I sat in the car for a while trying to process what had just happened and as it sank in, a stream of quiet tears began to flow down my cheeks and drip from my chin. As fast as I wiped them away more would fall, and eventually Christopher noticed and asked me what was wrong. 'Someone was nice to me' I said without thinking. 'But that's a good thing, isn't it?' he asked. 'Yes, yes – these are happy tears' I told him, but the truth is they were so much more.

I've often wondered if that lady, whose name I never even knew, remembers anything about our snatched conversation in the car park. I wonder if she has any idea of the impact our meeting had on me, and to be honest I'd be very surprised if she did. By now I was single-handedly parenting three young boys in the grip of full-blown autism, so being judged and criticised by family and strangers alike was very much part of my day to day life. I'd had to learn how to deal with the constant rejection by now or I'd have gone under, but someone being publicly kind to me and actually *complimenting* me on my parenting skills was so unexpected it caught me off guard. It's hard to put into words the relief I felt as I realised I wasn't universally despised after all; that at least one mother at the club had noticed what I did and wasn't offended by it.

Never underestimate the depths of loneliness and isolation parents of autistic children can feel, and if you're ever in a position to give a bit of encouragement to another mum or dad who's clearly struggling, please, don't hold back, just go ahead and do it. The repercussions of a small act of kindness and solidarity like this from one parent to another can genuinely change the course of someone's life, so never underestimate your ability to do good in this world either – you're a lot more powerful than you might think.

Dark clouds, silver linings

Day to day life continued along these lines for a couple of years and I rarely thought about the future, being too busy trying to survive the present most of the time, so finding love again was the last thing on my mind, but as always, Life had other plans and this time it set about achieving them in a pretty spectacular way. On September 11th 2001, New York's Twin Towers were destroyed in an appalling attack that sent shockwaves around the world. I was deeply affected by the tragedy (not least because Pat had been working in the buildings a week or so beforehand) and felt, as so many of us did when we heard the news, totally helpless. I'd finally started to get to grips with the computer and it was such a dark time that I decided to write a message of hope in my internet provider's online Book of Sympathy because, to be honest, it was all I could think of to do. Lots of people contacted me to say how much it had inspired them which I found very moving, and one of those people was a young man called Nigel.

They say every cloud has a silver lining and this one certainly did for my little family. Nigel and I started to chat by email and against all the odds his online messages turned to phone calls, his phone calls to visits, and before long we were deeply in love. Sometimes truth really is stranger than fiction and that terrible, heart-breaking event was directly responsible for the meeting of two soulmates, neither of whom were interested in finding a partner at the time, but both of whom were overwhelmed by what can only be described as 'love at first message'. Nigel is five years younger than I am and was studying geology at university as a mature student. He was a seasoned adventurer who'd travelled the world, with no children of his own and no experience of autism at all as far as he was aware. You can imagine what his friends and family thought of this strange woman with three autistic children who'd suddenly appeared out of thin air and stolen the heart of such a free-spirited explorer - they certainly weren't shy in telling him our relationship was an incredibly bad idea.

I didn't let him meet the boys until I was sure this was going to be a permanent thing, and during that time he was told all kinds of horror stories by the people around him, about how badly they'd behave and how restricted his life would be if he took on all this 'baggage'. Interestingly several people thought it was okay to tell me the same thing, and my answer was always the same: 'My children are *not* baggage, they're amazing, and any man would be lucky to know them.' And I meant it. Neither Nigel nor I ever felt he was doing us some kind of favour by becoming a step-dad to my boys, but rather that *he* was the fortunate one to be welcomed into such a wonderfully loving (if rather unique) family.

The boys' reactions to hearing I had a boyfriend after being single for so long were varied to say the least. Aidan was a bit young to understand of course, and although Dominic listened, it was always difficult to tell whether or not he'd taken something in at this stage because he rarely answered when you spoke to him and this time was no exception. Christopher on the other hand, left me in no doubt as to how he felt. He declared himself 'Very pleased' and proceeded to run up and down the garden for several minutes before informing me that he'd never dreamed this could happen because (and I quote) 'You're fat, you've got braces and you talk too much.'

Having full train track braces in your thirties isn't the most glamorous thing in the world and I was already struggling with my feelings about the other two points as well, having not had a relationship for such a long time, so naturally this did wonders for my self-confidence. Still, it can never be said that my children are anything but honest! Christopher then produced a detailed drawing of Spider-man (Nigel's favourite superhero) to give him as a 'welcome to the family' gift and spent the rest of the day asking endless questions about everything from what he looked like to his favourite foods.

Falling in love as a family

The first weekend we spent with Nigel was a pretty steep learning curve for us all. Christopher chatted excitedly about art, LEGO and superheroes and was delighted to find that Nigel shared his enthusiasm for all three; meanwhile Aidan, highly suspicious of this random intruder, crouched silently on the kitchen countertop dressed as Spider-man and shot him with imaginary webs whenever he came within range. For me though, it was Nigel's first meeting with Dominic that made the biggest impact.

As he often did back then, Dominic was sitting cross-legged in front of the television engrossed in a Scooby Doo PlayStation game with his back to the door when Nigel and I came into the room behind him and said hello. Naturally he ignored us both. Before I could warn him that Dominic had a three foot exclusion zone around him which couldn't be crossed without triggering an immediate meltdown, Nigel strolled into the room and said 'Scooby Doo! Cool! Can I play?' I was just about to explain why this was *never* going to happen when without taking his eyes from the screen, Dominic placed another controller on the floor beside him and calmly continued with his game. I watched with my heart in my mouth as Nigel plonked himself down on the carpet leaving no more than half an inch between them, and braced myself for the inevitable mayhem I knew from bitter experience was just about to explode in his face.

Only it didn't.

To say I was confused by this reaction (or lack of reaction, I should say) would be an understatement, but my confusion quickly turned to amazement when Dominic leant over and rested his head on Nigel's shoulder, leaving it there for the remainder of the game. Without a word being spoken, he'd accepted Nigel as one of the family. I really couldn't have imagined anything better and I'm sure it's no surprise to you that I shed more than a few tears of happiness and relief that day. When the time came for Nigel to leave, he said something I'll never forget. His exact words were 'I knew I'd fallen in love with you, but I didn't expect to fall in love with your family as well.' If I'd had any doubts he was 'the one', that was the moment when they evaporated for good.

A clash of cultures

I'd love to say it was all plain sailing when Nigel moved in with us but the difference between staying for that initial weekend and actually living in the heart of an autism family was enormous, and we struggled for several years to find a balance that kept everyone happy.

Nigel was from a strict military background where children were told (not asked) to do things and expected to do them correctly first time without question or face the consequences. Unsurprisingly then, moving in with us was a huge culture shock.

What Nigel saw (or thought he saw) were three strong, healthy boys whose mother never expected them to clean the house or run the kind of important errands he did as a child, but instead gave them only minor tasks to complete which they generally half-finished or forgot about entirely because they couldn't be bothered and had no respect for her. They'd receive no punishment for what he saw as their laziness and disobedience, only encouragement for anything they'd actually managed, and gentle guidance on how to do things a bit better next time. It's fair to say it drove him wild with frustration. He was convinced I was the weakest parent he'd ever met and that the boys simply lacked discipline and routine. Yes, that old chestnut!

The fact they had no set mealtimes, never ate the same food and didn't sit at the dinner table together only added to his conviction that they were manipulating me and I just wasn't strong enough to stand up to them. In his opinion I was in serious need of some military style guidance on how to just *make* them do what I wanted (why didn't I think of that?) and never held back on telling me how this could be achieved.

What he missed of course, through no fault of his own, was that the boys were in fact doing *exactly* what I wanted, because they were constantly learning, each at their own pace, while being reassured that it was okay to make mistakes, to be different, to be respected as individuals and that they could rely on my unquestioning support whenever they struggled. Of course they were years behind other children when it came to taking responsibility for chores, so I could understand why he worried so much about how they'd cope as adults, but they were all making progress in their own ways and I was confident they'd get there in the end if we didn't push them too hard. We clashed terribly during those early years and having faced me in a number of very heated arguments, Nigel quickly realised there was nothing weak about me at all, which only confused him even more.

Having not been around during the worst times when the boys were small, Nigel had no idea how much progress they'd already made using this parenting style, so trying to explain why giving any of them a direct order was guaranteed to result in a meltdown was almost impossible. The idea that it takes far more strength to be patient and kind than to shout and bully wasn't something he'd experienced before and he often said he felt like we were all playing some complicated game with rules he just couldn't understand. It's a pretty good analogy really, but despite his confusion - all credit to him - he loved us dearly and did his best to do things our way despite his understandable reservations.

He went on to become an incredibly supportive stepdad who's hugely proud of all the boys' achievements. It still drives him insane that they can't cook a meal without wrecking the kitchen or remember to bring their plates down from their bedrooms despite years of being reminded, but he doesn't take it to heart or see it as disrespectful anymore, and although it doesn't solve the problems (is there *anyone* who knows how to solve issues like these?) it really does make all the difference.

Surprise, surprise!

After six years together we'd become a strong family unit and Nigel and I were married in a beautiful 12th century castle in Wales. We had a full medieval wedding which included some heartfelt touches from The Lord of the Rings (which happens to be Nigel's favourite book too – what are the odds?) with a little bit of Shrek thrown in for good measure.

Christopher walked me down the aisle and by the time he'd finished his after-dinner speech welcoming Nigel to the family, the entire congregation was in tears, as were most of the serving staff.

Three weeks before the wedding, Life decided to spring a couple of pretty big surprises on me, because, you know, it probably felt I didn't have enough to do already. The first was when I woke up one morning and the right side of my face had completely collapsed, which isn't exactly ideal when you're about to get married. I was diagnosed with Bell's palsy and although the doctors couldn't be sure what had caused it, they were pretty certain it was stress related. 'Was I under any particular pressure at the moment?' they wondered. Well, I was working full time as a therapist, bringing up three autistic boys, running a home and planning a wedding, so yes, I was under a *bit* of pressure, but I certainly wasn't stressed about it, just a little more tired than usual, I told them. 'How much more tired than usual?' they asked suspiciously, and sure enough, surprise number two revealed itself soon afterwards when the test results came back and confirmed I was expecting another baby. Wow!

Nigel and I had always planned to have a child of our own, so although it was a shock, it was a wonderfully welcome one. I decided to keep the news secret until the wedding day, which means we're now fortunate enough to own a YouTube-worthy video of the whole room erupting (and Nigel bursting into tears) when I announce the identity of our 'very special and very surprise guest: Baby Wallace-Iles.'

It was one of those truly unforgettable moments, but Life hadn't quite finished with the surprises yet, and several months later when we went for a scan, we discovered that 'Baby Wallace-Iles' who was *obviously* going to be a boy like his brothers, was in fact a little girl.

Autism's Ten Commandments

1. Thou shalt not sleep.
2. Thou shalt not eat food which has made contact with other food.
3. Thou shalt not accept minuscule changes to thy routine.
4. Thou shalt take everything literally.
5. Thou shalt not socialise in the anticipated manner.
6. Thou shalt repeat thy mother & thy father's private conversations loudly in public.
7. Thou shalt not wear suitable clothing for the weather.
8. Though shalt not tolerate any attempts at nail or hair cutting.
9. Though shalt not allow thyself to be strapped into a car seat or buggy.
10. Thou shalt not find something amusing unless it is totally inappropriate.

So the Princess learned that sometimes having sensory processing disorder was a real advantage...

Chapter Nine

The Female of the Species

'Don't you know that it's different for girls?'
Joe Jackson

The following July we welcomed another new performer into the ring, making our little circus troupe complete. Isabelle was (and still is) the very image of her dad and so much like him in character that if her hair didn't have a distinct tinge of copper when the light hits it, I'd wonder whether she was mine at all! Naturally everyone told me how wonderful it would be to have a dainty little girl in the family and I did think it might be nice to have someone to share my love of sparkly clothes with at last, but as always, Life had other ideas and sent me instead a tough, outdoorsy tomboy with a passionate hatred of anything lacy, glittery or sequinned who'd rather die than suffer the indignity of wearing something pink, least of all anything resembling a dress. Sigh.

Is she or isn't she?

As a newborn, Isabelle made perfect eye contact with everyone and even returned their smiles (something none of her brothers had done) so although I realised how unlikely it was, to start with I did wonder whether I'd somehow managed to produce a child who *didn't* have autism this time.

She would watch my lips when I spoke and mirror the movements I made; she was happy to follow the sound of a chiming rattle and absolutely beamed whenever she was cuddled, so something was definitely different about how she was responding to the world. From the way she interacted with the hospital staff, she seemed to be a 'people person' which was the absolute opposite to all three of her brothers at this age. She was more than happy to be handled by the midwives, but unlike Dominic who didn't object because he was happily lost in his own thoughts, she cooed and smiled and interacted with them all. At the time I knew very little about how autism affects girls, so as we made our way home from hospital a few days later I genuinely didn't know whether she was autistic or not. I didn't want to make any assumptions just yet, so I treated her like any other newborn and waited to see how things would pan out.

Within a week of course, any illusions of Isabelle being neurotypical had been unceremoniously shattered. Right from the start she had serious problems with her digestion; sudden noises above a whisper would make her hysterical and unless she was constantly occupied she'd scream the place down. It was all looking very familiar and there were too many other signs to go into here, but one of the major giveaways was something I hadn't encountered before: the huge amount of stimming she did ('stimming' is short for 'self-stimulatory behaviours' i.e. unusual and specific things such as sounds or rhythmic movements that stimulate good feelings in an autistic – or sometimes neurotypical - person).

A particular favourite of hers was to lie in her cot and lift her right leg up at an angle so it was suspended in mid-air; she'd leave it hanging there for around five minutes at a time, then slowly lower it onto the mattress and let out a little sigh of happiness. This would be followed by a flurry of movements from both legs that can only be described as looking like a grasshopper jumping up and down on the spot, something she'd keep up for ages before suddenly falling asleep. I use the term 'falling asleep' loosely of course because she never did anything more than cat nap.

It'd been sixteen years since I'd dealt with a sleep disorder as severe as Christopher's but Isabelle's was definitely in the same league and during those early years with her my exhausted body would regularly scream at me 'What on earth made you think *this* was a good idea?! Don't you realise we're over forty now?! What is *wrong* with you?!'

A whole new world

We made the decision to send Isabelle to full time nursery from a very young age because firstly she loved meeting new people and secondly we felt that mixing with neurotypical children would give her a chance to learn different ways of interacting than we could teach her at home.

Soon after she started I got a very concerned phone call from the nursery manager telling me she'd suffered some kind of seizure. 'Oh,' I said 'did she sit in her highchair, move her legs like a grasshopper for a while then suddenly go unconscious?' When it turned out that yes, that's exactly what she'd done, I said 'Don't worry, she's just stimming.' Trying to explain that this friendly, outgoing little girl was in fact on the autism spectrum proved next to impossible, and the nursery were highly sceptical about what I told them. More incidents followed and whenever she displayed any unusual behaviours they'd ask 'Are you sure she's not just copying her brothers?' I'd explain every time that none of her brothers' behaviours were anything like Isabelle's, so there was no question of her copying them, and assured them she was just being herself, doing what she'd done since she was born. Nonetheless I soon got labelled as 'that woman who thinks her daughter is autistic when she's really not' which was a whole new world for me as I was more used to being 'that woman who thinks her sons aren't as autistic as they really are'.

The little philosopher

As soon as she could walk, Isabelle followed the nursery teachers around like a tiny, brown-eyed shadow. She happily copied whatever they did and spent her time doing everything from clearing up (she has a love of cleaning and arranging things in straight lines which was very useful in a busy teaching environment as you can imagine) to helping out with the new babies and sitting in the staff room having a pretend chat. They adored her and she adored them right back, so I completely understood why they thought she couldn't be on the spectrum. I remember how touched they were by the way she instinctively 'knew' if one of them was upset and would offer hugs and kisses to help them feel better, stopping whatever she was doing and rushing over to offer them comfort because she could somehow feel their sadness even if nothing had been mentioned.
What they didn't realise was that in both cases she was displaying classic female autistic behaviour. Mimicking things she saw the adults doing - acting out the grown up role rather than simply being a child like the other little girls – and displaying 'hyper-empathy' are both well-known characteristics in young autistic girls, and so was pretty much everything else she did.
When she played, it was always with the boys and she'd quickly take charge of their games, organising things according to her rules and making sure they all played 'properly' (another classic sign) which they usually did rather than risk having to face her legendary temper. It *could* be argued she was bossy, but I prefer to think of her as showing excellent leadership skills, just like her mother's!
Young girls on the spectrum are frequently referred to as 'little philosophers' because of the slightly otherworldly way they express their deep connection with, and interest in, the world and people around them. They often come across as being unusually wise beyond their years and have a heightened level of empathy

with people and animals that's rarely seen in such tiny children. Young autistic boys, on the other hand, are sometimes known as 'little professors' owing to their fascination with facts and objects and their ability to understand the intricate mechanics of how their world (and the world in general) actually works.

It's all in the wiring

In the fifty or so years I've been on the planet, attitudes towards the differences between men and women have changed beyond all recognition, and talking about anything to do with gender nowadays has become a bit of a minefield where it's very easy to upset people and make them feel excluded or offended. That being the case, I do want to make something very clear here: human beings are all unique and no two brains are made exactly alike, so the potential for diversity when it comes to everything (including gender identity) is endless. What I'm talking about here isn't to do with gender identity though, it's to do with brain wiring, and the bottom line is this: at a neurological level, male and female brains *do* work differently because that's just the way they're designed.

Here's how it works: Every human brain is made up of two separate hemispheres known (unsurprisingly) as the Left Brain and the Right Brain, and it used to be believed that everyone's brain had a dominant side which meant their character was heavily influenced by whichever side was in charge. The Left Brain was thought to be responsible for dealing with language, logic, reasoning and numbers, making a 'left brained' person more analytical and objective, while the Right Brain was supposedly in charge of recognising faces, expressing and reading emotions, appreciating music, colour and images and controlling all aspects of creativity, making a 'right brained' person more thoughtful, intuitive and subjective. It was also believed that men were more 'left brained' and women more 'right brained'. In fact, it's now understood that both sides of the brain work *together* on most things, communicating through a dense bundle of fibres which connect the two halves together, called the corpus callosum. It's the way they communicate through these fibres that's different depending on whether a brain is male or female, which is why girls' and boys' brains work differently whether they have autism or not. It really is nothing to do with gender identity or sexism and everything to do with science.

Meanwhile, there's some fascinating research being carried out into the effects autism has on the corpus callosum which I won't go into here, but suffice to say that although no one has all the answers yet, at the moment it appears both autistic and neurotypical girls use their corpus callosum in a different way to boys when they process information.

As a general rule, girls tend to be more focussed on relationships rather than objects and better at picking up social cues and blending in. They also have better verbal skills and are likely to show much more of an interest in imaginative play than boys, which explains a lot about why there's such a big difference between the number of boys and girls who currently receive an autism diagnosis.

To add to the difficulties they experience when it comes to being diagnosed, the tests developed in the 1940's by Leo Kanner and Hans Asperger really weren't designed to accommodate girls, and don't take into account the different ways autism presents itself in females. As a result most autistic girls simply don't tick the right boxes when they're assessed and end up being misdiagnosed with anything from anxiety to OCD or bipolar disorder, all of which can often develop later on as a result of struggling to live a 'normal' life while feeling so completely different to other women, but none of which are the original cause of their challenges. This can lead to older girls and women feeling like they're constantly failing because despite years of therapy and even drug treatment for depression, they just don't feel any different.

The invisible girl

Even from a very young age, fitting in and doing what was expected of her outside the house was hugely important to Isabelle. At nursery she'd pay close attention to the rules and do her very best to follow them, and if she ever felt she stood out from the other children for some reason, she'd quickly change what she was doing in order to blend in.

A good example of this was when the nursery staff realised that, like many autistic children, no matter how many times she spun around she never got dizzy. They found this quite incredible and would ask her to spin and spin then walk towards them across the room (which she duly did in a perfect straight line) giving her lots of cuddles and praise for her special skill when she reached them. Rather than being pleased about this extra attention, Isabelle realised she was being singled out and became worried there was something odd about her. Her solution was to start crossing her eyes every time she was asked to spin, which had the effect of making her become just as dizzy as the other children. Once she started responding the same way as everybody else she was happy because, she told me, it meant she was doing things 'properly'. Standing out in any way has always been hard for Isabelle to handle, and this trait, known as 'exposure anxiety' is another very common feature in girls with autism.

The older she got, the more she understood what was expected of her, and the harder she worked at getting things right, which made her hugely popular with both the children and staff, and she positively thrived in such a highly structured environment. What the nursery staff didn't see of course was the huge toll it was taking on her emotionally as she desperately struggled to follow so many unwritten social rules while not really understanding why.

This was nothing to do with not liking or enjoying nursery, in fact it was the opposite: she loved being there and since she understood it was a safe, welcoming environment *because* everybody followed the rules and got along with each other, she was constantly working as hard as she could to make sure everyone understood this and got things right. As we all know, there's bound to be a certain degree of chaos involved when it comes to large groups of young children, but to Isabelle's ultra-logical way of thinking, they should all follow the rules to the letter otherwise they might be putting themselves in danger. Despite taking on the role of a mini member of staff to help make sure this happened, resisting the urge to stage a coup and take charge of the entire nursery at three years old really was a daily struggle for her.

At home she was steadily becoming more anxious, constantly melting down and regularly self-harming. She was violent, aggressive and terribly destructive, struggling to cope with the slightest changes to any routine and unable to follow even the simplest of instructions unless they were carefully phrased to allow her to think she was still in charge.

Every evening when we collected her from nursery, she'd happily hug and kiss both her friends and the staff goodbye and head towards the car with lots of waves and smiles, only to transform – literally within an instant – into a screaming, kicking, hysterical monster the second they were all out of sight.

I appreciate some people reading this will say 'Oh, she was just playing you up. All children do that to their parents' and believe me, I understand that, but this was on a whole different level - the intensity of her rage and frustration was really quite shocking, even to me.

After a twenty minute struggle we'd finally get her into her car seat, where she'd sit, furiously stimming, randomly pointing at the air and shouting at no-one in particular 'You do that! You go there! Not like that, like this!' 'You naughty!' as if she'd been saving up her frustrations about children doing things 'wrong' all day, only to have them burst out of her like a box of live fireworks when she could finally relax.

Although a lot of her behaviour with us was similar to that of her brothers at the same age, the fact she was totally cooperative outside the house while she was still so young was something completely new. It put me, once again, on unfamiliar ground as I struggled to explain my concerns about her development to people who only ever saw her on her very best behaviour and wondered what on earth I was worrying about.

Nigel was terribly upset by this enormous difference in her behaviour as soon as we were alone with her and was certain we were doing something wrong, but I'd seen it before with her brothers (albeit when they were much older and had been taught how to control themselves) and realised it was actually because we were doing something *right* and she felt safe enough with us to relax and let go of all her anxieties.

It's something called the 'delayed after effect' and this is how it works: Every human brain, whether it's autistic or not, contains an area called the pre-frontal cortex that's in charge of controlling impulses. When someone is anxious, the pre-frontal cortex is very active and works hard to keep their impulses under control, stopping them from lashing out verbally or physically if something upsets them and helping them follow society's rules to the best of their ability. When the anxiety eventually disappears, the pre-frontal cortex relaxes and allows emotions like fear, anger and sadness to be processed, which is why everyone is different when they're feeling safe in their home environment, away from the public eye. Because autistic people struggle to process emotion and find social rules so confusing and frustrating, they can easily become overwhelmed when they're suddenly able to relax after a hard day of doing their best to fit in. While the boys had to be taught this strategy over many years, Isabelle has always done it instinctively because she's female.

It's something that's extremely common in autistic girls and is known as 'passing' or 'camouflaging' - in other words doing whatever it takes to be invisible in a crowd no matter how much stress it's creating inside you. The pressures of living this way inevitably build as girls get older and it's often during the teenage years, when the social rules change so dramatically, that autistic girls really struggle. I'll talk a lot more about this in my next book (covering autism, Asperger's and adolescence) but suffice to say that teenage girls on the spectrum can be very vulnerable when it comes to low self-esteem, self-harm and eating disorders in their never-ending quest to fit in, so this is definitely something worth tackling while they're young if you can.

If your child is displaying this kind of behaviour, the best advice I can give you is to make sure they're given plenty of opportunity to just be themselves and do their own thing when they get home. If they want to sit in front of the TV or play a video game by themselves rather than talk to anyone, make time for them to do this. Alternatively, if they want to do something active like bike riding, or talk to you non-stop about anything and everything, just let them. Whichever way works best for them, they'll be instinctively drawn to it and it will help them decompress, giving them a chance to process everything they've been experiencing during the day.

Diagnosis and beyond

Although she was clearly as bright as a button, Isabelle's speech didn't develop at the same time as her friends' and the older she got, the more her frustrations grew. Her meltdowns were becoming dangerous: she'd often try to throw herself down the stairs and regularly punched herself in the face, slashed at the skin on her arms and tore her hair out at the roots. Although she was still behaving perfectly outside the house, I could see trouble ahead if this behaviour wasn't acknowledged, and insisted she be given an assessment by a paediatrician. Naturally people thought I was insane and once again I found myself having to do my 'polite, consistent and annoyingly persistent parent' routine until she was given a referral.

Needless to say, Isabelle behaved like an absolute dream at her appointment and initially I thought there was no chance she'd be diagnosed, but the paediatrician clearly knew her stuff and assured me that yes, she could see Isabelle was on the spectrum, which was a huge relief after being doubted by so many people for so long.

Speech-wise she reassured me that although there was indeed a delay, her language development was still within the accepted boundaries and as it turned out, her speech did eventually come in, all at once in a huge rush, and nowadays she has an incredible vocabulary for her age.

Although the paediatrician recognised and understood exactly what was going on at home, as she rightly pointed out, what mattered *educationally* was how Isabelle could function at school. As harsh as it sounds, the education system simply isn't equipped to deal with what's going on outside the classroom, so helping her deal with her anxieties at home was pretty much always going to be my responsibility unless things got worse for any reason. As things stood, she was more than capable of coping without any extra help at school but that could always change in the future, so we'd need to be a bit creative when it came to her diagnosis.

If Isabelle had simply been diagnosed as 'autistic', the SEN department would have been obliged to give her help in the classroom, which at this stage she didn't show any sign of needing. Since we both agreed there were other children out there who needed the support far more than Isabelle (like her brothers had at the same age) we came up with a diagnosis that could stay on her records and be referred to if anything became a problem in the future, but wouldn't automatically start the process of getting her a level of support she clearly didn't require.

Her official diagnosis then, is 'Strong family history of autism;' (understatement) 'shows autistic tendencies when under stress.' Naturally, 'stress' can be defined as anything from trying to brush her hair (an unutterable nightmare) to convincing her that wearing a sock with a bumpy seam will *not* in fact kill her, even though it clearly feels as if it might.

When Isabelle started school at four a distinct change came over her. Whereas before she'd been supremely confident and outgoing, suddenly she was shy and withdrawn, so much so that the school spoke to me about their concerns. It seemed she wasn't playing with the other children and would sit alone in the book corner whenever she could, where she appeared to be watching everything from a safe distance instead. I told them it was nothing to worry about, described her diagnosis and explained she was simply taking her time to process her new environment. Having never dealt with an autistic girl before, they were unconvinced, so I came up with the idea of enrolling her into their newly-formed After School Club which happened to be held in her classroom, to give her the chance to explore things without so many other children being around.

As it turned out, the club was so new she was often the only child there, and this allowed her to interact with the teachers on a one to one basis which was what she was used to at nursery. It worked like a charm and she quickly found her confidence.

So far *touches wood* at ten years old there've only been a handful of times I've had to refer to her diagnosis and ask, not so much for extra help, but for a bit of extra understanding. On the whole her teachers have been fantastic about it, although there have been one or two who've said 'Oh, she's not really autistic, just spoilt' and told me I lack discipline. Nothing I can't handle after what I've been through with her brothers, but still highly irritating nonetheless.

Nowadays there are so many children like Isabelle in the education system who don't need a full SEN Statement but need a bit of extra consideration instead, that I think it's becoming a bit old fashioned to assume every child who doesn't need teaching assistants and a specified budget to help them learn can't actually be autistic. I'd love to see the teachers who refuse to accept this start to open their minds a little and realise that being autistic is about *way* more than just your ability to function in a classroom.

Similarities and differences

The interesting thing about girls on the spectrum is how they can appear similar to, yet distinctly different from, both autistic boys and neurotypical girls, which is what makes them so fascinating, complicated and notoriously difficult to diagnose.

When it comes to boys...

In the same way autistic boys do, girls on the spectrum have challenges with processing sensory information, handling emotions, dealing with change and understanding social rules, but how they *respond* to these challenges will often be quite different. In addition to the usual five senses, girls will often seem to have a finely tuned 'sixth sense' that allows them to intuitively know things other people don't.

Although girls are likely to ask endless questions about the world just as boys do, their questions will often focus on deeper issues than the mechanics of how the world works. Subjects such as animal abuse, the destruction of the natural world or even what happens after death can fascinate autistic girls because of their heightened sense of empathy, which gives them a deep connection with, and concern for, these types of issues.

They'll usually enjoy collecting and categorising certain objects, something that's very common in both genders, but whereas boys will arrange their favourite items in long straight lines, girls will often sort them into size, shape and colour order, making beautiful displays and becoming distressed if they're changed in any way. Cuddly toys and stationery are both firm favourites with girls on the spectrum, but they'll be organised and admired rather than being played with or used as they're designed to be.

Autistic girls tend to be ahead of boys when it comes to communication skills, but may show some unusual traits such as singing rather than speaking or developing an intense interest in language, including writing stories and poetry or studying the rules of grammar. They can find it easier to stand up and address a group of people rather than having a one to one conversation, and often have a serious aversion to speaking on the phone, a trait they definitely share with a large number of autistic boys.

When it comes to girls...

Like neurotypical girls, they'll often have an interest in fantasy fiction and can sometimes take things to the extreme and retreat into a complicated fantasy world filled with imaginary friends. They frequently have a deep love of nature and animals, particularly horses, which aren't uncommon in girls, but it's the *intensity* of their interests – bordering on obsession – that's unusual rather than the interests themselves. They're likely to become experts in the subjects that fascinate them, reading everything they can find and memorising large amounts of information about them just for fun. Autistic girls are often hyperlexic too: learning to read very early and enjoying books generally considered far too advanced for them to understand.

Many have quite remarkable creative talents and show a great flair for theatre, art or dance, which they'll practice tirelessly until they're happy with the results. Another area where girls on the spectrum can excel is in the STEM subjects (science, technology, engineering and maths) as many of them prefer 'purposeful play' where everything is categorised, ordered and investigated. Jigsaws, LEGO and gaming are all very popular pastimes too.

Having an interest in clothing is very common in girls, and those on the spectrum are no exception, but their interest can be expressed rather differently. They'll either tend to be tomboys who'll happily wear the same clothes day after day, being uninterested in fashion but still very particular about what they like and dislike, or they'll be intensely feminine 'princessy' types who love to dress up in the latest styles and can't bear getting dirty. Whichever is the case, they like their clothes to be a certain way (more often than not with all the tags removed!) and can become very distressed about any suggested changes.

Shyness is also something a lot of young girls experience, as is separation anxiety, but for autistic girls these feelings can be so powerful they become a full blown social phobia. On the other hand, some neurotypical girls have a tendency to be bossy, and again, in the case of autistic girls this can be exaggerated by their need to control things, often meaning they form better relationships with adults than children when they're small, because adults are better at following the rules. This can lead to them being labelled a 'teacher's pet' and make finding friends of their own age even more difficult.

Society tends to expect girls to be quieter, neater and better behaved than boys when they're young and this can be a real struggle for girls on the spectrum who often have trouble with manual dexterity (doing up buttons or shoelaces) and bilateral coordination (learning dance moves or riding a bike). This can cause a lot of unnecessary stress for autistic girls, as they're usually total perfectionists who can't rest until they've completed every task flawlessly. As a result they may avoid trying new activities due to how much anxiety the fear of failure causes them, and can be diagnosed as having pathological demand avoidance (PDA) as a result.

Encouraging self-acceptance

Whether you're male or female, autistic or neurotypical, the most important part of living a happy, productive life is learning to like, love and accept yourself for who you are. The world will be very quick to point out your supposed flaws (you're too fat, too thin, too tall, too short, too loud, too quiet etc.) so having a good, strong understanding that in actual fact *you are enough*, just as you are, really is vital if you're ever going to flourish.

Girls on the spectrum are notoriously hard on themselves and it can be heart-breaking to watch them pull themselves apart trying to be perfect, but there's plenty you can do to help them feel better, so don't despair. Telling them to 'just stop caring about what other people think' isn't really going to help much because they're simply not wired that way. Instead, point out the fact that caring about other people's ideas and opinions is a wonderful quality to have but isn't the same thing as letting other people's attitudes rule your life, because *everyone's* opinions and ideas matter including theirs. It may seem like a small point to make, but believe me, when an autistic girl has spent her life trying to be like everyone else, she can quickly lose sight of herself as an individual and see herself instead as some kind of inferior, faulty reflection of the other girls around her.

Where do I begin?

Well, first and foremost you're going to need to get informed about exactly how autism affects girls, and although I've written some of the basics here, there just isn't room to write everything, so I'd highly recommend you invest in some books about females on the spectrum. Get familiar with all the little things you might have thought were just what made your daughter a bit quirky or oversensitive and find out the real reasons behind them so you can either teach her to accept them or, if they're causing her distress, work on them together and find some solutions. I've listed several books in the 'Further Reading' section, but the best place to start in my opinion is with Jennifer O'Toole's book 'Sisterhood of the Spectrum' and a book called 'Aspergirls' by Rudy Simone. Obviously this book is about my children when they were small so it's largely written from the perspective of someone with a young family, but some of these other books cover some more adult themes. Personally I feel you can never be too prepared for the future when it comes to bringing up your children, so they're definitely worth reading even if you can't share them with your daughter just yet.

Next you need to teach her how to deal with her emotions. Most girls will struggle with their feelings at some point or another, but girls on the spectrum will experience them at a far deeper level and can easily become overwhelmed as a result. Anger, sadness, frustration and disappointment are all things she'll struggle with way more than most girls, so teaching her a variety of coping strategies before the dreaded teenage hormones arrive is a seriously good idea.

Help her learn relaxation and anger management techniques and explain the difference between being aggressive and assertive. When she was very young, Isabelle had some serious anger issues and we read a book together called 'The Red Beast' by K.I Al-Ghani which really helped her visualise her anger as something separate from herself so she could take charge of it. There are plenty of great books about reducing anxiety and getting to grips with rage and I've listed some excellent ones in the 'Further Reading' section so do check them out if these are the kind of difficulties your daughter (or son) is facing.

Since the age of seven I've worked on these issues with Isabelle using a book called 'How to Be Angry' by Signe Whitson. Because it's designed to be used by quite a large group of children in an informal classroom setting, I adapted some of the content and we converted our spare room into a little schoolroom where I'd stand up and give presentations with a flip chart like an old-fashioned teacher while she and Nigel sat at their desks and asked or answered questions. We still do it to this day and as you can imagine, Isabelle absolutely loves it. Whenever we hold a 'class' she learns so much, not only about herself but about how to respect differences of opinion and identify difficult behaviours in people like passive-aggression, social exclusion and intimidation.

Obviously giving talks and presentations is something I'm used to because of my job, so I'm not expecting everyone to approach things the same way, because that would be unrealistic. It's just an example really of thinking outside the box and using whatever you've got to help your child understand themselves. Never be afraid to dig deep and do things other people might find strange because trust me, if you're on this wildly colourful, unpredictable journey called 'autism parenting' you're going to need to get creative every now and again or you'll go under.

When it comes to tackling anxiety, the first thing to do is accept that feeling it is a real, genuine part of life on the spectrum and not just your daughter being dramatic or overreacting to things. If she feels her concerns are being taken seriously, her anxiety will automatically reduce a little and you can start working on ways to lessen its negative impact on her life; to do this I'd recommend using the techniques I talk about in the 'There Is No Magic Wand' chapter. While nothing can ever be 100% guaranteed to work for everyone, using them has quite literally transformed my life and the lives of my children, not to mention the hundreds and hundreds of clients I've successfully treated with them over the years, so they're definitely worth considering if you're struggling.

I'd also suggest using complimentary treatments like the Bach Flower Remedies, especially Rescue Remedy which works like a charm on Isabelle and is something she's taken since she was very young. If your daughter is approaching the teenage years, think about giving her an Evening Primrose Oil supplement once a day as well to help regulate her hormones.

In case anyone was worried, I don't use these products because I'm some kind of hippy-dippy weirdo, I use them because they genuinely work and make a difference to her peace of mind. Looking after your daughter's emotional and psychological health is every bit as important as taking care of her physically if she's on the spectrum and the younger she is when you start supporting her this way, the more normal it will seem to her and the easier it will be for her to self-regulate as she gets older.

Accepting her individuality

One thing you can guarantee if your daughter is on the spectrum is that she'll be an individual. Whether she's a creative, sensitive introvert, a loud, forceful extrovert or a mixture of both like Isabelle, she'll be an out-of-the-box thinker who interacts with the world in her own unique way. Encouraging her to be proud of who she is, rather than expecting her to automatically fit in and conform, is one of the most empowering things you can do for your daughter whether she's autistic or not, but if she is, you might have to work a little harder before you get the balance right.

As I mentioned before, she's bound to have her own ideas when it comes to what she wears, and encouraging her to experiment with clothes and create her own unique style is a great way to teach her about self-expression.

In Isabelle's case, 'unique' means her clothes are chosen purely on how soft they feel against her skin, and some of her colour and pattern combinations are, well, interesting to say the least. If an outfit doesn't consist of a t-shirt, joggers and flat, comfortable shoes, she's really not interested, and I've left many girls' clothes shops feeling most disappointed after all the beautiful, delicate dresses have been firmly rejected in favour of yet more Star Wars t-shirts and leggings.

Not that it's a total loss on the girly front: When she was four, she went through a phase of wearing a sparkly party dress and cardboard hat whenever she went to the shops, just in case anyone was having a birthday party and might ask her to join in. Personally I thought it showed great initiative on her part because she was (and still is) well known for loving a bit of a get-together. I reminded myself several times back then that I was clearly winning at this whole parenting lark, because she wasn't dressing as a padded dinosaur every day like her brother had.

Something else that's absolutely vital is to make sure your daughter understands there's no 'right' way to be a girl, so play to her strengths whenever you can. If she's an introvert and prefers spending time alone, instead of forcing her to socialise, encourage her to find friends who share her interests and when she's older, talk about career options where being quiet and sensitive can be a bonus. The world is full of opportunities for people of all personality types and there are countless jobs that might suit her temperament, including becoming a writer or editor, a counsellor or an interior designer. If she's an extrovert and has a tendency to be controlling, rather than calling her bossy, explain that she's got great leadership skills and help her refine them a bit so she learns not to upset people. Becoming an entrepreneur, a police-woman or a teacher are all options she might like to explore, as they're great careers for extroverted women. There are so many more, and if you can find something that appeals to her character and incorporates her special interests too, she'll enjoy a wonderfully fulfilling career doing what she loves, while making her own unique contribution to the world. Isabelle's special interest is animals and at the moment she's planning to become a pet shop owner and get a full tattoo sleeve on her left arm, showing all the wildlife in the Amazonian rainforest in full colour. Gulp. Still, I can't deny that she's showing some seriously individual self-expression with that particular idea.

Dealing with self-doubt

All parents of daughters are painfully aware of just how many negative, destructive messages are aimed at women every day by the media and advertising industries. Making women feel like there's something wrong with them is what sells products so the message is loud and clear: You must weigh *this* much and wear *these* clothes, have *these* opinions and *this* many friends if you want to be accepted by society, and however many possessions you already have, you must have *more* or you're just not good enough. Young girls the world over are crippled by self-doubt as a result, and that's without the added pressures of being on the spectrum, so for our daughters it can be a serious problem that literally stops them in their tracks when they're looking for the courage to tackle something new.

It first happened to Isabelle when she was four years old. We were at the local park and she saw a group of children playing football. Being her usual friendly self, she decided to join in and started running across the field, only to stop abruptly, mid-stride and become as rigid as a poker. She looked like she'd been paralysed and after she'd slowly and awkwardly made her way back towards me, she whispered urgently in my ear 'Oh no, Mummy, I think I might be shy!' It broke my heart because I knew just where she'd inherited this one from: I was exactly the same until I was well into my twenties and had to do some serious work on myself to overcome it.

Sadly it's a trait that's increased as she's got older and although she's supremely confident with people she knows well, in front of strangers or even friends she hasn't seen for a while, she'll still only communicate by whispering directly into my ear. It's something we're working on and I've never criticised her for it because it's such a common trait in autistic girls, but it has caused a few raised eyebrows over the years as you'd expect.

Isabelle is hugely self-conscious in a way her brothers have never been. When Dominic was eleven, he bought himself a shocking pink, glittery cowboy hat which he wore round the town on a shopping trip with his friends. He came home positively beaming and told me how everyone he met had absolutely loved it. 'How do you know?' I asked 'Well' he said 'they all shouted "Nice hat, mate!" as I went past.' Isabelle would have shrivelled with embarrassment at being singled out like that, not to mention that she would've understood that they weren't being serious.

A great way to inspire any girl is to introduce her to confident, successful women who fire her imagination and help her visualise what she might achieve as she grows up. If she's a reader, find positive fictional role models like Hermione Granger from Harry Potter and Roald Dahl's Matilda. If she's an active, outdoorsy type, introduce her to Princess Leia from Star Wars and when she's a bit older, Katniss Everdeen from The Hunger Games.

Remember there are countless real-life role models to inspire young girls nowadays too. It's easy to find examples of women succeeding in every career from athletics to astrophysics, or working in fields as diverse as aeronautics and high profile politics. A fantastic resource for inspirational stories about women of all ages, races and backgrounds is a website (and Facebook page) called 'A Mighty Girl'. Details are in the 'Further Reading' section and I'd really recommend checking it out whatever your daughter's age, because it's one of those sites that's got something for everyone.

Be aware of celebrating home, family and motherhood too because if that's what she's drawn to, making a success of those is every bit as valuable a contribution to the world as having a glittering career. Just make sure she's aware of all her options, give her some gentle guidance and she'll get there. Her choices may surprise you and you probably won't approve of them all, but if she does something with her life that makes her truly happy then as a parent, what more can you really ask?

It's perfectly understandable that even with all these positive role models, your daughter might get concerned about her autism holding her back and whether it might stop her achieving her dreams, so always tell her about famous women with autism as well. International superstar Susan Boyle, Hollywood actress Darryl Hannah, Professor of Animal Science and autism advocate Temple Grandin and Paralympic gold medallist Jessica-Jane Applegate are just a few examples of women in the public eye who live with autism every day. Remind her there are many, many more autistic women out there leading positive, rewarding lives, a lot of whom aren't even diagnosed. They've all worked out how to deal with the inevitable struggles of living with autism and managed to make a success of things in their own way, and with the support you're willing to give her, there's every chance she'll do exactly the same.

Handling the haters

With the best will in the world, it's highly unlikely that everyone will embrace your daughter's differences and respond to her with kindness, so at some point you can expect her to experience a bit of jealousy, bitchiness or criticism. As I said before, telling her to ignore other people's negativity just isn't going to work, because this kind of thing has the potential to hurt her. A lot. The best way to deal with it is by doing everything you can from a very young age to teach her self-respect, and explaining how this is way more important than anyone else's opinion of her. The techniques in the 'Magic Wand' chapter will help with this no end, but it's the small, everyday reinforcements she gets from you that will do the most to boost her self-esteem. Lead by example and show her how you admire women of all shapes and sizes (including yourself), let her see you respecting and celebrating inventors and original thinkers and admiring people with an unusual sense of style. Be open minded and creative when it comes to praise. Search 'ways to praise a child' and 'boosting your child's self-esteem' on Google and get busy putting the ideas you'll find into practice. There are *so* many more ways to praise a girl than just focussing on her physical appearance, so learn to nourish her spirit too; it really will make all the difference.

A good friend of mine has a daughter with a very unique sense of style and when she was a teenager, a group of girls approached her at school with the sole intention of criticising her for being different. 'You're weird' the ringleader told her with a sneer. Because she's been brought up to respect herself and celebrate her individuality, she looked the other girl in the eye and said 'Thank you.' 'It wasn't meant to be a compliment' came the girl's reply. 'Oh I know,' said my friend's daughter, 'but I chose to take it as one.'

And that, my friends, is the best comeback ever.

Anyway

(The Paradoxical Commandments)
by Kent M. Keith

People are illogical, unreasonable and self-centred.
Love them anyway.
If you do good, people will accuse you of selfish ulterior motives.
Do good anyway.
If you are successful, you will win false friends and true enemies.
Succeed anyway.
The good you do today will be forgotten tomorrow.
Do good anyway.
Honesty and frankness make you vulnerable.
Be honest and frank anyway.
The biggest men and women with the biggest ideas can be shot down by the
smallest men and women with the smallest minds.
Think big anyway.
People favour underdogs but follow only top dogs.
Fight for a few underdogs anyway.
What you spend years building may be destroyed overnight.
Build anyway.
People really need help but may attack you if you do help them.
Help people anyway.
Give the world the best you have and you'll get kicked in the teeth.
Give the world the best you have anyway.

Chapter Ten

Tackling the Tough Stuff

'Whoever said the small things don't matter
has never seen a match start a wildfire.'

Beau Taplin

When it comes to autism parenting there's such a variety of day to day struggles that no-one could ever list them all. Everyone's lives are different, everyone's expectations are different and everyone's children are different, so the number of potential problems you could come up against at any given moment is so vast it would be impossible to discuss them all in one book, let alone one chapter.
I've chosen instead to focus on four of the most challenging issues you're likely to face if your son or daughter is on the spectrum, offer some insight into what might be causing them, and more importantly explain how you can handle them without losing your mind.
Behavioural meltdowns, refusal to cooperate, food aversion and sleep disturbances can all be part and parcel of living with autism, and how you deal with them can make all the difference to both your peace of mind and your child's progress.

Well that makes sense

Understanding how your child makes sense of their world is absolutely vital if you're going to successfully ride the rollercoaster of emotions that come with life on the spectrum. Being autistic means your brain is wired to process information differently to non-autistic people, so inevitably an autistic person's experience of life will be very different too.
Whatever we do in our lives, whether we're awake or asleep, our brains are constantly processing information and deciding how best to respond to it. We take this information in through our senses: by seeing, hearing, smelling, tasting and touching. These are the best known senses, but we also collect data in other ways including understanding what our muscles, joints, tendons and ligaments are doing (known as proprioceptive input) and through our sense of balance,

movement and our relationship to gravity (known as vestibular input).

We collect information in all these different ways at the same time, wherever we are and whatever we're doing, whether we want to or not. For non-autistic (neurotypical) people this doesn't present much of a problem because they can easily prioritise each bit of information as it comes in and automatically ignore those sights, sounds, smells etc. which aren't relevant to what they're doing at the time, but autistic people can really struggle with this process.

They have something called sensory processing disorder (SPD) which means their brains are trying to process an absolute torrent of information from every direction at once without being able to block any out, and this can quickly lead to them becoming upset and overwhelmed in a situation most people would simply take in their stride.

Imagine you're climbing a hill. Although you might usually do it without thinking, your brain will be constantly processing all kinds of sensory information: anything from the surrounding temperature to moving the muscles in your arms and legs; from keeping your balance to feeling the touch of your clothing on your skin. For an autistic person, not only is every little scrap of information just as important as all the rest, so they're all competing for attention at once, but that information can be distorted to the point where a bird singing sounds like a train whistle going off inside their ear and the label in their trousers feels like it's made from rose thorns. Make no mistake: being autistic is hard work, and making sense of the world can be incredibly difficult, painful and often downright scary.

The good news is there's plenty you can do to help reduce the difficulties, pain and fear your child might be experiencing; you just have to learn to spot what's going on as quickly as possible and do whatever you can to put it right.

Reading the signs

So how can you tell if your child is having trouble processing specific types of information, especially if they're non-verbal? Well, once you know what you're looking for, their behaviour will give it away every time. As with everything about the autism spectrum, nothing is straightforward (of course) so they might display their processing problems in one of two ways: either by disliking too much sensory input (known as sensory avoidance) or by craving it (known as sensory seeking). Oh, and just to make it a bit *more* confusing, they often display symptoms of both avoidance *and* seeking at the same time, and these will change depending on where they are and how they feel. Brilliant. Nothing difficult there then.

So, these are just a few of the ways SPD can manifest:

Sensory avoidance behaviours

- Disliking being touched particularly when having their teeth brushed, nails cut, hair washed, being given a bath or being dressed because it causes them physical pain.
- Being unable to tolerate labels in clothing or specific types of material which aren't extremely soft because they feel irritating and scratchy.
- Having an unusual response to pain: either over or under responsive depending on their perception of why the pain occurred rather than the actual injury itself.
- Refusing to eat foods which have certain textures, flavours or smells. Preferring soft, bland food that's easy to swallow and gagging if they try foods they don't like.
- Being afraid of changing their position in relation to gravity, meaning they dislike slides, swings, fairground rides or anything involving their head being tipped backwards.
- Having very bad motion sickness.
- Being oversensitive to light: asking to wear sunglasses indoors and having trouble with the flickering of overhead lighting.
- Refusing to make eye contact because it causes them physical discomfort.
- Covering their ears and becoming upset when they hear loud sounds such as vacuum cleaners, hand dryers, toilets flushing etc. and being unable to concentrate if the television is too loud.
- Feeling nauseous or being physically sick when they're exposed to certain smells including food smells, paint, cleaning products or perfume.
- Building small dens or forts that provide a safe, dark, quiet space to block out sensory input.

Sensory seeking behaviours

- Wanting to touch everything, particularly certain textures which can become obsessions.
- Preferring very spicy or crunchy foods that provide a strong sensation in the mouth and eating them obsessively.

- Enjoying being held upside down, spinning around without getting dizzy, and rough play including tight hugs.
- Needing to be constantly in motion: showing thrill seeking behaviour such as climbing and jumping without showing any fear of injury.
- Staring closely at bright lights or spinning objects.
- Constantly humming or singing to themselves.
- Turning the television or their music up much louder than other people can tolerate.
- Needing background music to concentrate.
- Speaking in a very loud voice or making random sounds just to hear them.
- Pulling on their fingers and cracking their knuckles.
- Chewing and twisting their clothes or any small objects such as pencils or items of jewellery.
- Walking with a heavy 'stomping' movement so they can feel their feet hitting the ground.
- Being a very active, restless sleeper and often falling out of bed.

These are only a few of the signs of SPD but hopefully you'll have seen something you recognise here. If not, look the condition up online and you'll find plenty more.

Another very common result of SPD is something Christopher did from the first time he stood up: walking on tiptoe. 'Toe walking', as it's called, isn't directly caused by either sensory seeking or sensory avoidance, but instead by an immaturity in a child's neural circuitry which leads to a dysfunction in the vestibular system. That's a technical way of saying there's a glitch in the feedback loop that sends messages from the brain to the feet about balance, movement and so on.

The most important thing is to get to know your child's individual triggers and how their brain is processing sensory information, because once you know how SPD is affecting them you'll be in a much better position to handle whatever it can throw at you. If your child has any specific behaviours you don't understand, notice when they happen and see if you can trace them back to a potential sensory problem; you might be surprised how much a few simple changes to their environment can improve their ability to cope, but remember to make them one at a time and do each one very slowly or you'll be asking for trouble.

Managing meltdowns

Something every autism parent dreads is their child becoming overwhelmed and going into meltdown. Meltdowns are terribly upsetting to watch and even more upsetting for the autistic person themselves, so they're definitely worth avoiding if at all possible.

The most important thing to understand about meltdowns is although they can look a lot like tantrums, they're actually completely different. Tantrums are massive outbursts of anger which happen when a child (or adult) can't get their own way. They're designed to manipulate and control situations by creating such uproar that whoever's having the tantrum immediately gets whatever they want. When someone's having a tantrum they might be extremely upset but they'll still be in control of their actions and won't do anything to deliberately harm themselves. A tantrum will stop once a person gets the result they're looking for, so tantrums always need an audience otherwise there's no point having one because there's no-one there to sort things out.

A meltdown on the other hand is nothing to do with anger and everything to do with frustration, anxiety and fear. Meltdowns happen when an autistic person is trying to process too much information too quickly and they go into overload, a bit like a computer when it glitches. They lose the ability to process any more information and lose all control over their own behaviour too. This is a result of the incoming information getting backed up in their brain like paper getting jammed in a printer, and because of their communication difficulties, they can't get any of this information back out in the form of words to tell you what's wrong. Trying to force them to focus on something else can send them into a blind panic, activate their fight or flight response and actually cause them physical pain. Before a meltdown there'll definitely be signs it's coming, and these will be specific to your child so I can't tell you exactly what to look for, but they'll most likely include behavioural signs like pacing, hitting their ears with their palms, flapping their hands, rocking or asking you constant questions because they need extra reassurance, plus physical signs like sweating, going rigid, turning pale or becoming very still and staring into space.

When the meltdown hits, they'll lose all control and will scream, break things, attack people and usually start self-harming in some way, often by banging their head on the nearest surface or pulling at their hair or skin. As it progresses they'll go into the second stage where they shut down and try to block everything out, often by curling up in a ball, closing their eyes, making rhythmic movements and becoming mute. This can last for hours or even days as their system gradually reboots, a bit like a computer that's crashed.

Are meltdowns always avoidable?

With the best will in the world it's not always going to be possible to prevent a meltdown as I know only too well. When Dominic was two he went through a phase of wanting to continually smash his head into the white lines in the middle of the road (I never found out why) and funnily enough, I wouldn't let him. If I had, I could've avoided hours and hours of screaming and self-mutilation, but no matter why he felt the need to do it, this definitely wasn't a behaviour I'd allow, so I just had to grit my teeth and get on with things.

Every day we'd collect his brother from school and every day I'd wrestle him across the road while he kicked, screamed, scratched and bit me as hard as he could. If he happened to be holding something at the time he'd aim it at the nearest passing car. If you're ever in a situation where your child is melting down in public and people are giving you dirty looks, just think of me and the withering death stare I got from an outraged BMW driver as a die-cast Thomas the Tank Engine bounced off his windscreen; or the time, covered in mud, vomit, blood and bruises, that I had to be rescued by a passing fireman because Dominic had thrown himself into a thorn bush and I couldn't get him out. Oh, the glamour!

What causes meltdowns?

As I've mentioned, meltdowns happen when an autistic person's senses become overloaded, they're unable to deal with the situation and they become completely overwhelmed. The overload can affect more than one of their senses at the same time, so if you're going to prevent or at least lessen the intensity of a meltdown, you'll have to work out exactly which directions the problems are coming from when you first notice your child is getting anxious. If possible, get them to express how they're feeling either by speaking, using visual aids like PECS (Picture Exchange Communication System) or a suitable app, and see what you can do to help them sort the problems out before things escalate.

Here are some potential triggers to look out for and a few ideas for reducing your child's likelihood to go into meltdown:

Sensory information overload

This is caused by too much noise, light or movement, textures (clothes or food), scents etc. needing to be processed at once. Too much information will be coming in too fast and this can be information from any of their senses. Ideas for reducing sensory information overload include:

- Turning the TV/radio/computer game down.
- Investing in ear defenders.
- Checking for rough seams on socks or tights.
- Checking labels and textures on clothes.
- Buying some 'fidgets' to provide different sensory input.
- Reducing lighting. Be very aware of overhead strip lighting as this is a major trigger for lots of autistic people.
- Using sunglasses or coloured lenses to reduce visual stress (this helped Christopher no end) I've put a link to the appropriate website in the 'Post-Diagnosis Survival Pack' chapter.
- Checking for any unusual scents from cooking/road resurfacing/cleaning products/fuel/the dentist's surgery etc.
- Giving your child something familiar to focus on which can act as an extension of their comfort zone.
- Getting into your child's mind-set as best you can and thinking of all the different information they're having to process. For instance, in a supermarket there's the sound and flicker of the strip lights, the endless rows of brightly coloured packaging, the random movements of other shoppers, the squeaking of trolley wheels, the tannoy announcements, the smells from the bakery counter, seafood and butcher's sections and so much more.
- Doing 'dummy runs' to places you can't avoid like the doctor's surgery, with no agenda other than to get your child used to being there, and taking a friend for moral support if possible.

Emotional overload

Sudden surges of emotion, whether they're considered negative or positive, can overload the processing centres in your child's brain. Being too happy or excited can lead to a meltdown just as easily as being upset or frustrated.
Ideas for reducing emotional overload include:

- Making their environment as peaceful, predictable and consistent as possible.
- Developing emotional management strategies together when they're calm and using them before they get too upset.
- Becoming progressively calmer as they become more agitated.
- Avoiding people who upset or over-excite your child.
- Using the strategies I suggest in the 'There Is No Magic Wand' chapter.

Exposure anxiety

Lots of autistic people find expressing themselves directly to other people very intense because of the changing emotions involved in a two-way conversation. Communicating directly makes them feel vulnerable and exposed, and for this reason they can easily go into shut-down when they're asked a direct question. Ideas for reducing exposure anxiety include:

- Speaking via a toy or puppet: for example if they have a favourite teddy bear, you could ask 'What does Teddy think we should do next?' They can then answer you indirectly by explaining that 'Teddy would like to go on the swings'.
- Understanding their need to quote film scripts, speak in rhyme or sing their answers. People on the spectrum often find patterns in letters, sounds and melodies that neurotypical people miss, and focussing on these makes the information less emotionally charged, letting the quote, poetry or song act as a kind of barrier between you.
- Using pictures or written words including PECS, apps, texts or e-mails to speak to each other. A huge number of autistic people prefer writing as a form of communication rather than speaking on the phone or face to face

because it gives them time to review and properly process what's being said.

- Using physical signals instead of verbal commands, such as tapping a specific rhythm on their arm or touching their hand in a certain way (if they'll allow it) to let them know when something's about to happen.
- Allowing them to look away or use their peripheral vision when they're talking to you. This reduces the emotional and physical discomfort of making direct eye contact and allows them to focus on what's being said rather than struggling to process the emotions involved.

Task performance anxiety

If your child doesn't understand what's expected of them, it can lead to high levels of anxiety about getting into trouble or being laughed at for doing something wrong.
Ideas for reducing task performance anxiety include:

- Breaking tasks down into different steps and not missing any out. Remember how many steps it takes to make a cup of tea! When you struggle to apply context to what you're learning, building new neural circuits is hard work and it will take time.
- Allowing extra time for your child to process instructions because of the difficulties they have interpreting spoken language.
- Being absolutely literal about what you want them to do.
- Explaining the concept of 'practice makes perfect' and how it's the same for everyone, not just autistic people. Praise them for the skills they've already learned and point out that everybody struggles with some things more than others, so it's these things that'll need lots of extra practice.

Intense frustration

This can be caused by a lack of communication skills or the feeling that they need to control an uncontrollable environment.

Ideas for reducing intense frustration include:

- Remembering the world is chaotic, unpredictable and uncontrollable on every level whether you have autism or not; it's therefore utterly terrifying if you can't understand what's going on. Imagine not having an information filter, so you can't prioritise what needs to be controlled because you can't identify what's dangerous. This can lead to the feeling that *everything* needs to be controlled otherwise something terrible might happen. Be patient with your child when they display controlling behaviour – it's not done out of naughtiness but out of fear.

- Doing your best to help your child express themselves using PECS or a suitable app. Alternatively, you could work out your own unique system of communication using objects, toys, hand gestures or something different. It doesn't have to make sense to anyone else as long as you both understand how it works.

- Helping your child learn about theory of mind (ToM) which is the ability to understand that other people's knowledge, beliefs and desires are different to their own. Autistic people can have something called 'mind blindness' and firmly believe that if *they* know something then *you* know it too. Teach them that it's important to explain things to you so you're able to help them.
Dominic almost died from double pneumonia when he was eight because although he'd had a persistent cough, he hadn't mentioned it was also agonisingly painful. When we found out how serious things were, I asked him why he hadn't told me he was in such intense pain; he said 'I thought you already knew.' To his totally logical way of thinking, since I already knew and wasn't doing anything about it, there clearly wasn't anything that *could* be done, so there was no point mentioning it. If he'd applied some context such as 'Mum always helps me when I'm in pain so perhaps she hasn't realised how much this is hurting' he might have told me, but of course, it was only *implied* that I didn't know otherwise I'd be helping, therefore the idea was beyond him. Naturally the doctor thought I was a monster and I spent months feeling like the worst mother on the planet yet again for not realising how ill he was.

Sudden changes in expectation

Changes to your child's routine and what they predict is going to happen can easily trigger a meltdown. This can apply to anything, no matter how insignificant the change seems to other people.
Ideas for dealing with changes in expectation include:

- Realising the trigger could be a change in their routine or simply that something they feel 'should' have happened hasn't happened after all.
- Using timers and verbal reminders to give them plenty of warning when a change of activity is about to happen.
- Using a visual timetable or suitable app to show the different stages of your day and allowing them to choose the order of certain activities.
- Being as flexible as possible about the order they choose. Pick your battles and be willing to change your own expectations of how something like a shopping trip 'should' progress.
- Avoiding giving direct orders when it's time to do something new and using indirect suggestions instead as much as possible.

The delayed after effect

As I discussed in the previous chapter, sometimes your child will have been in an environment like school where they've had to struggle to control their emotional responses, or they might have had an upsetting experience earlier in the day that they haven't processed properly yet. These stressful feelings can build up like water in a barrel and when a few more drops of stress are added on top, the barrel can overflow, sending them into instant meltdown.
This sudden change in behaviour is very common in autistic children and is known as the 'delayed after effect'. It often leads teachers to doubt what parents are telling them when their child is anxious about school, because while they're in class they'll be following the rules and behaving impeccably, only to melt down as soon as they get home. Everyone behaves differently in public and in private and this is just a more extreme version, where all their built up stress comes pouring out in one go. Despite how it appears, it's actually a good sign that your child feels safe and relaxed enough at home to finally let go. I appreciate it doesn't help much but at least you know you're not doing anything wrong.

Christopher used to physically attack me every night when he got in from school: ripping my clothes, scratching and biting me, even blacking my eye and breaking my front tooth during a couple of particularly violent outbursts, yet at school he was beautifully behaved. Naturally, at the time I thought he hated me but as it turns out, it was the exact opposite.

The only way to manage this particular trigger is to ask your child how their day has been and encourage them to communicate using words, pictures etc. rather than their fists and feet, and inevitably this behaviour will take quite a while to change. If they're verbal, get used to asking open-ended questions like 'Who did you play with today?' rather than 'Did you play with anyone?' otherwise all you'll get are yes or no answers. I have to say that getting *any* information out of my children after a day at school has always been virtually impossible, so I wish you more luck than I had on this one, but I did find checking their body language, inspecting their clothes for any holes they might have chewed in their cuffs or any missing elastic they'd pulled out of their socks, plus scanning their bodies for injuries, to be pretty useful techniques when looking for clues.

Remember it can take a long time for your child to process strong emotions so if something has upset them earlier in the day or even earlier in the week, it could suddenly upset them now without warning. Although they'll appear to go into meltdown for nothing, it's just their brain making sense of things and working through the emotional overload they experienced when it originally happened. Clearly you need to add 'mind reader' to your list of talents to successfully work this one out every time!

Being tired or hungry

Autistic people can become very agitated when they feel the sensation of tiredness as it makes them feel out of control. This can cause a release of adrenalin which makes them suddenly appear hyperactive. Like everyone else, your child's blood sugar regulates their ability to control their impulses. If they're hungry and their blood sugar levels are low, they're much more likely to lash out or behave unreasonably. This is really common and is affectionately known as suffering from 'hanger'.

Ideas for tackling tiredness and hunger issues include:

- Getting to know your child's sleep pattern (if they have one!) and avoiding shopping trips, doctor's appointments etc. when you know they'll be at their most tired.
- Taking a buggy if they're small enough to fit in one, so they can have a rest or a nap while you get on with your day. Larger buggies are available from your local disability supplies store and can sometimes be provided free of charge by the local authority. Speak to your health visitor about this if you think it might be useful.
- Making sure your child has plenty of snacks, preferably ones that release their sugar slowly, and allowing them to eat little and often to keep their blood sugar stable.
- Keeping stimulants like chocolate and fizzy drinks to a minimum. These will intensify their sensory issues and make things worse in the long run, not better. Giving your child sugar will make them feel better to start with, but around twenty minutes later their blood sugar levels will drop sharply and they can become very upset without understanding why.

So, now you're armed with all this information, public meltdowns are going to be a lot easier to understand. To make them easier to *handle* though, you'll also need to arm yourself with plenty of mental resources and a whole variety of physical ones as well. I'd strongly recommend you use the strategies I talk about in the 'There Is No Magic Wand' chapter, especially the 'post-hypnotic triggers' which have saved my sanity more times than I care to remember. They'll help you hold yourself to a higher standard than people who know nothing about the condition and deal with the inevitable disapproval you'll get from many, but not all, passers-by. People will stare, that's to be expected, but they won't all be staring for the same reason, and in my experience there's usually someone who'll smile and offer you a bit of quiet solidarity just when you need it most.

Now, I don't want to give you the impression that autistic children will only misbehave because of some kind of overload, because at the end of the day they're still children, and all children feel cranky and have tantrums at times, just like adults do. Adults can have 'off' days or be in a bad mood sometimes and it's seen as acceptable, yet many people think it's okay to punish children for showing those same emotions, which isn't really fair when you think about it. All children are capable of playing you up of course, but in my experience autistic children don't tend to be deliberately defiant or naughty, because they don't really understand the 'battle of wills' thing the way most children do.

Before my children were born, I swore I'd never bribe them to do anything, because they were all going to behave perfectly all the time, so there really wouldn't be any need. Life soon put a stop to that little delusion for me as you know, and nowadays I never leave home without at least one pocket full of bribes to be handed out in emergencies.

Below is a list of items I've found invaluable over the years for helping my children cope on days out. Yours will no doubt be different because your child's needs will be different, but it's a good place to start and hopefully it'll give you some new ideas for reducing everyone's stress levels. Invest in a good quality shoulder bag or backpack to carry everything around in; baby changing bags are great for this and some of them are really stylish nowadays.

Survival Kit for Days Out

- Visual timetable showing what you're going to do and in which order. If possible, make it flexible. Phone or tablet apps such as the Grace App for Autism are really useful for this kind of thing. Full details here: www.graceapp.com

- Hand-held timer to explain the transition from one activity to another.

- Preferred foods, ideally finger food and small snacks to help regulate blood sugar. If you're eating a meal while you're out, take cutlery and crockery they're familiar with.

- Fidgets like a stress ball or a small, soft terry cloth blanket; bubble wrap or any number of specially designed items. Search 'autism fidgets' online.

- Weighted vest or a small weighted blanket.

- Phone, tablet, Gameboy or DS with their favourite games installed.

- Charger and spare batteries.

- Small bag of LEGO.

- Puzzle books and creative toys like coloured pencils and a small colouring book or a note pad and pen for playing games like noughts and crosses.

- Sunglasses to reduce visual overload.

- Ear defenders or an iPod with ear buds, containing music they find soothing or maybe a favourite audio book. Ideally use one or more of the subliminal programmes I talk about in the 'There Is No Magic Wand' chapter.

- Hoodie or hooded coat/cardigan to block out excess light and noise and create a kind of portable safe space.

- Something that smells familiar like a small bar of soap, some hand lotion or a piece of cloth sprayed with a particular fragrance they enjoy.

- Your contact details for them to carry in some way in case they wander off, maybe on a bracelet or in their pocket.

- A basic first aid kit for the inevitable bumps and bruises.

- Bribes! Be prepared with some of their absolute favourites to offer in case of emergency.

- If possible, allow your child to take the lead in deciding when to take sensory breaks and which items to use. This helps them learn about their own sensory needs and teaches them how to self-regulate so they can become more independent as they get older.

Encouraging cooperation

My boys have all been described many times as naughty, belligerent, defiant, stubborn and uncooperative, none of which they actually are; nonetheless I can see why people might have thought this about them. Carrying three screaming, kicking children along the street could certainly give people that impression, but the trick is to understand what's going on beneath the surface when they get agitated and refuse to cooperate. Once you understand their reasons for resisting whatever's going on, you realise their motivation isn't that they're trying to be awkward but is often an overwhelming anxiety about being out of control.

Literally going back to basics

The first thing to do if your child is being uncooperative is to keep a very strict watch on exactly what it is you're saying to them. Autistic people are very literal so it could be that they've not understood your instructions correctly.

All language has two layers of meaning: what words *actually* mean (their literal meaning) and what we *want* them to mean (their figurative meaning) which is where the expression 'figure of speech' comes from (when someone says one thing but means something else). Autistic people, as I've said before, learn in fragments so they're often unable to match the literal meaning of a word or phrase to the figurative or intended meaning, which can lead to a lot of stress and confusion.

For example, if you tell your child you're going to catch the bus and they become upset and resistant, think about what you've just said in a *literal* sense. A bus is a huge, heavy vehicle which would undoubtedly crush you to death if you tried to catch it, so is it any wonder they're agitated by this idea? What you *meant* to say was that you're going to board the bus, sit in the seats and ride into town inside it (not *on* it because then you'd be sitting on the roof) but autistic people don't make these connections automatically because their minds don't put words and phrases like this into any context. That doesn't mean they can't learn to apply context to figures of speech, it just means you have to explain things properly to start with. I've taught my children to ask themselves 'how likely is that?' if they ever feel confused over something like this, and it's really helped them make sense of things like sarcasm, idioms and metaphors.

Autistic people have a lot of difficulty picking up both verbal and non-verbal clues like body language and tone of voice during a conversation, so instead of realising that a wry smile and a raised eyebrow means someone is being sarcastic when they say 'That was the best film I've *ever* seen', they'll take it literally and believe it really *was* the best film they've ever seen. Neurotypical people can get very frustrated when autistic people misunderstand things or never seem to 'get the joke' and often think they're either stupid or are being deliberately obtuse, but this very much works both ways. Dyslexic people always ask 'Why can't words just be spelled the way they sound?' while autistic people ask 'Why can't people just say what they mean?' It's one of the main reasons people on the spectrum struggle so much with social situations, but with a little understanding and patience, it's easily resolved. The best way to deal with this is to remember autistic people don't understand what's *implied*, only what's actually *said*.

When Dominic was sixteen his friend's brother had open heart surgery and he asked how the operation had gone. His friend said 'Well, they were in the theatre much longer than expected' to which Dominic replied 'Wow! They went to the *theatre*? He must have been feeling better.' Without missing a beat, his friend said 'Not *that* kind of theatre, Dom' and they carried on with their conversation. That it was an *operating* theatre was clearly implied by the fact an operation had just taken place, so Dominic's friend didn't bother to say the word 'operating', only the word 'theatre'. To Dominic's mind though, a theatre is where you watch a play, and because he couldn't add the right context to what he'd been told, it seemed perfectly logical (if rather surprising) that the lad must have suddenly gone on a night out. Instead of making fun of Dominic for this, his friend realised he actually hadn't explained himself clearly enough, and dealt with it as if it was the most natural thing in the world. Autism acceptance at its best!

So, if possible, work with your child and build up a reference library of euphemisms and figures of speech - sitting on the fence, it's raining cats and dogs, please take a seat etc. - and laugh together about how funny they can sound. Learning to laugh about things like this is a great way to bond, and can really help with their social skills. Obviously there's a whole world of difference between laughing *about* something and laughing *at* someone for not understanding it, so be very sure your child understands that you're not laughing at their expense (I've had to explain this to Aidan many, *many* times). In our house we have a whole set of books looking at the origins of phrases like 'mad as a hatter' and 'Bob's your uncle' and we all find them fascinating. Lots of autistic people develop a real love of puns and word play once they understand the ideas behind them, so never be afraid to appeal to their sense of humour when it comes to language.

Processing delays

Another reason your child might seem to be uncooperative is that they're having trouble processing what you're asking them to do. Autistic people take a bit longer to process spoken language and apply the correct meaning to each word, because their brain doesn't automatically group commands together in the right way, even if they've heard them several times before. Give them a little extra processing time and make sure they've understood you before giving them any more instructions, otherwise they can become overwhelmed and go into meltdown.

When we concentrate on things we really love, we can 'lose ourselves' in the process – literally losing track of time and forgetting about everything else – and one of the wonderful things about autism is that this ability is much more intense, meaning autistic people can find endless pleasure in their special interests long after other people would've become bored by them. The frustrating thing about this however, is that they lose themselves so completely that it takes a while to come back to reality and focus on something else, so moving from one task to another can be incredibly stressful for them because doing it too quickly feels like such a huge wrench.

If your child has trouble with this, I'd suggest using visual timetables to explain exactly what you're doing and what you're going to do next, as well as timers to show them how long they have left at each activity. If possible give them ten minute, five minute and two minute warnings when you're going to start doing something new so they've got time to disengage from whatever they're doing and start engaging with something else. It might sound obvious but helping them deal with this processing difficulty (known as cognitive delay) really can make all the difference.

Pathological demand avoidance

Some people on the spectrum have a condition called pathological demand avoidance (PDA). If your child has this, it will seem as if they'll do anything at all rather than what you're asking them to, even if it goes against their best interests. Aidan has PDA which he manages incredibly well outside of the house, but not so much at home, so if we ask him to do anything he'll instantly make excuses and refuse, even if it's something he enjoys. The trick is to work out why your child might be refusing your request and learn how to ask them in a different way. People with PDA will use some or all of the following tactics to avoid doing what they've been asked:

- becoming hysterical and physically attacking you
- acknowledging you've made the demand but refusing to complete it
- distracting you (often with difficult behaviour) so you forget about the demand you've just made
- procrastinating or negotiating with you to let them complete it later
- disappearing into a fantasy world and pretending not to hear you

The reason they behave this way isn't because they're naughty or uncooperative, although it can certainly seem that way, it's simply because they experience huge levels of anxiety whenever they feel they're out of control, and being asked to do something while they're focussing on something else makes them feel this way. As I've said before, autistic people can really struggle with applying context, not only to what you're saying but to situations and what might happen as a result of sudden, unexpected changes. People with PDA will panic when they're given a direct instruction, and this can be for a variety of reasons: anything from fear of making a mistake to misunderstanding what's been said. Remember that when you ask them to do something, it's *implied* they can finish what they're doing first, but unless you actually *say* this, they'll assume you mean they need to do it immediately, even if they're in the middle of doing something else. When I ask Aidan to do anything, I always start the sentence with 'When you've finished doing what you're doing, would you...' It really does make all the difference.

Autistic people like things to be safe and predictable, but as we all know, life just isn't like that sometimes. An interesting feature of PDA is that children can behave very differently in different environments, depending on whether or not they feel safe and in control. Aidan, for instance, will follow any instruction to the letter when he's at school because those are the rules and they make him feel safe. At home however, things are more relaxed which means there's more room for doubt, and if there's room for doubt, there's room for anxiety.

The best way I've found to handle PDA is to give indirect (but very literal) requests rather than direct instructions and as I said before, always make it quite clear those suggestions don't have to be followed immediately. Don't fall into the trap of making things a power struggle between you and your child. They're not resisting to be defiant, they're resisting because they're afraid. See if you can work out why: are they having trouble with the language you're using? Are they afraid they'll make a mistake and get into trouble? Are they panicking because they haven't had enough warning that it's time to change activities? Whatever it is, always approach the situation with love and compassion rather than anger and frustration. It won't be easy and it won't be quick, but over time you'll get to know what's triggering them, and can change your approach accordingly.

Remember, your child thinks in a very rigid way so *they* can't be the one to initiate any changes here, it has to be you. Don't focus on winning the battle or feel like you're giving in if you can't get them to do what you're asking, focus on winning the war and helping them to feel more secure about their place in the world. Believe me, it's definitely worth it.

Food, glorious food

Not every child on the spectrum has issues with food, but the vast majority of them certainly do. Isabelle, for instance, can be a bit picky about what she eats, but her brothers took food aversion to a totally different level.

Christopher never gave me any cause for concern when he was bottle fed, but when we reached the weaning stage things really took a turn for the worse. The first time I put a spoon of baby rice in his mouth he went completely hysterical and took several hours to calm down. This went on for about six weeks during which time I began to wonder if perhaps I'd poisoned him in a previous life, but we persevered and eventually he got the hang of it. He had an incredibly restricted diet and no foods were allowed to touch on his plate unless we wanted hours of hysterical screaming, but with a lot of creative thinking and a fair degree of mess, I managed to keep him alive, healthy and growing faster than most other children his age, so I considered my efforts at weaning to be a success. Dominic, however, was another matter entirely.

Dominic also did brilliantly while he was bottle fed, putting on the right amount of weight and growing taller and stronger every day. When it came to weaning though, we hit a major problem: he couldn't work out how to chew and couldn't physically swallow anything other than liquid. He'd sit in his highchair with a mouthful of baby rice looking utterly confused until it started to run down his throat, at which point he'd choke so badly it was terrifying.

Despite my superb efforts at miming a chewing motion, he just didn't pick it up, and even if he had, he still couldn't swallow anything even vaguely solid. This went on for months and we made no progress at all, so in the end I resorted to dipping my finger into slightly rice-thickened milk and dribbling it into his mouth one drop at a time, gradually thickening it up in the hope his brain would eventually make the connection. At first these drops were unceremoniously spat back at me or pulled out with his fingers, but over time he got used to the new sensation and instead of choking, he started to gulp them down. Nowadays I know this was something called dysphagia (a difficulty with swallowing) which is part of aphasia (a communication disorder affecting speech and language but not intelligence) which affects autistic people to varying degrees, but at the time I had no idea about any of this so I simply did whatever it took to stop him from starving to death.

To say it was a long road from there to proper solids would be a huge understatement but once he'd got the hang of this swallowing lark, there was no stopping him. The first things on the menu were an assortment of dead spiders and flies, which he'd hunt for around the house and garden all day. Next came mud, washing up liquid, cigarette butts and when, to his absolute delight, he managed to undo the lock on the toilet, a small chunk of the bleach block. That one didn't end well as you can imagine.

He'd also eat soft, white bread by now, which was full of added vitamins and minerals, thank God, but only if no-one saw him do it. Helpfully he wouldn't eat anything he felt I actually *wanted* him to, only things he wasn't allowed to, and wouldn't even *think* about eating something if anyone else could see him doing it, so over time I developed an unusual strategy to help solve the problem.

Every morning I'd put a couple of slices of bread in a bowl, leave it on the living room floor and walk into the kitchen, saying 'That is *not* your bread and you can't eat it!' Within minutes he'd eat the whole lot, but unfortunately this only lasted a few weeks because I didn't seem upset enough about what he'd done so he quickly realised he was being conned and stopped eating it altogether. Back then I knew nothing about exposure anxiety, so I just let him take the lead and did whatever it took to get him to eat. More than one visitor asked me if we'd bought a cat; telling them the bowl on the floor was in fact Dominic's and he only ate dry bread from it did absolutely nothing to improve their opinion of my parenting skills as you can imagine.

Unsurprisingly he didn't carry any excess weight, but what little weight he did carry quickly began to drop off, and he developed big dark circles under his eyes, so in desperation I filled a bag with fresh bread and took it to the park on the pretext of feeding it to the ducks.

It was made perfectly clear to him that once again this was *not* his bread and he wasn't to touch it under any circumstances. I'd then pretend to be engrossed in feeding the ducks while he ripped a big hole in the bread bag and stuffed full slices in his mouth as quickly as he could. It worked perfectly and this soon became our daily routine. He was clearly undernourished and ate like a ravenous, wild-eyed beast, yet while he was eating I'd tell him off loudly and pretend to wrestle the bread out of his hands until it was all gone.

Oddly enough, I wasn't too popular with the other mums at the duck pond.

Different needs, different agenda

Until the age of five the majority of Dominic's diet was goat's milk which I dosed heavily with multi-vitamins (he'd been allergic to cow's milk since birth), but over time he also started eating ready salted Pringles and McDonald's chips, which although not terribly nutritious, did at least help him practice his chewing and swallowing. He carried a full bottle of milk permanently clamped between his front teeth for so long that eventually one of them snapped in half, and at nursery he'd sit in the corner by himself with his back to the classroom, while eating only the Pringles I'd sent him in with.

By now the disapproval rating of my parenting skills from family, health professionals and strangers was about an eleven out of ten. Tutting, whispering and death stares became so normal I hardly noticed them, and helpful statements and suggestions like 'surely his growth will be stunted by his awful diet', 'if you only gave him vegetables he'd eat them when he got hungry enough' and 'can't you just *make* him eat?' were a daily occurrence, but still I held my ground. Neither I nor the nursery staff wanted him to eat this way – we felt awful seeing him sitting on the 'time out chair' all by himself - but we understood he was dealing with *so* much more than these dietary complications, so what he ate was nowhere near the top of our agenda. I didn't understand why he wasn't developing like the other children but I knew he was making progress in his own way, so instead of focussing on what he 'should' have been doing by now, I focussed on what he *was* doing and celebrated every tiny step in the right direction no matter how long it took to achieve.

Today Dominic eats a healthy, varied diet. He's a strict vegetarian and although he still has his favourite foods (Pringles included), he's happy to try new flavours and textures. At six foot two with size 14 feet, his growth doesn't appear to have been stunted much either!

Making sense of food aversion

As with so many things, a lot of food aversion is to do with difficulties processing sensory information.

Firstly there's the taste, smell and texture of the food. Are the foods you're offering too strong? Perhaps they're too bland and your child needs something more stimulating. If you look at their favourite foods you'll often see a pattern: do they prefer spicy, salty, crunchy food or soft, slippery, plain food? Does the food they eat tend to be the same colour? Your child is an individual so there could be any number of reasons why they're refusing to eat, but with a bit of detective work you can figure it out and change how you're approaching meal times accordingly.

Autistic people can often have something called synaesthesia, which means the sensations coming in through one of their senses, such as hearing, can trigger a sensation in another sense, such as taste. As bizarre as it sounds, some people with synaesthesia can actually hear colours or taste numbers. Yes, you did read that correctly.

What you need to work out is how the eating environment is affecting your child. People on the spectrum will often eat one thing quite happily in one place but refuse to touch it in another. This isn't about being awkward, it's because the sensory input they're getting from their location has changed and this can make the food taste quite different.

In Dominic's case, once we'd got past the physical difficulties he had with chewing and swallowing, his main trigger was emotional overload from being too near other people. Once this had been removed he was able to relax enough to digest his food and I was gradually able to work through this with him until he could tolerate it. We went from me leaving the room, to me looking away at the duck pond, to sitting on his own at nursery, to being able to sit at a table for family meals and yes, there were plenty of bumps in the road but we got there in the end.

In your child's case it could be that they're overly sensitive to sound, so if that's what it is, make sure the television or radio are turned off whenever they eat. They could also have an over-sensitivity to visual information (all of my children have this) so always use plain crockery rather than patterned, to reduce visual stimulation. The list of potential triggers is endless, and just when you think you've cracked it something else will probably crop up, so expect plenty of setbacks, but keep going because when it comes to autistic people and food, the normal rules just don't apply. You can't *make* them eat and yes, they *will* starve themselves despite what people might tell you, so do what's right for your child, keep taking those small steps and eventually you'll make some progress.

Sleep is for wimps

Studies suggest over 80% of children on the autism spectrum have difficulty either falling asleep, staying asleep or both. Just for the record, 100% of my children have severe sleeping difficulties, which means I haven't had a full night's sleep in over twenty-five years. This makes me an expert on surviving without sleep, and anything *but* an expert on how to tackle sleep disorders. Still, I know a lot more about it today than I did twenty-five years ago and there's some great advice available from specialists nowadays, so I'll do my best to help with this one and hopefully you'll have a bit more success than I did when my children were small. As I'm sure you're aware, all young children take time to get into a proper sleep routine, so if you have a young baby or toddler and they're struggling to settle at night it doesn't necessarily mean you need to be concerned. If however, you have a child who sleeps for no more than twenty minutes at a time then wakes up full of energy and runs screaming round the house at all hours of the day and night (Christopher) or is still wide awake at 2am then falls asleep until 4am before getting up to start their day in the worst mood imaginable (Isabelle) there might be something that needs looking into.

All living things have a natural 24 hour wake/sleep cycle known as their circadian rhythm or body clock, and autistic people are much more likely to have circadian rhythm disturbances. The hormone that regulates sleep (melatonin) is something autistic people are also likely to have difficulty producing in the right quantities at the right times to give them a decent night's rest. Add to this their sensitivity to light and sound, and their general difficulty switching off when they're over-stimulated by day to day life, and you've got a recipe for sleep deprivation the likes of which only experienced autism parents can truly understand.

For the first eighteen months of Christopher's life I tried every self-help strategy I could lay my hands on. Despite being told it was the only way forward, leaving him to cry was never an option for me and I'm happy to say this isn't recommended as a course of action for autistic children anymore because it just increases their anxiety levels. Other than that I tried everything, but despite my best efforts he didn't sleep the night until he was fourteen, by which time both of his brothers didn't sleep either, so unfortunately I never really felt the benefit.

Every evening I'd go to bed hoping against hope this would be the night he finally slept, and each time I'd be disappointed, frustrated and exhausted by what I saw as my own failure to settle him. When I had my sudden realisation that he was different to other children for some unknown reason, not only did I start doing things very differently during the day but I also changed my expectation of getting a night's sleep. Interestingly it really helped. It didn't help Christopher to sleep any more regularly of course, but waking up knowing I'd done the best I could and not beating myself up over it any more was a huge relief.

When I first met Nigel he found it quite extraordinary just how little sleep I needed to survive and wondered where on earth I got my energy from. The truth is I was using the techniques I talk about in the 'There Is No Magic Wand' chapter and I can honestly say they've transformed my ability to keep going to the point where people still ask me if I have some kind of superpowers, even at fifty one years old. More on that later, but for now here are some ideas that might help your child get a better night's sleep:

- As always, check whether your child is being over-stimulated by their environment. If they are, very gradually reduce the stimulation (don't do it all at once unless you want to create absolute mayhem) and establish a new bedtime routine with less intense sensory input.

- Think about investing in a weighted blanket or an enclosed bed that looks like a den. Both can be easily found online and could really help.

- Make a visual timetable with pictures covering every stage of going to bed, sleeping and waking up in the morning. Many autistic children don't pick up the social cues when their family starts settling down to sleep at night and can be startled by what they see as a sudden and unexpected change from moving freely around the house to being expected to stay in their bedroom.

- Reassure your child every step of the way at bedtime, even if you don't understand what they're anxious about. Lots of autistic people dislike the feeling of letting go and being out of control and can panic when they feel themselves falling asleep, leading to lots of sudden anxiety (all of my children did this).

- Buy a CD of calming music to play as they fall asleep or better still use one or more of the therapy CD's I talk about in the 'There Is No Magic Wand' chapter.

- If things are really severe, consider asking your GP for a referral to a paediatrician or sleep specialist. We eventually gave Isabelle a melatonin supplement on the advice of a paediatrician and she's slept the night ever since. She has plenty of proprioceptive and vestibular issues so she regularly twists herself into a knot inside her duvet or falls out of bed, meaning I still have to get up and sort things out for her, but she sleeps through and doesn't remember anything about it in the morning. Going on melatonin was a real turning point for Isabelle, and her meltdowns, self-harm and emotional outbursts reduced enormously once she was getting enough sleep. Aidan was a teenager by now and still hadn't slept the night, so we tried melatonin supplements on him as well. They made no difference whatsoever, so they clearly don't work for everyone, but are definitely still worth a try.

When nothing works

When you're doing your best to tackle the tough stuff there'll be times when nothing seems to work and that's not because you're a failure, it's because that's just the way it is for every parent on the planet. The important thing to remember is that you *are* doing your best and that's all anyone can expect from you, and most importantly, all you can expect from yourself. How do I know? Because you're still reading, so you're investing your time looking for answers to make your child's life easier, which is something so many other parents won't bother doing. So, always be every bit as patient, kind and loving *with yourself* as you are with your child, because it really is just as important, and what's more, you totally deserve it.

'Stones
in the road?
I save
every single
one,
and one day
I'll build
a castle.'

Fernando Pessoa

Chapter Eleven

And the Good News Is...

'We can complain because rose bushes have thorns,
or rejoice because thorn bushes have roses.'

Abraham Lincoln

After reading about all that tough stuff, I'm sure you could do with a bit of good news about autism, so this chapter focusses on some of the wonderful, inspirational and uniquely exceptional qualities shown by people on the spectrum.

Autism and evolution

Ever since humans have existed, autistic humans have existed too. Some genetic research even suggests that certain autism genes were around before our evolutionary split from the apes. As Temple Grandin puts it: "What would happen if the autism gene was eliminated from the gene pool? You would have a bunch of people standing around in a cave, chatting and socializing and not getting anything done." While that might be overstating things a bit, she's certainly got a point. Early communities of humans lived in unbelievably harsh and dangerous environments, so to survive they had to rely on those members of their group with particular talents and skills.

First of all there'd be a need to pass on the wisdom of the tribe. Information about medicine, shelter building, crop planting etc. would be handed from generation to generation by the village 'wise man' (or woman) and in an age before written history, people would naturally turn to those with exceptionally good memories who could recall the tiny details most people would forget. Frequently described as eccentrics who preferred to live a somewhat secluded life, these people were nonetheless treated with huge respect, and often this talent would run in families, which suggests they may well have been autistic.

Another area where exceptional memory skills would have been highly prized was in the arts. Actors and musicians have entertained and enlightened humanity since long before writing was invented, and it's well known that autistic people can be hugely talented in writing and reciting poetry, remembering songs and playing complicated musical pieces.

Members of the clan with a natural gift for the intricate patterns of mathematics, engineering and design would also have been invaluable to early humans, and it would've been the out-of-the-box thinkers who were responsible for creating the ever more sophisticated forms of shelter, drainage and sanitation that moved civilisation forward.

Those with an instinctive connection to animals (a very common autistic trait) would have provided the group with another important set of specialist skills, being responsible for anything from taming horses to rearing livestock. Because of their unique way of processing sensory input, people on the spectrum are often very in tune with the weather too, sensing changes in barometric pressure long before others become aware of them. This would have been enormously useful to early tribes-people when planning hunting expeditions or planting crops.

When humanity first evolved, we were much more in tune with ourselves and our surroundings, and spirituality played an enormous part in many early societies. Tribes would have a 'shaman' or 'medicine man/woman' to offer spiritual wisdom and guidance; they'd generally live in isolation and wear unusual clothing of some kind to represent their status. They'd gather large collections of very specific 'sacred' objects which they considered hugely important, and communicate with the spirits of both nature and their ancestors, relaying messages which affected the destiny of the entire group. Having a heightened sense of taste, smell, vision and touch would have been important in this role, as would having a 'sixth sense' – an ability to somehow know things other people didn't - as well as a natural tendency to focus on objects and go into meditative states, all of which are recognised autistic traits.

I'm not saying these roles were *always* filled by autistic people, just that I suspect the natural talents of people on the spectrum were both incorporated into, and celebrated by, these early human tribes-people, making autistic people essential to the survival and development of their societies.

Autism and celebrity

So, if autism has been around forever, what were all the autistic people doing? Well, most of them were simply getting on with their lives, but with such a unique set of talents it's inevitable that some of them would become celebrated public figures. Hans Asperger once said 'It seems that for success in science and art, a dash of autism is essential', and looking at this list I can definitely see what he meant.

The term 'autism' wasn't used until well after many of these amazing and highly influential people had lived and died, so of course describing them as being on the autism spectrum is open to debate. Ultimately you'll have to decide for yourself, but I've studied them, and feel (along with many, many others who've done the same) that they were indeed people who dealt with autism every day of their lives. This list is here to inspire and uplift people who struggle with social and sensory issues, just as those on the list did (and in many cases still do), and to assure them that being on the spectrum is something that will often help you *succeed* in life, rather than holding you back as so many people would have you believe. Remember that for every famous autistic person, there have always been thousands upon thousands of highly respected autistic specialists out there working in the fields of art, science and a whole lot more, whose unique approach to life has been quietly making a difference to the world and improving the future for us all.

- Michelangelo Buonarroti (1475-1564) - Painter, Sculptor, Architect
- Isaac Newton (1642 - 1727) – Physicist
- Henry Cavendish (1731 – 1810) – Philosopher, Chemist, Physicist
- Thomas Jefferson (1743 - 1826) - American Founding Father
- Wolfgang Amadeus Mozart (1756 - 1791) - Composer
- Hans Christian Anderson (1805 - 1875) - Author
- Charles Darwin (1809 - 1882) - Naturalist
- Emily Dickinson (1830 - 1886) - Poet
- Marie Curie (1867 - 1934) - Physicist, Chemist
- Lewis Carroll (1832 - 1898) - Author, Mathematician
- Vincent van Gogh (1853 -1890) - Artist
- Nikola Tesla (1856 - 1943) - Engineer, Inventor
- Albert Einstein (1879 - 1955) - Theoretical Physicist
- Béla Bartók (1881 - 1945) - Composer
- Pablo Picasso (1881 - 1973) - Artist, Sculptor
- Paul Dirac (1902 – 1984) – Theoretical Physicist
- Andy Warhol (1928 - 1987) - Artist, Filmmaker
- Wassily Kandinsky (1866 - 1944) - Artist
- Dian Fossey (1932 - 1985) – Naturalist, Photographer
- Jim Henson (1936 - 1990) – Entertainer, Puppeteer

- Peter Tork (1942 -) – Musician, Actor
- Temple Grandin (1947 -) – Author, Livestock Specialist
- Dan Aykroyd (1952 -) – Actor, Comedian
- David Byrne (1952 -) - Musician
- Gary Numan (1958 -) - Singer
- Tim Burton (1958 -) - Film Director & Producer, Artist, Author, Animator
- Daryl Hannah (1960 -) – Actress, Activist
- Satoshi Tajiri (1965 -) - Inventor of Pokemon
- Susan Boyle (1961 -) - Singer, International Superstar
- Chris Packham (1961 -) - Photographer, Naturalist, Author

I've listed two books in the 'Further Reading' section which go into much more detail about autistic people through history. They're well worth a look.

Autism and friendship

While the majority of autistic people struggle to make and maintain friendships, once you take the time to get to know them, they really can make the most amazing friends.

Firstly they're incredibly honest, not just about their opinions, but about who they are as well. They're very unlikely to be manipulative or play mind games; people on the spectrum have no hidden agendas so it really is a case of what you see is what you get. Knowing where you stand with a friend is incredibly important, and another benefit of their honesty is that they're not the sort of people who'll ever lie, cheat or steal from you.

They're not bullies or scam artists either, and won't take advantage of other people if they sense any weakness in them. Autistic people tend to value everyone (and everything) equally, and are generally very accepting of other people's quirks and differences, so you don't have to worry about whether they'll run you down behind your back or spread nasty rumours about you, because they're simply not wired that way. In my experience, the vast majority of people on the spectrum are highly sensitive and compassionate, and even though they can sometimes make mistakes when expressing their opinions, their intention is never to be malicious or upset anyone.

People with autism are also some of the least judgemental individuals on the planet. They have no interest in criticising others, and their opinions are based solely on someone's behaviour towards them; things like age, race, gender, wealth or social standing really don't come into the equation when autistic people are making friends. Their values are shaped by their own specific experiences of life, and even if they've had a difficult start, with terrible role models or a lack of moral guidance, more often than not they'll form their own unique opinions and in spite of everything, they'll usually develop an optimistic, imaginative view of the world that makes them a joy to be around.

Peer pressure is mostly wasted on people with autism and if they believe an activity is ethically wrong, no amount of persuasion will make them join in. Many of them can be a little naïve however, and there's always a danger that if they become socially isolated they could fall in with the wrong crowd and be manipulated into doing things they'll come to regret later on. What I've found however, is that they're often instinctively drawn towards decent, honest people who share their values, so if an autistic person wants to be friends with you, you can definitely take it as a compliment. Do give them a chance, even if they seem a little unusual to begin with.

People on the spectrum find small talk and gossip a bit pointless, but they'll always be willing to talk about more meaningful subjects, and since their knowledge about the world can be phenomenal, they're certainly fascinating company. They're out-of-the-box thinkers who bring a whole new dimension to everyday life, so if you have a friend with autism, you can guarantee things will never get boring.

Autistic people are notorious for their inappropriate sense of humour too – often enjoying the comedy of Jimmy Carr, Ricky Gervais, South Park and Rick and Morty - and if you appreciate these things too, they can be absolutely hilarious company. They often love puns and figures of speech and will usually have an endless supply of TV and movie quotes to use at the appropriate (or inappropriate) time in a conversation just to liven things up a little. Inevitably there'll sometimes be misunderstandings caused by their communication difficulties, so if anything like this ever happens, do take the time to talk it through together. You'll find people on the spectrum are very quick to forgive and move on in their friendships. They're loyal to a fault and have no interest in degrading or embarrassing anyone, so although it might initially take a bit of extra work to get things going because of their social problems, being friends with an autistic person really can be a hugely rewarding experience.

Autism and employment

While I realise it's not possible for every autistic person to be employed, with a bit of extra understanding, those who choose to enter the workplace often have the potential to become excellent employees.

People with autism can be extremely hard working and tend to take their responsibilities very seriously, so if they're given a task to complete, you can rely on them to get it done. They're not afraid to go the extra mile, and enjoy researching subjects down to the smallest detail, making them a fantastic source of information for the people they work with. Although it's widely believed that autistic people only want to work by themselves, many of them are very sociable and can thrive in a happy, supportive environment just as much as neurotypical people do.

If they're working on something that interests them their enthusiasm is endless, and they bring a fresh perspective when it comes to problem solving that can be quite inspirational to their co-workers. Since they don't instinctively understand the idea of cause and effect, they have a tendency to think without boundaries when it comes to new ideas, and this can lead to some amazing discoveries and inventions that can really benefit their employers.

Nowadays many autistic people continue their education to university level, and they often have outstanding computer skills which are greatly valued in the workplace. With their preference for routine and their exceptional memories, many people on the spectrum can make fantastic IT workers and quite a few companies are starting to realise this. Recently I've seen a variety of large corporations introducing schemes to encourage autistic people to apply to them for jobs, which really is quite brilliant news.

Since they're naturally honest, reliable and conscientious, many employers have been pleasantly surprised by how much their autistic staff members can contribute to the company. Sometimes (but not always) they might need a few adjustments to their working environments like a change in lighting or being seated a suitable distance away from any noisy machines, but the benefits of having them on the pay roll far outweigh any inconvenience these minor tweaks can cause.

Autism and talent

The autism spectrum is so vast and contains so many unique individuals that people with autism have been able to succeed in every walk of life imaginable. Some places they often shine however are in the areas of science, technology, engineering and maths, plus anything related to the arts.

With their love of patterns and predictability, they often have a natural talent for the STEM subjects, finding satisfaction and security in the complicated formulas and techniques so many other people find confusing. Not all STEM specialists are on the spectrum, and not all autistic people particularly like those subjects, but there's certainly a high percentage who excel in them. It's lovely to see these abilities becoming more accepted and even celebrated nowadays. The science nerds and computer geeks who were once universally despised have now become cool in their own way with the advent of 'Geek Chic' and in today's society, intellectual intelligence is finally being seen as something to be proud of.

Autistic people aren't generally all that concerned about being thought of as cool of course, but a culture that encourages them to pursue their talents and take pride in their achievements rather than being embarrassed by them can be a very positive environment to grow up in. Today we're seeing more people on the spectrum continue their education to college and university level, receiving the kind of support we could only have dreamed of when I was a child in the 1960's. Not that people with autism are anything new in the world of academia. It's widely believed that the stereotype of the 'absent-minded professor' comes from the high number of autistic adults working as specialists in the field of further education, so they've always been there; it's just that nowadays they're recognised as being anything but 'absent-minded'.

Surprisingly, given their struggles with bilateral coordination, autistic people can also make superb dancers and even athletes, generally preferring solo pursuits such as cycling, swimming or gymnastics over team sports.

Many have increased flexibility and this, along with their determination to practice tirelessly until they've mastered everything they set their mind to, can really give them an edge when it comes to competitions. Often the sheer love of what they're doing and the desire to perfect their skills is more of an incentive for them than winning rosettes or medals, but being outstanding in their chosen field is definitely something they'll feel proud of, and rightly so.

When it comes to other forms of artistic expression, features of being on the spectrum such as having a highly complex imagination and being acutely sensitive can be extremely useful. Many autistic people love to perform on stage, feeling far safer reading from a script (knowing exactly what to say and when to say it) than they do when interacting with people in the outside world. Their hyper-empathy makes it easy for them to understand and represent different characters, and they often become 'method actors', tuning into and experiencing their characters' emotions to bring a greater sense of realism to their performances.

As I mentioned before, autistic people are often hugely talented when it comes to writing poetry and songs too, and their ability to memorise long passages and recite them by heart can be very familiar to anyone who knows them. They can also excel as musicians, composing exquisite songs and playing them flawlessly with little or no training, and their ability to lose themselves in their music is truly inspirational to watch.

Their creative thinking often leads to unusual forms of self-expression, and people on the spectrum can become incredible artists, sculptures, puppeteers, dressmakers or designers, bringing a distinctly original style to their work that both inspires and challenges their audience. They'll often work with highly unusual materials or mix different textures in a fresh, unique way, and produce breathtakingly intricate pieces that really push the boundaries and help no end in moving society's appreciation of art and beauty forward.

Film-making is another area they can apply these principles, and a great example of this is the rise in popularity of the science fiction and comic book genres. Years ago, these were very much the domain of the uber-nerd, but over the last ten years the Star Wars, DC and Marvel universes have been embraced by the mainstream public to such an extent that 'cosplay' (dressing up in an elaborate, screen accurate costume as your favourite film or comic book character) and 'Comic Cons' (conventions where those who appreciate such things can gather together and celebrate them) have become recognised parts of our culture.

The term 'geek and proud' is regularly used nowadays by people who, rather than apologising for their quirkiness, choose to celebrate it instead. Now that's something this particular nerd never thought she'd live to see!

Autism and spirituality

Spirituality is a tricky subject to discuss because obviously it can mean completely different things to different people, but I'll give it a go nonetheless. What I'm describing here are the general, underlying traits I've noticed in many (although obviously not all) autistic people and how I feel they reflect the inner workings of their personalities in a spiritually enlightened way.

One of the main examples comes from the difficulties they have in understanding cause and effect. Most people have a little voice inside their head that says 'Oh, you can't do *that* because *this* will happen…' whenever they consider trying something unusual, and often it stops them from expanding their minds and experiencing new things. As I've said before, autistic people simply aren't wired that way, and although this can cause problems for them in their day to day lives, when it comes to original thinking, it definitely gives them an advantage.

People on the spectrum don't see boundaries in the same way neurotypical people do, and this allows their minds to explore ideas and concepts most people would automatically dismiss. As a result they're often drawn to philosophical and spiritual teachings which they can appear to understand very early on, at a far deeper level than would usually be expected for someone of their age.

Something else I've already mentioned is their heightened sense of intuition – a kind of 'knowing' that goes beyond logical thought – which means they're much more in tune with their environment and the individuals around them. Many autistic people have a tendency to tune into other people's energy and focus on that rather than on what they're saying or doing, which is one of the reasons they find social interaction, with all its fake smiles and false friendships, so difficult to understand.

Their finely-tuned instincts are often combined with a hugely increased sense of empathy and compassion, not only for other people, but for whatever they come into contact with. They have a profound connection with the natural world and believe everyone (even an inanimate object) deserves kindness and consideration. It's well known that many of them have a deep connection with animals as well, and show respect for *all* creatures, including those most people tend to overlook such as reptiles and insects. Interestingly, animals seem to respond positively to autistic people too, as if they sense something kind and non-threatening about them.

In my experience, people with autism find it easy to see the good in others, often when they don't see it in themselves, and can make wonderful therapists or life coaches, teaching people to look beyond their supposed shortcomings and focus on the positives instead; something promoted by all the great spiritual teachers. It's not only people they view this way though, it can be anything from patterns of information to mathematical equations; everything has its own innate beauty in their eyes, which gives them an appreciation of the world that most people could never even imagine.

As a result they often become experts in their chosen field, and their choices might be a bit, well, *unusual*, meaning people on the spectrum can be a mine of information about anything from archaeology to zoology. They can make incredible progress in specific areas other people haven't even considered researching, and often dedicate their entire lives to their work, losing themselves in their passions but finding themselves too, by entering a kind of meditative state when they're working, where they live entirely in the present moment and the outside world ceases to exist.

Another wonderful thing about them is that since they're not jealous or competitive people, they love to share their wisdom and discoveries freely. A prime example of this was Nikola Tesla who was responsible for many of the most revolutionary inventions the world has ever seen, yet often let others take credit for them. When Marconi sent the first transatlantic message, Tesla had this to say: 'Marconi is a good fellow. Let him continue. He is using seventeen of my patents.' So much of Tesla's behaviour can be explained if you accept he was on the spectrum, but he was born before the concept even existed, and was generally considered to be some kind of strange, eccentric genius. If he was around today however, I'm sure things would've been very different.

Lessons to be learned

Modern society seems to be largely based on the idea of needing to amass more and more things while somehow managing to convince you that all those things will never be *quite* enough to make you happy, which is a bit odd when you think about it.

Supermarkets, for instance, are designed by a whole series of consultants, specifically to stimulate your brain. These people are experts in the field of sound, vision and all sorts of other areas you've probably never even considered. From packaging sizes and colours to aisle widths and acoustics, everything is carefully designed and constructed, all with the sole intention of exciting your senses and steering you towards whatever it is the shop owners want you to buy. Taking note of how autistic people respond in these environments can make us all stop and think about just how much we're being manipulated here.

Imagine people from the 1800's trying to cope in today's high-octane society. It wouldn't be long before they'd be completely overwhelmed by the sheer chaotic speed of everything, let alone the bright lighting and the noise. I'm sure relaxed theatre performances and shopping times would be something they'd appreciate just as much as autistic people do.

Everyday life may be whirlwind fast, deafeningly loud and frighteningly out of control, and let's face it, you don't have to be autistic to notice those things any more, but the world itself is still an immensely, profoundly beautiful place with so much true happiness to offer us.

We're often advised to 'stop and smell the roses' – to make time to appreciate the beauty of the world before it's too late - but autistic people don't just stop and smell the roses, they *connect* with them. They experience the nuances of every leaf, luxuriate in the texture of every petal and lose themselves in their delightful scent, because to autistic people, those things are so beautiful and powerful they simply can't be ignored. When you think about it, it's no wonder society and all its bright, glitzy glamour has so little appeal to them.

Being able to lose yourself in the pure, unadulterated joy of a single moment or feel totally blissful about the magnificence of the tiny details most people simply overlook really is priceless. Finding the magic in the everyday is something so many people aspire towards their whole lives, yet autistic people are born hard-wired to do just that.

These details go largely unappreciated by the majority of people; drowned out by the endless clamour of society telling them what's important. HD humans know what's important though: it's the stuff that makes them feel good inside. The stuff that brings their souls to life and makes their spirits dance. The real stuff. And yes, it might not be the same stuff everyone else thinks of as beautiful, but remember, they can see and experience things in ways that standard definition humans can't. People with autism are the living embodiment of what it means to slow down and really appreciate the unique properties of *every* item that makes up life, the universe and everything. Perhaps they're here to teach us to slow down and notice the details; to find the magic in our day to day lives just as they do so easily in theirs. Maybe by following their lead we can learn how to find the magic inside ourselves as well; the childlike wonder all of us once possessed, that gets lost somewhere along the way and can only reveal itself again when we take the time to catch our breath and quieten our minds.

No single human brain can understand the whole of creation, but perhaps by tapping into their perspective and recognising the potential of autistic brains, we can reap the benefits of their increased, hyper-focussed understanding, and together we can expand our collective consciousness. It's definitely going be a group effort, and it can only happen if we apply new ways of thinking while building on established ones; working together as a team. A quantum leap in human evolution isn't something we'll ever achieve by being separate, but instead by recognising and celebrating how autistic people have *always* been an integral part of who we are as a species.

Listen to their voices, whether they're verbal or not. Watch, observe, and learn. Think outside the box like they do, and expand your mind. Appreciate the gifts they have to offer and encourage them to appreciate the world as you experience it too. When *all* of our special interests and points of view are seen as valuable contributions to society, we'll make more progress as a species than we have in a very long time.

If we look at things from this perspective, there are some really valuable lessons to be learned here. Well, when I think about it, there are quite a few, and in my opinion that's very good news indeed.

Top Ten Social Tips for People with Autism

1. Never, under any circumstances barring an absolute emergency, speak to anyone on the phone.

2. Always use the 'Self Service' check out at the supermarket to avoid unnecessary human interaction.

3. If a person has repeated themselves three times and you still haven't understood them, just nod, give a small laugh and hope to God it wasn't a question.

4. Make sure everyone understands that even though you won't actually attend them, you'd still appreciate being invited to parties.

5. Resign yourself to the fact that if something amusing occurs to you while you're alone in a public place, you will have no option but to laugh hysterically for no discernible reason, making you appear to be clinically insane.

6. Should the doorbell ring unexpectedly when you're alone in the house, remain perfectly quiet and still until whoever's there has left.

7. Spend at least 99% of your time planning witty conversations in your head and the remaining 1% forgetting everything you'd planned to say when the chance to use them arises.

8. When someone you know approaches you in the street, pretend you're sending a text and haven't noticed them, then walk quickly in the opposite direction.

9. Be continually prepared to have your day ruined by a random passing thought about something embarrassing you said or did several years ago.

10. Should you ever find yourself at a social gathering, always do your best to locate an animal of some sort and spend the evening petting it to avoid making small talk with other humans.

Courage
doesn't
always
roar.

Sometimes
courage
is the little
voice at
the end
of the day
that says
'I'll try again tomorrow'.

Mary Anne Radmacher

Chapter Twelve

Being Your Own Hero

'...there is something you must always remember: You are braver than you believe, stronger than you seem, and smarter than you think...'

A.A. Milne

To be honest I'm always a bit taken aback when people describe me as being 'inspirational' yet it happens to me quite a lot, so I've concluded there must be something in it, even if I don't always see it myself. It does sound a bit grand to be described that way though, doesn't it?

Since what inspires each of us is a purely personal thing, something that one person finds inspirational, another could just as easily find repulsive, so I'm quite certain there are some people who are repulsed by me too, and although that's not a particularly pleasant thought for anyone to have about themselves, at least it's an honest one.

The other thing I'm often described as is 'intimidating' although in over fifty years on this planet I can honestly say no-one has ever said to my face, 'I find you intimidating'- well, apart from my husband of course. Any man who's married to a redhead will understand that one! Instead I'm often told by third parties that 'He/she finds you very intimidating...' which would make sense I suppose, because presumably whoever he/she is, they're far too intimidated by me to let me know about it themselves - unless I happen to be married to them of course.

Instead I can get all kinds of negative reactions from people who feel this way, including jealousy, bitchiness and what I call 'the look' where I'm greeted with lowered eyes and a general air of awkwardness as they silently withdraw from me without taking the time to get to know me first. One thing's for certain: whether people find you inspiring or intimidating has much less to do with you personally than it has to do with them and their preconceived ideas of who you are.

In good news, the vast majority of people don't react to me like that at all and will happily accept me for who I am, and as a result I have some wonderful friends who genuinely mean the world to me.

So why am I telling you this? Well I don't want anyone to read this book and think

'Oh, she's so inspirational and/or intimidating, I could never be like that...' because actually, you could. In fact, you already have the potential to handle everything that happens on this crazy autism journey, you just might not have realised it yet. There's no denying that I'm a strong woman, and maybe you don't feel very strong yourself at the moment (I certainly didn't when I started out on this path) so I can understand why you might be feeling that way, but the important thing to remember here is that I'm a *strong* woman, not a *hard* one.

Many of the lessons I learned in my early life were impossibly hard, it's true, and could easily fill a book all by themselves. They began long before my children were born and offered me, time and again, the choice of becoming harder myself as a result, or becoming stronger in spite of them. Fortunately I chose strength, and it's a choice I'd urge you to make every single time. Don't let my old adversary Life make you hard, because being hard makes you brittle and when you're brittle, you're so much more likely to break.

Learn how to let it make you strong instead; strong enough to take whatever it throws at you, process things at your own pace and come up with the solution that works best for you and your family.

The myth of the super-parent

When I first meet people and mention I've got four children on the autism spectrum, the most common reaction I get is 'Oh, I'm so sorry.' This is followed by either 'Are they all yours?' or 'Are they genetically related?' both of which are asking the same thing: 'Did you adopt them?' Well, as you already know, I didn't adopt them, so once this has been confirmed to whoever's asking, a puzzled expression tends to appear on their face and they'll ask, quite innocently 'Why on earth did you have *four* then?'

Apart from the fact this is unbelievably rude, it tells you a lot about why people assume I've had four autistic children. It seems if I'd adopted them it would be understandable in some way (probably because I'd be some kind of martyr or hero) whereas the reason I've deliberately chosen to have four of my *own* children, presumably knowing at some point that they'd all be autistic, is really quite beyond them. When they realise they are indeed speaking to a woman who's intentionally given birth to four children on the autism spectrum (gasp!) their eyes widen and they say one of two things: either 'Wow! You're amazing!' or 'I could never do that.' But are either of those statements really true?

When Christopher was born, without warning I found myself in a whole new dimension of extreme-parenting I hadn't even realised existed. What I *did* realise though, was that he was mine and I loved him more than I'd ever dreamed possible. I didn't know my eldest son would be autistic, and I lived during those early years in a permanent state of exhaustion and terror, wishing with all my heart that I could understand why my child was reacting so differently to everyone else's.

Despite things being impossibly hard, as I've said before, I chose to have three more children for pretty much the same reasons most people do: I adored the child I already had and hoped to have others who were similar yet uniquely themselves at the same time.

The answer to that all-too-familiar question about why I had four children is simple: It turns out I love autistic people more than anything in the world. If I wanted to have children of my own, which I very much did, then I had no choice but to produce more of these extraordinary little autistic people, and that's been something I wouldn't have missed for the world.

In our family, being autistic is our 'normal' and ultimately I think of myself as an ordinary mother doing the best I can to give my children the most rewarding lives possible. I'm always very moved when people tell me I inspire them of course, so over the years I've learned to take it as the compliment it's meant to be, rather than feeling excruciatingly embarrassed by it and wanting to run away like I used to.

Clearly I wouldn't be writing books on parenting autistic children if I didn't want to help people, and if they can identify with what I've been through and it makes them feel better or think in a more positive way, that's absolutely brilliant. I'm always really pleased to hear about it, and it spurs me on to help even more, but please don't think about me as someone who's all that different to you because I'm really not. Personally, I identify far more with the blogs and memes written by the frazzled, half-crazed mothers desperate for a few seconds to themselves than the preachy, humourless, holier-than-thou types who think they've got it all worked out.

There was virtually no decent autism support available when I first became a parent, so the truth is I got creative and made it up as I went along. As it happens, the things I did instinctively are now considered legitimate advice rather than proof that I was clinically insane, but I don't think that makes me some kind of unapproachable autism parenting expert. The only thing I'm an expert in is doing my best and keeping my head above water while bringing up my children. Being described as 'inspirational' or 'intimidating' as a parent implies that I float along effortlessly every day, managing every crisis as it occurs without missing a beat. Lots of people I meet think I'm always cheerful and positive and never lose my temper or cry or feel frustrated. I'm hoping that illusion was shattered pretty soon after you started reading this book.

My point here is this: I've lived an extreme life, so I've done some extreme things, and as a result I take lots of difficult situations in my stride. It's easy to see me as some iconic 'super parent' and think you could never cope with the kinds of things I do every day, but the reality is that I'm just an ordinary woman who happens to live an extraordinary life.

Most importantly, whoever you are and whatever your situation, you never know *what* you can cope with until you absolutely have to, so never underestimate just how much potential you really have, and just how much good you can do for your child, even on the days it seems like everything's collapsing around your ears. Believe me, I've been there too and I've had many moments of utter despair along the way, but here I am, sharing my story and being all 'inspirational' or 'intimidating' depending on your point of view, so there really is always hope.

Whatever you tell yourself in your darkest moments, you really *can* do this, however impossible that might seem right now. Your children won't necessarily make progress in the ways society considers to be 'normal' – mine certainly haven't – but that doesn't mean their lives can't be happy and rewarding or that they can't make their own unique contribution to the world.

My advice would be to use the techniques described in this book and have just a little more faith in yourself than you did before you started reading it. You'll be amazed by what you can achieve; especially now you've got an inspirational, intimidating woman like me in your corner.

A Day at the Circus

August 2003

- 9am: It's Saturday. Family member offers to take Child 2 (age 7) out for the day with boy of similar age. This has never happened before. Am unsure but eventually agree.
- 1pm: Take Children 1 (age 11) and 3 (age 4) to fun day at local youth club.
- Child 3 spots lady with dwarfism. Begin to regret decision to introduce Children to Lord of the Rings when Child 3 shouts at top of voice 'Look, Mum! It's a real dwarf! They really do exist!'
- Seeing woman's understandably angry face, Child 1 grabs his brother and drags him away, shouting 'Look out! She could have an axe like Gimli's!'
- Wish for ground to open up and swallow me while offering an apology which is promptly rejected. Hurry Children 1 and 3 back to car and make quick getaway. #PoliticallyCorrectAsAlways
- 4pm: Family member returns Child 2. Both pockets of his jeans are bulging with coins.
- Family member explains the two boys were allowed to visit an arcade, where Child 2 was given £1 and told to spend it as he wished.
- Apparently Child 2 spent some time working out which machine to use, finally deciding on one he felt was paying out the most.
- He now possessed a hundred penny pieces, having enjoyed a fun afternoon working the Change machine. #FinancialGenius
- 8pm: Despite terrible rain storm, food shopping must be bought. Leave Children 2 and 3 with Boyfriend and set off for Tesco with Child 1.
- 9:30pm: Wheel two full trolleys back to car in pouring rain with help of Child 1. Open car and say 'I'll put some in the boot; you put the rest at the back of the car' meaning on back seat.
- Emerge from boot to find eight bags of shopping neatly laid out behind car, stretching in perfect straight line across wet car park. #ExactlyWhatIAskedHimToDo

Quantum LEAP

Launching Everyone's Amazing Potential

Chapter Thirteen

There Is No Magic Wand

'You've always had the power, my dear;
you just had to learn it for yourself.'

Glinda – The Wizard of Oz

Hopefully the last two chapters have given you some new insights into the positives of autism and made you feel a bit more optimistic about the future and about yourself in general, so now seems like a good time to show you the techniques I've been referring to throughout the book. So, the things that have helped me push on through the darkest days, survive the sleepless nights and keep things going in the right direction when everything around me was descending into chaos are about to be revealed... *cue dramatic music*

Promises, promises...

Now, you know one thing I really can't stand? Reading a book that constantly promises to give me the answer to all my problems then turns out to have been just one long advert for something ridiculously expensive that doesn't even work. When that happens I always feel like I've been conned, and over the years I've read way too many of those kinds of books. As a result I actually considered not mentioning these techniques at all, especially since some of them do cost a small amount of money, but when I thought about it a bit more, leaving them out didn't really make sense.

Whenever I meet new people they're always fascinated by how positive and proactive I am when it comes to living with autism, and the questions I get asked more than any others are 'How do you stay so cheerful?', 'How have you survived so long without any sleep?' and 'Can you teach me your secrets?' so it seemed a bit pointless for me to write a book like this and *not* include the things I've used every day to survive this incredible, exhausting life, hence they've made it into the final edit.

Whether you use them or not is up to you of course, although I'd definitely recommend that you do. They'll take a bit of effort on your part, but they'll be totally worth it, so even if you're short on time or motivation (and let's face it, who isn't?) making them part of your life is the only way they're going to help things improve. Look at it this way: I could give you the best set of gardening tools ever invented, the kind of equipment that's guaranteed to have your flowerbeds blooming in no time, but if you leave them in the shed they simply won't work. It's up to you to gather those tools together and use them to make things happen, and once you do, with a bit of commitment, you'll soon see the results you're after. The good news (apart from the obvious bit about the fact that these techniques actually *work*) is that the basics – the stuff that can really start transforming your life and the lives of your children and family – I'm giving you for free, because the whole point of writing this is to help as many people as possible, regardless of how much more they can afford to spend.

No magic required

Something I do need to make clear is that no matter what *anyone* promises you, *nothing* can make all your difficulties vanish in a puff of smoke because, well, when it comes to the kind of challenges Life is going to throw at you (whether you're an autism parent or not) like the title says, there is no magic wand. Fortunately, you don't actually *need* one, because the power to handle your problems is already inside you, you just have to learn how to harness it and set about using it to create a happier, healthier life for yourself.

I appreciate that sounds a bit too good to be true, but there it is nonetheless: none of the twists and turns Life has up its sleeve for you are a match for the kind of inner strength you already possess. So many of life's struggles are beyond our control, but what's always within our control is our reaction *to* those struggles, and tapping into the ability to react calmly and confidently when things get tough really can transform your life in the most incredible ways. The difficulty is that since our minds don't come with an instruction manual, unless you've studied this kind of thing, it's highly likely you don't have the first idea where to start looking for this mysterious ability. Don't panic though, because that's where I come in.

Trust me, I'm a therapist...

As I said before, I first started learning about the power of the human mind when I was expecting Aidan, and since as I'm writing this he's just turned eighteen, I've had plenty of time to study it. I may have mentioned once or twice that I'm a tiny bit obsessive (okay, maybe more than just a *tiny* bit) when it comes to collecting new information, so I'm sure you can imagine how much research I've actually done.

Over the years I've read thousands of books and articles and helped hundreds and hundreds of people change their lives for the better using what I've learned. On a different note, I've also walked barefoot across burning coals without feeling a thing and stuck large nappy pins through my arm without experiencing pain or losing a drop of blood and still, every step of the way, I've researched, analysed and questioned absolutely *everything*, because as you know, I'm a giant nerd so my main purpose in life is to know *why* things work, not just accept that they *do*. I've studied the evidence, both anecdotal and scientific, and invested years of my life in unlocking people's potential using these techniques, so all I can say is that if any of them seem a bit 'out there' to you, then I hope you'll trust me, take a small leap of faith and give them a go. Nothing in the world will work for every single person, but in my experience, if you're prepared to be open-minded and set aside a little time to use them, they can help you make real, lasting changes in your life more easily and quickly than you might expect.

Now, I'm going to hazard a guess that if you're an autism parent you haven't exactly got an excess of time on your hands. I know exactly how you feel. With that in mind, I've put together some of the most powerful and effective strategies I know and made sure that although you'll initially need an hour to complete a few of them, others you can do in five minutes, some in less than ten seconds, and some you can even do while you're busy doing something else.

Being human: a contradiction

When it comes to improving your life, it's important to have some idea about the needs that drive our behaviour. I could write a whole book about the mysteries of what human beings need to keep them happy (well, several actually) but after a considerable amount of work I've managed to condense things down to a reasonably short list of essentials that can be applied to everyone. Whether you're old, young, male or female and wherever you happen to be on the autism spectrum (if you're on it at all) your basic needs are going to be the same, even though each of us is an individual who requires those needs to be met in different ways. I know that sounds like a contradiction; believe me, you'll get used to contradictions as you read this section.

Since the human mind is incredibly helpful and easy to understand (not) it roughly

287

arranges the things that make it happy into opposing pairs, leaving you with the less than simple task of balancing yourself between each set of needs so you can find long-term happiness. Hey, nothing complicated about that then!

As you know, I've invested decades of my life in unravelling the mysterious workings of the human psyche, so I now have an excess of knowledge about people and their endlessly complicated needs, but that's not what's needed here. When you boil it all down, what follows is a list of some of the most useful information I've ever learned: simple, yes, but incredibly powerful and effective too. The idea of this section then is to briefly explain what your basic human needs are and why they're arranged in this particularly confusing way.

The bottom line is that all living things must have their own unique set of requirements met in order to survive, and human beings are no exception. People's needs take many forms, and range from the most basic, such as the need for food, water and shelter to the more complex emotional, psychological and spiritual needs which have to be successfully managed so they can lead happy, healthy, well-balanced lives. Like I said, this is a simplified list, but it's a very useful one nonetheless.

The need for certainty and comfort

If we have no certainty in our lives, no sense of somewhere to go or something to do that makes us feel safe and protected, we live in a constant state of 'Fight or Flight' and the resultant stress won't just considerably shorten our lives, but will also reduce the quality of any life we do have. As a result, we're all born with an instinctive desire to create certainty and comfort for ourselves and those we care for. Eating a healthy, balanced diet, getting enough good quality sleep and living in a secure, nurturing environment are all very basic ingredients when it comes to creating lasting contentment. However, too much certainty will leave us feeling bored and frustrated, so we're also born with...

The need for uncertainty and variety

Variety is, so we're told, 'the spice of life' but variety does much more than just add flavour to our lives, it actually prolongs them. The human brain is designed to constantly form new connections and works in the same way as your muscles: if it receives no new stimulation over prolonged periods of time, it becomes wasted and less efficient, so new experiences and stimuli are a vital part of keeping yourself young and vibrant both psychologically and physically. Once the brain has registered that there's no new stimulation to be had, nothing new to learn, no changes to be made, it begins to die, and once your brain makes that decision, you can guarantee your health will also deteriorate.

The need for significance, autonomy & control

Every one of us needs to feel special and unique in some way, and feel that who we are matters. Some of us are driven by an overwhelming desire to prove this to the whole world, while others want to be special and significant only to a select few people, or even just in the eyes of one other person; but still the need is there, and for a very good reason: without people who stand out from the crowd and see things from a fresh perspective, we'd never move forward as a species, we wouldn't have created any technology, and might not have survived at all. This trait gives us the need to experience a sense of autonomy and control in our lives, a feeling that we're the masters of our own destiny and that we can make some sense of both our day to day lives and the more unusual, unexpected events we encounter. However, being *too* unusual or controlling makes others shy away from us and leaves us lonely and isolated, so we're also born with...

The need for connection and love

Everyone is born with a need to connect to their environment at some level or another, for the simple reason that the survival of the human race depends on it. Sometimes, especially in the case of autistic children, this need can be difficult to identify, but however much the condition complicates things, however deeply this need is hidden, it's still there, and with time, courage and perseverance it can be uncovered and nurtured.

As we grow older, we unconsciously seek out other people who are similar to us so we can find a sense of belonging, a sense of connection, and ultimately, if it's what we want, to find a mate for ourselves and ensure the survival of the species. The need for an intimate connection with the world is a powerful one, and however we choose to achieve it, whether in person or by some other means, giving and receiving attention is an essential part of being a well-rounded person. Feeling that at least one person is on your side and that you can truly be yourself with them can be invaluable. We're also born with a need to spend time connecting with ourselves of course: our own quiet, inner moments, where we remember our hopes, dreams and aspirations, and this is equally important to the health of our minds, bodies and spirits.

The need for evolution

Put simply, anything that isn't evolving is dying. We all have an instinctive need to stretch ourselves; to push ourselves beyond yesterday's limitations, to find out just how amazing we really are. Increasing your self-esteem, noticing your own progress and enjoying a sense of achievement are definitely some of the most rewarding things you can do with your time. Once you feel you've achieved the success you've striven for however, if you don't continue to grow as a person, to challenge yourself to do more than you ever thought possible, then no matter how many people acknowledge you, no matter how much money you've made, you'll eventually begin to feel unhappy and unfulfilled. That's why we're also born with...

The need for contribution

Passing on information and wisdom to other people guarantees the evolution not only of the whole species, but also of each individual. Humans aren't designed to be solitary creatures otherwise the species would have died out before it began, so to some degree or another we're each born with a desire to go beyond ourselves and connect to something bigger: to create a better world for everyone. We somehow know, at a deep, instinctive level, that no matter how small our contribution may seem, when added to everyone else's, the sum of the parts really does equal more than the whole, and this keeps us evolving on all levels: as an individual, as a family, as a society, and as a species. Remembering to contribute to ourselves is also vitally important, as we can only give out what we already possess - physically, psychologically, emotionally and spiritually - so we need to look after ourselves for everyone's sake, not just our own.

Taking a Quantum LEAP

The best way I've ever found to fulfil these needs is by using a combination of approaches including various hypnotherapy, psychotherapy, neuro-linguistic programming (NLP) and emotional freedom technique (EFT) strategies, all delivered in safe, secure ways. I'll talk about EFT a bit later on, but for now I'm going to focus on the cornerstone of my therapy: powerful, effective programmes that gently support and encourage you, leading to more positive thinking and more proactive behaviour.

They work by relaxing you to the point where your conscious mind (the part that's in charge of rational thinking) lets go and your subconscious mind (the much bigger part that's in charge of everything else) takes over. I then deliver a series of positive instructions and suggestions directly to your subconscious which allows it to make beneficial changes for you at a very deep level. I also give you a trigger you can use afterwards that will instantly boost the effectiveness of the programme without putting you back into a deeply relaxed state, so you can use it whenever you need to.

During my years as a therapist I've seen some incredible results in people's lives when they use these programmes and as you know, I've used them myself too, so I really do speak from experience when I say they can be hugely powerful tools for change if you give them a chance.

Since I don't practice therapy one-to-one anymore - firstly because I'm busy running the charity, and secondly because I can help so many more people by doing things online - I've developed a very straightforward system that allows you to download programmes directly from my website. The web address is **www.autism-all-stars.org/quantum-leap** and you'll find lots more information there about my programmes, experience, qualifications and so on.

In case you were wondering about the name, I decided to call my practice Quantum LEAP for a number of reasons, the most obvious being that starting this kind of therapy really can be the beginning of some really big strides forward in your life. LEAP is written in capitals because it stands for 'Launching Everyone's Amazing Potential', and that really does mean *everyone*, whether they're young or old, autistic or neurotypical.

Many people are sceptical about entering therapy and they're quite right to be, because there are plenty of awful therapists out there who can do more harm than good; I know because over the years I've helped so many clients recover from the damage they've done. Fortunately I'm thoroughly trained and have an excellent track record, so you can relax when you use my programmes, knowing you're in very safe hands. The most important thing about this type of therapy isn't getting people to relax though, it's knowing what to say once you've done it, and that's what I've spent so many years learning how to do. Interestingly, I found being an autism parent quite an advantage when I was training, because the main thing you have to remember when dealing with the subconscious mind is that it will take whatever you say to it absolutely literally.

Quite literally doing as it's told

The subconscious mind is a 'doing' machine. It's in charge of keeping your blood pumping, making you breathe in and out, digesting your food and everything else you do automatically without thinking about it. Because of this, it simply doesn't understand the concept of *not* doing something, which is why it's so vitally important to tell it exactly what you want it to do, not what you don't.

For example, if I say 'Don't think about a penguin', what's the first thing you think about? Yep. A penguin; and the harder you try not to think about the penguin, the more you're going to think about it. The reason this happens is because your subconscious is programmed to 'do' not to 'not do', so it has to think about the penguin first in order to *not* think about it. Hopefully that doesn't sound too confusing. The point is that speaking to the subconscious is a lot like speaking to autistic people. Telling an autistic person not to think in literal, black and white terms is like telling a flower not to turn its face to the sun; they're just wired that way, and it's the same with the subconscious. As a result you'll notice the language I use in my programmes is very positive and also incredibly specific, plus it always gives your subconscious something to *do*, which is why so many of my clients have enjoyed such great results over the years.

Real world results

Using these programmes my life has improved in more ways than I could possibly talk about here, but I think a real life example of how they work is important so I've chosen to describe something that causes no end of stress to *so* many parents: coping with the dreaded school run.

When the boys were small we lived less than five minutes' walk from Christopher and Dominic's school and a short drive away from Aidan's nursery. To get them in by nine o'clock, I had to get up at five and face four hours of constant screaming, kicking, biting and general hysterics while I struggled to get them all washed, dressed and out the door with enough time to spare. It was a horrible way to start the day, and every morning I'd open my eyes, take a breath and feel a massive surge of adrenaline shoot through me in preparation for the upcoming battle. By the time I got home, I'd be sweating, shaking and close to tears (often I'd collapse onto the sofa and sob just to get rid of some of the tension) and it would be hours before I was able to calm down again.

When I discovered this form of therapy, reducing my anxiety levels on the school run was pretty high up on my list of priorities as you can imagine.

When I sat and thought about it, I realised I was stuck in a vicious cycle: I knew I was going to get stressed, so I was anticipating it and getting stressed before it even began. The boys were then picking up on my stress and becoming more stressed themselves as a result, which lead to even *more* stress for all of us. What I needed was something to not only break this vicious cycle but to replace it with a virtuous one instead, where I could lead by example and show them it was possible to survive the school run by behaving easily and calmly. But how?

The answer came with a programme called Increasing Inner Calm. It worked on improving everything from mental calmness to physical relaxation, confidence to the quality of my sleep, but most importantly it included a post-hypnotic suggestion (a posh way of describing something you say outside of hypnosis to bring back the good feelings without re-hypnotising yourself) that I could use in less than ten seconds to make me feel wonderfully calm and relaxed. I listened to the programme, memorised the trigger and started using it straight away. It worked like a charm. To begin with the boys' behaviour was exactly the same, but whenever I felt my tension levels rising, I'd stop and use the trigger then carry on with a renewed sense of calm, dealing with the chaos far more easily than I'd ever have thought possible. After a few weeks the boys started to calm down too, and we'd get through the school run with so much less aggravation that I actually stopped dreading it and started taking it in my stride. I can honestly say I'd never have believed it could happen and I genuinely believe it wouldn't have done without the programme.

Several years later, Nigel offered to do the school run for me, and without thinking I said 'Sure. Thanks.' When he got home, he burst through the door and literally roared with frustration, threw his car keys at the wall and shouted 'Oh my GOD! How do you stay so *calm*?' The interesting thing is that until that moment, the transition from chaos to calm had been so smooth and gradual that I'd never really stopped to think about how far I'd come.

It had been years since I'd used my trigger and I suddenly realised why: every time my stress levels had risen, I'd instantly used it to change my reactions, and after a while my mind had said 'Oh, I see! *That's* how you want to feel' and set about reprogramming my responses to difficult situations. To say I'm calm in a crisis nowadays would be an understatement. Every time my children hurt themselves, get upset or become overly demanding, my mind automatically floods my whole system with wonderful feelings of calm and confidence, allowing me to deal with the situation in the best way possible while showing them there's no need to panic which helps keep them feel calmer too, and that, I'm sure you'll agree, is pretty life-changing stuff.

The best news of all is that because you've bought this book I'm giving you this programme completely free. Just visit the website **www.autism-all-stars.org/quantum-leap** and follow the 'Therapy Programmes' link to see what's available. Choose 'Increasing Inner Calm'; use the code **RMTIIC** at the checkout and it's all yours. Yes, I'm good to you, I know!

Questions, questions...

When people first use my therapy programmes it's perfectly understandable they'll have lots of questions about how everything works, so if you're unsure about anything, do feel free to ask using the contact form on the website. These are the questions I've heard most often since I've been a therapist, so hopefully you'll find the answers you're looking for somewhere on this list. If your question hasn't been answered here, please feel free to contact me through the website and I'll be happy to explain things. Believe me, I asked a million questions (at least) while I was training, so I have plenty of answers to share!

Is it safe to go into hypnosis?

Absolutely: the routines I use have very strict safety procedures. You go into hypnosis using a deep relaxation technique and your exit is safe, monitored and controlled at all times.

Will I be under your power?

No, you're always the one in charge. You can't be forced to do anything and you can't be taken into hypnosis against your will. It's your experience and you're always in control. Unlike stage hypnotists, I have no desire to make you do anything silly or humiliating, so the answer to the question I've been asked more than any other - 'Will you turn me into a chicken?' - is a definite 'No.'

What if I can't be hypnotised?

You can; everyone can. As long as you want to enter hypnosis, you will. It's an easy, enjoyable and thoroughly relaxing experience.

Will I be asleep under hypnosis?

No you won't. You'll be fully awake and alert, aware of everything that's happening throughout the session. At the end of your programme I'll give your subconscious mind the option to wake you up or allow you to drift off to sleep so you can use it with confidence either during the day or at night.

Will I be able to drive afterwards?

Definitely. The last thing any good hypnotherapist wants is to do you harm, and obviously it would be very dangerous to let you drive while still hypnotised, so you can rest assured that you'll be wide awake, fully alert, refreshed and relaxed in every way before you exit hypnosis. There are a number of strict safety procedures ensuring this, which I always follow to the letter.

What does hypnosis feel like?

You might be surprised to hear you already know the answer to this one, because you experience hypnosis many times every day: watching television, reading, driving, painting or doing anything that absorbs your attention is deeply hypnotic. The problem with this kind of hypnosis (natural hypnosis) is it's unintentional and therefore, although it can be relaxing, it's very unpredictable.

Hypnotherapy (using intended hypnosis) is an extremely safe, controlled way to access your subconscious mind and make profound changes quickly and easily. During hypnosis you're deeply relaxed and comfortable, yet completely aware of everything going on around you, experiencing a pleasant feeling similar to daydreaming or drifting off to sleep. Many people fear being 'out of control' during hypnosis, but the truth is that you're always in complete control of yourself and can come out of hypnosis whenever you want to. You'll remember everything afterwards, and the words used in every subliminal session are there for you to read when ordering your programme.

During intended hypnosis you might feel warm, cool, heavy or light, or you might feel none of these things. It's an entirely personal experience, and the most usual comment I get from clients afterwards is 'I felt like I could open my eyes if I wanted to, but I couldn't be bothered.' So you can be sure that whatever you experience consciously, you're doing just fine.

What's the difference between a normal session and a subliminal session?

A normal session of hypnotherapy contains lots of powerful suggestions to deeply relax you, so you'll need to take time out of your day to complete one and it can't be used when you're doing anything requiring your full attention, especially driving or operating machinery. Subliminal sessions contain no suggestions for sleep or relaxation, only positive affirmations, so these can be used while you're doing something else like cooking, reading or watching TV. Don't use them when you need your full attention on anything though, so definitely not while you're driving.

Will the effects wear off over time?

Absolutely not; in fact you'll find that with my therapy the opposite is true because the progressive hypnotherapy and psychotherapy techniques I practice are specially designed to become more and more powerful over time. They simply continue to work, quietly and consistently, in harmony with your subconscious mind, creating a beautiful ripple effect of positive change throughout your life. Your subconscious mind has looked after you since before you were born, and it knows exactly how to keep you safe. It always has your best interests at heart and will make sure any changes happen at your own individual pace, easily and comfortably fitting them into your daily routines, making this a wonderfully smooth, automatic procedure. All you have to do is trust the process and enjoy the results.

Can your programmes do me any harm?

Not at all - they can only bring about safe, positive changes in your life. Many people get confused about what hypnotherapy actually is, thinking it's the same as stage hypnosis or even some form of brainwashing, but honestly, it's very different. I'm highly skilled in both hypnotherapy and psychotherapy, and everything I do is designed to help, not harm you.

Are there any age restrictions for using your programmes?

None at all. People of all ages have benefitted from my therapy sessions over the years, so feel free to use them no matter how old you are. If you're worried you may be too young to use them, remember that the suggestions I use are carefully crafted to unfold and become more powerful over time, so starting young gives your subconscious mind some fantastic tools to use as you mature.

I'm not autistic; can I still use your programmes?

Yes, definitely. The important thing to remember is although the *brains* of people with autism may be wired differently to yours, I'm dealing with people's *minds*, and all my programmes are designed to work for everybody. Autistic people have some very specific issues which I understand and focus on because it's my specialist area, but my therapy works in exactly the same way for everyone, so it's safe to use any of my programmes whether you have autism or not.

Can I share my programme with other people?

If you're using a pre-recorded programme then lots of safety procedures will already be in place to make sure anyone can use it, so technically you *can* share these ones with others, but obviously I'd rather you didn't! A percentage of the profits from every programme I sell goes directly to my charity Autism All Stars, so sharing them around is a bit like buying one red nose for Comic Relief and letting everyone wear it. Feel free to recommend the programmes to everyone you meet though, and let them know where to buy their own, then everybody benefits.

How often can I use my programme?

The simple answer to this one is: as often as you like. You can't overdose on these programmes so it's entirely up to you how often you listen to them. What I would recommend though is that you use them at least once a day for the first two weeks, then once every other day for the following two.

Can I use more than one programme at the same time?

Definitely; I always mix and match programmes when I'm using them myself, so you can certainly do the same. All my therapy programmes are specifically designed to work with each other and each one supports and strengthens the others, so feel free to listen to any recordings you've got, in any order. Incidentally, this process of linking suggestions from one programme to another is called 'Quantum Looping' which, in part, inspired the name of my practice.

Will the programme still work if I fall asleep with it on?

Yes it will; in fact I highly recommend using your programme to help you relax and drift off to sleep at night. Your subconscious mind never sleeps, it's always awake and working to keep you safe and secure, so listening to a therapy programme while you sleep is a great idea because your subconscious mind can absorb and use the suggestions I give it, without any conscious interference. Each session contains a suggestion for you to either wake up or go to sleep at the end, and your subconscious will decide which response is correct, so you can simply relax and enjoy your sleep.

If someone doesn't speak, how can they understand what's on your programmes?

I can see why people would ask this question, and the simple answer is that although many people with autism are non-verbal, they're often aware of what's being said to them, even if they can't communicate this fact. The challenges they have with processing and translating language come from wiring issues within their brains, not their minds, which is often the cause of much of their anger and frustration. Everyone's subconscious mind absorbs far more than they realise and the same goes for autistic people too. The subconscious communicates in all kinds of ways, many of which still aren't fully understood, and over the years I've seen some remarkable changes happen in the lives of the non-verbal children and adults I've treated, so I know my therapy works in these instances, even if I can't tell you exactly how just yet.

What kind of subjects do your programmes cover?

In the past I've written thousands of programmes covering everything from stopping smoking to curing phobias, but the ones I've put together for you on the website cover the things I feel can be most useful for people living with autism. There are eleven listed at the moment and I'll give you a brief outline of each one in the list below. All hypnotic programmes except one include a very discreet trigger you can use afterwards (no-one will realise you're doing it) and these are described in full on the website.

Increasing Inner Calm

This programme is the foundation of all my therapy and is the result of many years of work in the field of human development. It works by increasing your mental calmness, physical relaxation, confidence and competence as well as promoting better quality hypnosis (which makes it more and more powerful as time goes by) and better quality sleep. A real life-changing programme that you can download for free as a thank you for buying my book.

Instant Calm, Confidence and Relaxation

This programme contains a powerful visualisation that introduces you to a calmer, more confident and more relaxed version of yourself and gives you the ability to instantly tap into these qualities whenever you need them. Highly recommended for people who struggle with public speaking or general anxiety, it's helped so many of my clients (as well as being incredibly useful on the school run) that it's another essential programme I use all the time.

Embracing Autism

This is the only programme without a trigger and is designed to be used by people on the spectrum to help them accept and celebrate who they are, while tackling some of the common issues many autistic people have to deal with. The main areas covered are learning to accept and cope with changes to your routine, keeping clean and healthy, enjoying new foods, liking and accepting yourself while respecting other people's opinions, exploring new relationships and environments, improving hand-eye coordination, expressing yourself verbally and in writing, understanding body language and establishing better sleep patterns. It's a long programme and I'd recommend people listen to this one at night while they fall asleep.

Clear, Capable Communication

This programme deals exclusively with communication skills and covers all aspects of conversations, with a focus on relaxing and enjoying them as much as possible. Topics covered include processing streams of information, shifting focus between different topics and processing verbal language, body language, facial expressions, tones of voice and gestures. It also deals with using appropriate volume when speaking, making comfortable eye contact, tuning our extraneous noise, being confident enough to ask questions, understanding humour and picking up subtle clues that help with taking turns in conversations.

Social Self-Confidence

This programme is specifically designed to tackle social awkwardness and deals with issues including how to feel safe and relaxed in social situations, letting go of past mistakes, liking and respecting yourself, celebrating your unique qualities and focusing on social achievements and success. It also concentrates on understanding boundaries, instinctively choosing people and situations that support and encourage you, and radiating confidence and friendship to those around you.

Peaceful, Healing Sleep

Although getting better quality sleep forms part of all my hypnotic programmes, this one focuses exclusively on the benefits of sleep and is designed to be used at night. It begins with a deep relaxation technique and covers topics including focusing on positive thoughts as you fall asleep, releasing the right chemicals to induce peaceful sleep, entering sleep more easily, finding the best temperature and sleeping positions, trusting your subconscious mind to keep you safe while you sleep and finding it easier to go back to sleep if you're woken up before you're ready.

Vibrant, Natural Energy

This programme was a real life-saver for me and is the answer to another question I'm often asked: 'Where do you get all your energy from?' It works on increasing your natural energy levels, having a more energised and focused mind, taking charge of your emotional responses and changing your posture to conserve energy. It also deal with increasing your circulation and general health, getting the most benefit from what you eat and drink, and encouraging your body's systems to work more efficiently and harmoniously. The trigger is great to use when you need an instant energy boost too.

Being an Exceptional Parent

This is the first of two programmes designed exclusively for parents of children with additional needs. The word 'autism' isn't actually mentioned so it's suitable for parents of all children in this position and will work equally well whatever issues you're facing. The main focus of the programme is on accepting things as they are and being confident as a parent. Topics covered include handling your emotions and responding more calmly to stressful situations, understanding that your child is so much more than their diagnosis, knowing you are enough as both a parent and a person, focussing on the positives and learning to laugh about things, recognising and responding to your child's non-verbal communication, being less affected by other people's negativity and having the confidence to ask for and accept appropriate help.

Succeeding with Support Services

This is a fantastic programme for anyone who's struggling to deal with the frustrations of the SEN system and has helped me enormously over the years. It contains help on subjects including finding it easier to understand and accept how the support services work, dealing with health professionals calmly and confidently, building a strong working relationship with your support team, dealing with difficult people appropriately, having confidence in your parenting skills and recognising *yourself* as an important part of your child's support network. It also deals with handling complaints firmly and reasonably, accepting delays and finding opportunities for change while you're waiting. Since no-one else has to know when you're activating your trigger, it's ideal to use just before or even during difficult meetings and can really make a difference to how much is achieved.

The Subliminal Recordings

There are two different subliminal recordings: one focusing on motivation and activity and the other on being calm and relaxed. They're both set to music and contain a series of positive statements (known as affirmations) which have been specially recorded at a very low frequency, allowing your subconscious mind to pick them up and use them, while bypassing any objections from your conscious mind.

All of the affirmations are listed on the website so there are no surprises, and they include statements like 'You feel motivated and excited about your life' and 'You handle every situation with ease'.

Everything is said in the present tense because to your subconscious, everything is happening 'now' and if it realises that you're *not* feeling or behaving in the way I'm telling it you are, it will recognise this and set about changing your thought patterns and behaviour to allow you to do so.

These recordings don't contain any suggestions about being relaxed or sleepy, but they're still not recommended for use when driving or operating machinery as you need to focus your full attention on those things at all times. Still, there's no need to take time out of your day to listen to the subliminal recordings, so you can use them as a form of background music that the whole family can benefit from.

The Emotional Freedom Technique

The emotional freedom technique (EFT) is something you can use in less than five minutes to bring you relief from stress, fear and anxiety as well as physical discomfort and pain. It's a fantastic stand-alone technique and is also very useful when practiced as a complimentary procedure alongside my programmes.

I'm a qualified EFT practitioner so I know lots about it, but to keep things brief, EFT is based on the subtle energy system of acupuncture meridians discovered by the Chinese more than 5,000 years ago and works using Einstein's theory that *everything* is composed of energy.

Anyone who knows something about acupuncture, acupressure or internal martial arts like Tai Chi will understand the principals of EFT straight away, but if this kind of thing is new to you, I do realise it can seem a bit strange at first. Nonetheless, it's very effective, so again I'm asking you to trust me, take a small leap of faith and see what happens.

As I said before, all living things need energy to survive, and as you can see from the list of contradictory things we humans need to make us happy, it's not just physical energy we need in order to thrive, but emotional, psychological and spiritual energy too.

Energy takes many forms and can uplift us (positive energy) or leave us feeling drained (negative energy) but to your subconscious mind it's all just energy, which it constantly takes in from its surroundings and busily transports through your body in the form of information via your acupuncture meridians. The subconscious interprets stressful or upsetting information as disruptions to your energy and if there's too much for your meridians to cope with, it can lead to blockages which build up over time and make you feel completely overwhelmed. When energy gets stuck you'll first experience its effects as a sensation of unease, sadness, anxiety and so on, but if it's left unresolved it can lead to physical discomfort and even pain.

EFT works by combining the physical tapping of the energy points along your meridians with focussing the intention and attention of your mind during a specific pattern of tapping along particular points on your body, and as a result you can tap to release stuck emotions, reduce pain, relieve tension and a great deal more.

Using physical tapping at specific points along your energy meridians where an energy blockage is situated, along with the focussed power of your mind, EFT literally 'taps into' your energy systems to help balance them and restore the flow, allowing your body, mind and spirit to keep running smoothly. The strong connection between the body and mind when it comes to illness, emotions and trauma is well known nowadays and accepted by many highly qualified doctors, so when you think about it, the way EFT works isn't actually as 'out there' as it might first appear.

Without going into too many details about brain science, energy blockages can be triggered by anything from difficult memories to sudden traumatic events, all of which can put you into a state of 'Fight or Flight' – your body's red alert mode – and EFT works to deactivate this response and clear the blockages, returning your mind and body to a state of balance. If you'd like to know more about how it works, I'd highly recommend reading a book called 'Emotional Healing in Minutes' by Valerie and Paul Lynch or visiting this website: www.emofree.com, both of which explain things in much more detail.

The EFT tapping points

On the next page is an illustration to show the tapping points and the different stages of the technique. I made this diagram myself and it took me ages, so I really hope you'll find it useful. I know it can look a bit complicated when you first see it, but it's very easy to get to grips with and once you do, you'll be able to complete the whole sequence in less than five minutes.

THE EMOTIONAL FREEDOM TECHNIQUE

STEP ONE

Rub either of the sore spots or tap on the karate chop point continuously and REPEAT 3 TIMES:

'Even though I...(i.e. 'Have this fear of heights') I deeply and completely love and accept myself'

STEP TWO

Tap 5 or 6 times on each point, naming just the issue itself aloud, each time you tap (i.e. ' this fear of heights')

Tap the pressure points in the following order:
TOH, EB, SE, UE, UN, CH, CB, UA, Th, IF, MF, LF, KC

STEP THREE

Tap/rub the Gamut point continuously and repeat the phrase (i.e. ' this fear of heights') with:
Eyes closed. Eyes open. Eyes hard down right.
Eyes hard down left. Eyes going round in a circle.
Eyes going round in the other direction.
Hum 5 seconds of a song (i.e. Happy Birthday)
Count to 5.
Hum 5 seconds of a song again.

STEP FOUR

Repeat STEP TWO

Tapping all the pressure points as before:
TOH, EB, SE, UE, UN, CH, CB, UA,
Th, IF, MF, LF, KC

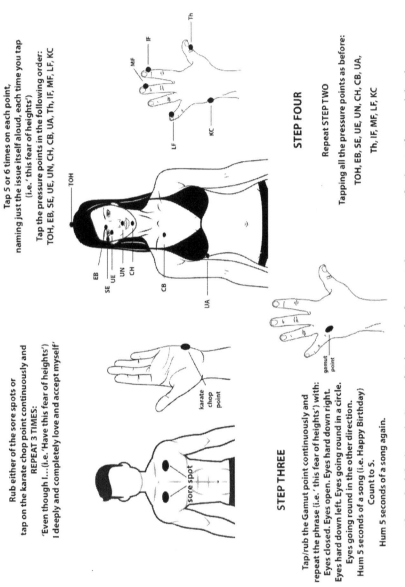

If you feel the issue isn't completely resolved, repeat the process, referring to the remaining issue
– i.e. 'Even though I have this *remaining* fear of heights, I deeply and completely love and accept myself.'
Name the issue as 'this *remaining* fear of heights' when tapping.

The tapping points

The Sore Spot: This spot is an acupuncture meridian associated with the lymphatic system and feels a bit tender when you rub it because lymphatic congestion happens here. When you rub it, you're helping your body disperse the congestion. Rub gently and firmly, but never hard enough to hurt or bruise yourself.
There are two 'sore spots' on your upper left and upper right chest. Find a U shaped indentation at the top of your breastbone and from the top of that indentation go down about 3 inches towards your waist and 3 inches over to the left (or right). You should now be in the upper left (or right) part of your chest. If you press firmly in that area you'll find a particular spot that feels a bit more tender than the rest.

Karate Chop point (KC): This is found at the centre of the fleshy part of the outside of both of your hands. It's basically the part you'd use to deliver a karate chop.

Top of the Head (TOH): Unsurprisingly this is found on the top of your head! It's the point at the very middle of your skull so it's pretty easy to find.

Beginning of the Eyebrow (EB): This point is found at the beginning of the eyebrow, just above and to one side of your nose.

Side of the Eye (SE): This point sits on the eye socket at the outside corner of your eye.

Under the Eye (UE): This is also located on the eye socket, in the middle of the bone about an inch below your pupil.

Under the Nose (UN): This point is found in the small area between the bottom of your nose and the top of your upper lip.

Chin (CH): This point is found in the dip halfway between the point of your chin and the bottom of your lower lip.

Collarbone (CB): This point sits at the junction where the breastbone, the collarbone and the first rib meet. To find it, put your forefinger on the U-shaped indentation at the top of your breastbone and from the bottom of the U, move your forefinger down an inch towards your waist, then go one inch to the left (or right).

Under the Arm (UA): This point is located about four inches below your armpit – around the point of a man's nipple or a woman's bra strap.

The Gamut point: The gamut point is the dip found on the back of either hand between the knuckles at the base of the ring finger and the little finger. The easiest way to find it is to make a fist, place your index finger in the gap between the knuckles then flatten your hand out.

Some tapping tips

- Always tap with two or more fingers so you've definitely covered the correct meridian points.
- You can tap with either hand, but most people use their dominant hand as it's more convenient.
- You need to tap approximately five or six times on each point apart from when you tap the Karate Chop point during Step One and the Gamut point during Step Three.

The basic EFT sequence

Firstly, decide what you want to work on and make sure you focus on one issue at a time otherwise you won't get such good results. You could work on something physical like a sore throat, or something emotional like an upsetting memory such as being rejected by a friend. You could also tackle something you're struggling with like playing better tennis or getting stuck when writing an essay. Secondly, concentrate on the issue you want to change and decide how much it's affecting you by giving it a score out of ten, where zero means it's not a problem at all and ten means it's the worst it's ever been. This is useful when you've completed each round of tapping because you can re-evaluate its intensity and give it a new number which will show you how much progress you're making. For physical pain you can just rate how much it hurts, for an emotional problem you can think about how uncomfortable it makes you feel, and for improving your performance at something, you can imagine being able to do it perfectly as being a 'ten' and see how close you are to achieving that ideal.

Step One

The main objective of this step is to acknowledge that there's a problem, then decide to love and accept yourself anyway. It's *really* important to remember that unlike other self-help strategies, when you're using EFT you need to focus on the *negative* aspects of whatever you're working on, and express these out loud. So, you start by continually tapping either of the Sore Spots or the Karate Chop point and saying *three times* 'Even though I _____, I deeply and completely love and accept myself.' Fill in the blank with whatever it is that's bothering you, so you could say something like 'Even though I have this awful sore throat...', 'Even though I'm embarrassed whenever I think about my singing voice...', or 'Even though I'm terrible at maths...' The important thing is to start with the words 'Even though I...' and make it about *you*, so rather than saying 'Even though my son has autism' you'll need to say something like 'Even though I feel frustrated that my son has autism.'

Step Two

This step is used to stimulate and balance the body's energy pathways and to complete it, you tap five or six times on each of the points shown in the diagram, always in the same order, and say a 'reminder phrase' to keep your mind focussed on the issue. Using the examples above, this could be something like 'This awful sore throat', 'I'm embarrassed by my singing voice', 'I'm terrible at maths', or 'I feel frustrated my son has autism'.

The sequence is always done as follows and is easy to remember because it starts at the top and works its way down your head, face and body.

Top of the Head (TOH)
Beginning of the Eyebrow (EB)
Side of the Eye (SE)
Under the Eye (UE)
Under the Nose (UN)
Chin (CH)
Collarbone (CB)
Under the Arm (UA)

Step Three

This step might seem really strange but it's invaluable for reprogramming your brain and releasing the problem. You might feel a bit silly when you first practice it, but it'll soon become second nature. To complete this step you'll need to rub or tap the Gamut point continuously and repeat your reminder phrase while completing different movements with your eyes, and activating different areas of your brain by counting out loud and humming a tune. First say the reminder phrase with your eyes closed, eyes open, eyes hard down right, eyes hard down left, eyes going round in a circle and eyes going round in the opposite direction. Next hum five seconds of a familiar song like Happy Birthday or Twinkle Twinkle Little Star, count to five out loud, and hum five seconds of the song again.

Step Four

Repeat Step Two, tapping all the points in order on your head, face, body and hand.

Once the sequence is complete

Test the intensity of the issue again and give it another score between one and ten. If you're not down to zero just yet, do another round of tapping and reassess how things are going. When you tap this time, change your phrase to 'Even though I have this *remaining*...' or 'Even though I'm *still*...' when talking about the problem.

If you complete three rounds of tapping and there's no noticeable improvement, it might be because you're not addressing the right issue, so stop and think about the phrase you're using and look for an underlying reason. 'Even though I'm panicking...' could change to 'Even though I hate confined spaces...' or 'Even though I can't stand crowds...'

In conclusion

Using these techniques has completely transformed not only my own life but my children's lives too, and I genuinely hope you'll allow them to do the same for you. I appreciate not everyone believes in complimentary therapies, but you've got nothing to lose and everything to gain by using them, so surely it's got to be worth giving them a chance. As I've said before, nothing can make your problems disappear - mine certainly haven't - but how you handle them can make *all* the difference to your quality of life, and on that you can trust me absolutely.

The Frogs in the Pit

A group of frogs were hopping contentedly through the woods when two of them fell into a deep pit.

All of the other frogs gathered around the pit to see what could be done to help their companions.

When they saw how deep the pit was, the rest of the group agreed that it was hopeless and told the two frogs in the pit they should prepare themselves for their fate, because they were as good as dead.

Unwilling to accept this terrible doom, the two frogs began to jump with all their might. Some of the frogs shouted into the pit that it was hopeless, and that the two frogs wouldn't be in that situation if they had been more careful and more responsible. They should save their energy and give up, since they were already as good as dead.

The two frogs continued jumping as hard as they could, and after several hours of desperate effort were quite drained. Finally, one of the frogs took heed of his fellows. Spent and disheartened, he quietly resolved himself to his fate, lay down at the bottom of the pit and died as the others looked on in helpless grief.

The other frog continued to jump with every ounce of energy he had, although his body was racked with pain and he was completely exhausted. His companions started again, yelling for him to accept his fate, stop the pain and just die.

The weary frog jumped harder and harder and - wonder of wonders - finally leapt so high that he sprang from the pit!

Amazed, the other frogs celebrated his miraculous freedom and then gathering around him asked, "Why did you continue jumping when we told you it was impossible?" Reading their lips, the astonished frog explained to them that he was deaf, and that when he saw their gestures and shouting, he thought they were cheering him on.

What he had perceived as encouragement inspired him to work even harder and to succeed against all the odds.

This simple story contains a powerful lesson: Your encouraging words can lift someone up and help them make it through the day. Your destructive words can cause deep wounds; they may be the weapons that destroy someone's desire to carry on - even their life. Be careful what you say, even to yourself - there is enormous power in words.

Chapter Fourteen

Post-Diagnosis Survival Pack

'If there is a book you want to read,
but it hasn't been written yet, then you must write it.'

Toni Morrison

I started reading books about autism when Christopher was really young and after reading the first chapter of the first book, I was already thinking 'How on earth do they know that about him...and that...and even *that*? Have they been in my house?' Realising all his strange, mysterious behaviours weren't actually 'just the funny little things he does' but were real, documented autistic traits, was a bit of a revelation to me to say the least.

It wasn't just the major things like his extreme sensitivity to sound and his lack of language, but all his little quirks like the way he watched TV sitting on his head or how he demolished my living room time and time again to build dens from the sofa cushions.

Everything I'd previously thought of as being Christopher's own personal eccentricities, including walking on his toes, refusing to let different foods touch on his plate and building large, complex structures from LEGO that were way beyond the usual abilities of a child his age, were all listed right there in black and white. 'This is great!' I thought 'Now I'm finally going to find out how to help him.' As it turned out though, *what* he was doing was listed, but *why* he was doing it just wasn't there.

Right then I began my search to discover as much as I could about autism, how it affects people and what I could do to help my son start living a happier life. Bear in mind this was in the very early 90's and not only did I have no idea the internet even existed at the time, but even if I'd been scouring it every day, there was precious little information around back then that could've helped explain things. It seemed like the health professionals who asked me all the right questions were pretty much in the same position I was. I remember his paediatrician asking 'Does he walk on his toes?' and when I said that yes, he'd always walked that way, she gave him a big tick in the 'autistic' box. When I asked her *why* he did it though, she said 'Well, to be honest we're not sure, we just know it's something autistic children do.'

Thankfully things have moved on a whole lot since those early days and *so* much research has been done into the condition over the years. Naturally, me being me, I've made it my business to follow the findings as they've been published, which is lucky for you because it means you don't have to go trawling through all the books, articles and internet posts that I have.

It's no exaggeration to say I've asked a million and one questions over the years, but obviously I can't answer quite that many here, so I'm going to focus on the things I found most confusing when my children were small. Some will already have been answered in this book, so I'll just redirect you to the appropriate sections for those, but others will be new, and hopefully this chapter will give you lots of the 'Oh, *that's* why!' moments I had to wait so long to experience.

Car trouble

Although it took me quite a while to work out the reasons behind many of the boys' behaviours, it was a *very* long time before I got to the bottom of one in particular.

Since he was the eldest, Christopher always rode in the front passenger seat of my car when we went out, and when he was three, he suddenly developed a new, and very disruptive, behaviour. Every now and then, for no apparent reason I could fathom, he'd suddenly go hysterical and attack me while I was driving. He'd kick, punch, bite and scream as if his life depended on it, and try as I might, I couldn't find a pattern to these attacks at all.

As he got bigger, things got so bad he had to sit in the back of the car instead, and I never found out what had caused him so much distress until one day many, many years later when he started learning to drive himself. 'You know what?' he said 'When I was younger, I used to think you changed gears just to annoy me.' Bingo! He'd believed I was deliberately moving my hand into his personal space just to irritate him and this was what was setting him off. The reason his outbursts were so random was because every time I touched the gear stick he'd sit and fume, his anger building more and more until eventually he'd explode into violence. If I'd realised at the time, I could've saved myself a lot of bruises! Ah well, we live and learn.

This chapter, then, covers the main questions I used to ask every day when I first became an autism parent. Since I only had the boys at this stage, I'll refer to 'my child' as 'he', but trust me, these could just as easily apply to Isabelle, so they're in no way exclusive to autistic boys.

Why does my child do that?

Why does my child have no spoken language yet?
Why does my child repeat what I've said or even what he's just said himself?
Why does my child take everything so literally?

Communication is about so much more than just spoken language, and children need to develop all kinds of social skills first before speech can develop. Pre-language skills act a bit like the roots and trunk of a tree, gradually developing until they can support a variety of different branches, one of which is recognisable speech. These skills include making eye contact, copying other people and using gestures such as pointing, as well as babbling and making other sounds with their voice. Autistic children struggle to process these early skills, which delays the onset of their speech to a greater or lesser degree, depending on how quickly they master each stage.

The tendency to repeat words and phrases, known as echolalia, is very common in autistic people of all ages and palilalia (the tendency to repeat something you've just said) also happens very frequently in people on the spectrum. Both can begin as glitches in the processing of spoken language and become a safe, comforting form of expression used when someone is under stress.

The reason autistic people take things so literally is discussed in more detail in the 'Tackling the Tough Stuff' chapter under the subheading *'Literally going back to basics'*.

Why does my child walk on his toes?
Why does my child watch TV on his head?
Why does my child keep getting naked all the time?
Why does my child keep building dens and forts?
Why does my child keep falling out of bed?
Why does my child refuse to put his coat on?
Why does my child keep making repetitive movements like flapping his hands?
Why does my child get so upset when I try to cut his nails or brush his teeth?
Why does my child insist on all the labels being removed from his clothes?

Why does my child spin round without getting dizzy?
Why does my child get furious when he hears people chewing their food?
Why does my child trip over his own feet?
Why does my child hate being cuddled?
Why does my child always shout, yet he can't stand loud noises?
Why does my child get hysterical in the supermarket?
Why does my child eat food in one place but refuse it in another?
Why does my child refuse to eat food that's touched other food?
Why does my child eat things that aren't food?

These may seem like a whole variety of different issues but in fact they can all be traced back to difficulties processing information that's coming in through the senses (sight, taste, touch, smell, hearing etc.) Each one of these behaviours is a direct result of sensory processing disorder which is explained in much more detail in the 'Tackling the Tough Stuff' chapter under the subheading *'Well that makes sense'*.

Why does my child always ruin days out?
This is also to do with sensory issues, and you'll find the very useful 'Survival Kit for Days Out' in the 'Tackling the Tough Stuff' chapter.

Why does my child get so upset when his routines are changed?
Why does my child get so upset when he has to change from one task to another?
Why does my child stare off into space?

These behaviours are explained in the 'Tackling the Tough Stuff' chapter under the subheading *'Processing delays'*.

Why does my child behave so differently at school?
Why does my child get angrier with me than with anyone else?

These behaviours are down to something called the 'delayed after effect' which is explained in the 'The Female of the Species' chapter under the subheading 'The invisible girl'.

Why does my child line things up?
Why does my child have such a fascination with numbers and patterns of information?

Autistic people of all ages absolutely love to line things up and organise similar items into colour, shape and size order. Many find it incredibly soothing and say it helps to keep their minds ordered. Racing, jumbled thoughts can be a real challenge for people living with autism and being able to arrange objects into categories or list things alphabetically can make them feel calm and safe.

Seeing patterns and shapes in their environment that most people miss is a very common trait in people on the spectrum, and they love to create their own patterns too, to bring some kind of order and familiarity to the chaotic world they're experiencing every day. Once they've created a pattern, they can become very distressed if it's changed in some way, even if no one else even realises it's there.

Why does my child keep repeating the same behaviours but expecting a different result?
Why does my child have no sense of danger?
Why does my child have such high anxiety levels?

These issues are discussed in the 'The ABC's to Elemenopee's of Autism' chapter, under the subheading *'How autistic brains learn'*.

Why does my child feel such an overwhelming emotional connection to inanimate objects?
Why does my child become hysterical when I clear up his toys?

Most young children form strong attachments to their favourite toys, often imagining they have human characteristics and feelings. That's really not what I'm talking about here. Autistic children (and adults) very often have a condition called 'personification' which takes the idea of inanimate objects having human emotions to an entirely different level. Because they can be incredibly compassionate and empathetic (known as having hyper-empathy) people on the spectrum often worry incessantly about 'upsetting' objects by treating them unfairly or making them feel left out.

I know this sounds strange but I've discovered it's a really common trait and it goes a long way to explain the lines and patterns autistic people create with their possessions, and why they get so upset when things are moved. Transferring emotions and creating whole scenarios about how an object might be feeling can lead to all kinds of unusual behaviour including being compelled to collect huge numbers of a certain type of rock or stick and having to make sure they're all receiving the same amount of attention in case they feel ignored, or using far too many paperclips on a batch of documents so they all get a chance to feel useful. It's important to remember that if your child feels this way towards objects, those feelings are just as intense as the ones they experience towards human beings, so always be patient and supportive because they really can get very distressed about this kind of thing.

Why does my child struggle to make friends?
Why does my child walk round and round the playground instead of playing with the other children?
Why does my child have such a connection with animals, nature and spirituality?

Autistic people struggle to understand so many things in life and for a lot of them, human beings are the most complicated, mysterious things of all. Being unsure about how to read other people's tone of voice, body language and facial expressions puts them at a distinct disadvantage when it comes to making friends, but fortunately it's nothing to do with not *wanting* to make friends, so it's definitely something they can work on.

Language is changeable; facial expressions lie; no two human beings are exactly alike, and social rules change depending on your age or your relationship to the person in question. All these factors can lead an autistic person to assume that humans are somehow being dishonest, when in fact they're just being, well, human.

Add to this the challenges of having a processing delay and a radically different sense of humour and how being unsure about whether or not to join in leads to frequently being rejected, and it's easy to see why people on the spectrum find it so hard to form close relationships outside the family unit.

Autistic children find it much easier being in a structured environment where they know what's expected of them, and a lot of the pressure to socialise is removed while they're in the classroom. At break times it's a different story, as they're expected to navigate a noisy, crowded playground full of fast-moving children all dressed the same way. From this blur of colours and shapes, they're somehow supposed to identify the people they know and form bonds with them by playing games which appear to them to be constantly changing for no particular reason. For children on the spectrum, once they find something they enjoy, they'll happily do it over and over again because it brings them comfort and makes them feel safe, so walking round the edges of the playground is very popular because it's totally predictable. They can count the number of paces it takes to walk from one side to the other, and experiment by taking larger or smaller steps. This may not seem like fun to most children, but if you're autistic it's a great way to unwind and reorder your thoughts, plus it gives you some much needed alone time.

I've often heard it said that autistic people have such a strong connection with animals and nature because they're both much simpler to understand than humans. While that could perhaps be a contributory factor, in my experience it's not the underlying reason. It seems to me that countless people on the spectrum are simply *born* with a deep connection to these things: a profound sensitivity, an instinctive appreciation of the environment and an inherent kindness towards those creatures they see as being more vulnerable than themselves.

Being so intuitive and having a heightened sense of empathy towards everything, whether it's alive or even inanimate, naturally draws a lot of autistic people towards exploring their spirituality. Many don't believe in organised religions because they find their teachings illogical, but they can still have a very philosophical view of the world and develop a spiritually enlightened outlook as a result.

Why does my child suddenly get upset when he feels really happy or excited?

This one took me a long time to work out and the answer is that autistic people have difficulties processing *all* emotions, not just the ones we think of as negative. Too much excitement or even laughter can overload them and lead to meltdowns, so it's important to keep things as consistent as possible while still giving them the chance to express themselves. After living with the condition for so many years, I know instinctively when things are getting a bit out of hand and will step in to calm things down. As a result, my boys now call me 'the fun sponge'. I'm *so* underappreciated around here!

Why does my child behave so differently when he has a high temperature?

Autism parents have known for years that their children often mysteriously change when they have a temperature, making better eye contact and being much more responsive than usual. Naturally nobody told me this when my children were small, so I used to think I was a terrible mother for making the most of Christopher being poorly and enjoying some cuddles instead of the constant physical attacks I was so used to. Obviously I didn't wish he'd get ill, but I certainly wished he'd stop battering me all the time, and without fail, every time his temperature went up, his aggression went down.

I genuinely believed this was something only my children did, but it turns out it's a real phenomenon known as 'the fever effect'. A scientific study conducted in 2007 concluded that for some reason (it's still being investigated) having a fever stimulates an autistic brain's ability to make connections and send information, so I can assure you if you've noticed your child showing this type of behaviour, it really is happening and you're not imagining things.

What on earth do all these initials mean?

If you're unfamiliar with the world of autism you'll have plenty of new information to process, and worrying about what all the different terms and abbreviations mean is the last thing you need. To save you hours of research, here are a few of the most common phrases and acronyms you're likely to come across when you're dealing with the condition. These are always changing so some may be out of date by the time you read this list, but they're all correct at the time of writing.

ABA: Applied Behaviour Analysis / Applied Behavioural Analysis

ABC: Autism Behaviour Checklist

ADD: Attention Deficit Disorder (short or erratic attention span without hyperactivity)

ADHD: Attention Deficit Hyperactivity Disorder (short or erratic attention span with hyperactivity)

ADOS: Autism Diagnostic Observation Schedule

APD: Auditory Processing Disorder (difficulty in recognising and interpreting sounds, especially those involved in speech)

AS: Asperger's Syndrome (very similar condition to autism but usually without any language delay)

ASC: Autism Spectrum Condition (another term for Autistic Spectrum Disorder)

ASD: Autism Spectrum Disorder (anything from classical autism to autistic tendencies)

CA: Classical Autism (autism which fits all of the diagnostic criteria)

CAMHS: Child and Adolescent Mental Health Services

CCG: Clinical Commissioning Groups

CDD: Childhood Disintegrative Disorder a.k.a. Heller's Syndrome (loss of previously learned communication, co-ordination and social skills)

DLA: Disability Living Allowance

DSM-V: Diagnostic Statistical Manual (edition V) the current version of this publication (lists the diagnostic criteria for all mental health disorders)

Dyscalculia: Specific difficulty with numbers, time and spatial reasoning

Dysgraphia: Specific difficulty with handwriting, processing letters and the movement of the muscles required when writing by hand

Dyslexia: Specific difficulty with reading and organisational skills

Dyspraxia a.k.a. **Developmental Co-ordination Disorder** (DCD) or **Motor Coordination Disorder**: (specific difficulty with co-ordination of movements and spacial awareness)

EHC: Education, Health and Care

EHCP: Education Health and Care Plan

EP: Educational Psychologist

ESCO: Early Support Care Co-ordination

EWO: Education Welfare Officer

GFCF: Gluten Free / Casein Free (specific dietary requirement associated with a number of autistic people's digestive systems)

HD: Hyperkinetic Disorder – hyperactivity without a poor or erratic attention span – (another term for ADHD)

HFA: High Functioning Autism (autism occurring with an IQ of 70 or over)

HI: Hearing Impairment

IEP: Individual Education Plan

LA: Local Authority

LFA: Low Functioning Autism (autism occurring with an IQ of 70 or below)

MLD: Moderate Learning Difficulty

MSI: Multi-Sensory Impairment

NOS: Not Otherwise Specified (usually seen in PDD-NOS)

NT: Neurologically Typical / Neuro Typical (no diagnosable neurological disorder a.k.a. 'normal people!')

NVLD: Non-verbal Learning Disorder (very similar to Asperger's but less severe)

OCD: Obsessive Compulsive Disorder (feelings of high anxiety that are relieved by repetitive behaviours)

ODD: Oppositional Defiant Disorder (disobedient, hostile and aggressive behaviour towards authority figures)

OT: Occupational Therapist / Occupational Therapy (enables people to engage in appropriate everyday activities, improving their quality of life)

PD: Physical Disability

PDA: Pathological Demand Avoidance (avoidance of everyday tasks and manipulative, socially inappropriate, sometimes aggressive behaviour)

PDD: Pervasive Developmental Disorder (a delay in social, communication and motor skills which does not meet the criteria for autism)

PDD-NOS: Pervasive Developmental Disorder Not Otherwise Specified a.k.a. Atypical Autism (almost classic autism or Asperger's but with some diagnostic criteria missing)

PMLD: Profound and Multiple Learning Difficulties

PR: Parental Responsibility

PT: Physiotherapy/Physiotherapist

RHLD: Right Hemisphere Learning Disorder (same as NVLD – non-verbal learning disorder)

SALT/SLT: Speech and Language Therapy/Therapist

SEN: Special Educational Needs

SENCo: Special Educational Needs Co-ordinator

SEND: Special Educational Needs and Disabilities

SIB: Self-Injurious Behaviour

SLCN: Speech, Language & Communication Needs

SLD: Severe Learning Difficulties

SPD: Sensory processing disorder (difficulties taking in and responding to sensory information) Also known as Proprioceptive Dysfunction

SPD: Semantic Pragmatic Disorder (difficulty understanding the meaning of language with little ability to use it appropriately in social situations)

SpLD: Specific Learning Difficulties

STAPS: Specialist Teacher and Psychology Service

TA: Teaching Assistant

TEACCH: Treatment and Education of Autistic and Related Communication Handicapped Children

ToM: Theory of Mind (the ability to understand that others have thoughts, feelings and desires which are different from your own)

TPA: Task Performance Anxiety

TS: Tourette's syndrome (sudden involuntary movements or 'tics' with vocal noises or inappropriate sounds which cannot be controlled)

VI: Visual Impairment

WTT: Working Together Team (outreach)

What can help me explain autism to my family and friends?

Films and TV shows are a great, non-threatening way of introducing autism to people who are new to the condition and showing them you're not the only ones going through these challenges.
They can be very useful for helping to explain autism to family and friends so I'd suggest you watch some by yourself, choose the ones you feel are most relevant to your situation, then make time to watch them together.

Films by release date
1969 – Change of Habit
1969 – Run Wild Run Free
1979 – Being There
1986 – The Boy Who Could Fly
1988 – Rain Man
1989 – The Wizard
1990 – Backstreet Dreams
1991 – Little Man Tate
1993 – What's Eating Gilbert Grape
1994 – Nell
1994 – David's Mother
1998 – Mercury Rising
1998 – Little Voice
1999 – Molly
2004 – Miracle Run
2004 – Killer Diller
2005 – Mozart and the Whale
2006 – Snow Cake
2006 – After Thomas
2007 – Her Name is Sabine
2007 – Ben X
2007 – Autism: The Musical

2008 – The Black Balloon

2009 – Adam

2009 – Mary and Max

2009 – The Horse Boy

2010 – Dear John

2010 – Temple Grandin

2010 – My Name is Khan

2011 – Extremely Loud & Incredibly Close

2011 – Fly Away

2011 – A Mile in His Shoes

2012 – The Story of Luke

2012 – White Frog

2015 – Autism in Love

2016 – Life, Animated

TV shows

Sherlock

The Big Bang Theory

Touch

Criminal Minds

The A Word

The Bridge

The Autistic Gardener

Yellow Peppers

Atypical

The Good Doctor

Who can help me understand the education system?

I've heard very good reports about all of these organisations:

Educational Equality - www.educationalequality.co.uk
This site is an amazing resource for helping families through the maze of special educational needs.

SOS!SEN - www.sossen.org.uk

This is a free, friendly, independent and confidential telephone helpline for parents and carers looking for information and advice on special educational needs.

IPSEA - www.ipsea.org.uk

This organisation is a real mine of information and deals with every aspect of the special educational needs process.

Can I get any financial help?

If you're struggling financially, it's definitely worth checking whether you're entitled to any benefits. Here are a few suggestions about where to start looking:

For Disability Living Allowance

www.gov.uk/disability-living-allowance-children

For Carers Allowance

www.gov.uk/carers-allowance

For help or advice about being a carer

www.carersuk.org

For Motability Allowance

www.motability.co.uk/about-the-scheme/allowances

For grants to help with day to day costs or holidays

www.familyfund.org.uk

Can anyone help my child get some sleep?

Both of these websites will be able to offer some good, practical advice:

ISIS (Infant Sleep Information Source) - www.isisonline.org.uk
The Children's Sleep Charity - www.thechildrenssleepcharity.org.uk

How can my child play Minecraft safely?

So many children on the spectrum love playing Minecraft and if you haven't
discovered it yet, it's a bit like building towns and cities out of LEGO on your
computer. There's a whole community of players, and as with anything like that,
there can sometimes be bullies on there too. To counteract this, an autism parent
named Stuart Duncan (who's also on the spectrum himself) created a version of
Minecraft that's exclusively for autistic children and adults. If this is something
your child might enjoy, I'd definitely recommend checking it out:

Autcraft - www.autcraft.com

How can I be proactive?

Waiting around between appointments can be incredibly frustrating, but there are
lots of people out there who'll guide you in the right direction. There's also plenty
you can do to help your child make progress and to help yourself cope better with
the day to day stresses of living with autism. Here are a few suggestions:

Quantum LEAP - www.autism-all-stars.org/quantum-leap
This is my therapy website where you can download programmes to help you
enjoy increased calmness and confidence, better quality sleep and a whole host of
other useful strategies. It's highly recommended, but then I would say that,
wouldn't I? Still, check it out because it really can change your life.

The Emotional Freedom Technique - www.emofree.com
Detailed information about the emotional freedom technique including
instructional videos.

Sutherland Cranial College of Osteopathy - www.scco.ac
This is a charitable organisation and a centre for shared learning, knowledge and
practice in the field of cranial osteopathy.

Irlen Syndrome website. - www.irlen.org.uk

If you're considering using coloured reading lenses to help reduce sensory overload in your child, these are the people to speak to.

National Autistic Society - www.autism.org.uk

The UK's leading charity for people with autism and Asperger's syndrome; providing information, support and specialist services for people on the spectrum and their families.

Adult Attention Deficit Disorder UK - www.aadduk.org/help-support/support-groups

This organisation works to raise the profile of attention deficit disorder (ADD) and attention deficit hyperactivity disorder (ADHD) in adults, providing information and advice on diagnosis and treatments. The link goes directly to a list of support groups for both children and adults.

OCD Action - www.ocdaction.org.uk

This is the largest national charity focusing on obsessive compulsive disorders. They provide information, support and help with diagnosis, while raising awareness of OCD.

British Dyslexia Association - www.bdadyslexia.org.uk

This is a charity working towards a 'dyslexia-friendly' society; providing information, support, activities and training for teachers, families and organisations.

Dyspraxia Foundation – www.dyspraxiafoundation.org.uk

This is a nationwide charity working to increase understanding and awareness of dyspraxia among the public and particularly professionals in the health and education fields.

Tourette's Action - www.tourettes-action.org.uk

This charity provides information and support, promoting research into better treatments, and fighting ignorance, misunderstanding and prejudice about Tourette's syndrome.

Allergy UK - www.allergyuk.org
This is the leading national charity providing support, advice and information for those living with allergies.

Coeliac UK - www.coeliac.org.uk
This is an independent charity who've been the UK experts on gluten intolerance (coeliac disease) and the gluten free diet for nearly 50 years.

HMSA Hypermobility Syndromes Association – http://hypermobility.org/ This organisation provides information on the heritable disorders of connective tissue (the 'Hypermobility Syndromes') including hypermobility spectrum disorder and Ehlers-Danlos syndrome.

Pinterest - uk.pinterest.com
Join this site and search for 'sensory rooms' for a whole world of ideas to help make your child's home and classroom more sensory friendly.

Where can I buy sensory toys and calming products?

Sensory Direct - www.sensorydirect.com
This company is one of the best resources I've found for sensory items. They sell everything from tiny fidgets to huge sensory dens, from weighted blankets to bean bags. They're very reasonably priced too. I use their products all the time and recommend them to so many people that I really should be on commission by now.

Jettproof - www.jettproof.co.uk
Originally started by two autism parents, this company provides some fantastic deep pressure and sensory-friendly clothing. The feedback I've heard about their products has been excellent.

Amazon – www.amazon.co.uk
If you visit Amazon and type in 'sensory products' or 'sensory toys' you'll find a

huge range of items to suit people of all ages and abilities. Their prices are great too.

Further reading

I appreciate you might not have an excess of time on your hands for reading, but knowledge really is power when it comes to autism, so even if you only manage to grab five minutes here and there, it's still worth finding out as much as you can about it.

Jessica Kingsley Publishers - www.jkp.com

These people offer one of the best resources for books on autism and Asperger's I've ever found. They have sections for children, parents and professionals devoted to all the relevant subjects linked to autism and its related conditions. I'd recommend using the 'Search' facility to look round the site because it's pretty big. Just type in 'anxiety', 'girls', 'siblings' or whatever else you're looking for and see which ones appeal to you. If you can't afford one of their books for any reason, you can always apply for a grant from the Family Fund or ask your local library to get you a copy. Below is a list of books I'd recommend as a great starting place.

Reference books for parents and carers

The Autistic Spectrum: A Guide for Parents and Professionals
Lorna Wing

The Complete Guide to Asperger's Syndrome
Tony Attwood

Books explaining autism

Thinking in Pictures
Temple Grandin

The 'Asperkids' series including The Asperkid's Game Plan
Jennifer O'Toole

10 Things Every Child With Autism Wishes You Knew
Ellen Notbohm

Asperger's Syndrome & High Achievement
Ioan James

Asperger's and Self Esteem: Insight & Hope Through Famous Role Models
Temple Grandin and Norm Ledgin

Information about girls on the spectrum

Aspergirls
Rudy Simone

Sisterhood of the Spectrum
Jennifer O'Toole

Asperger's and Girls
Tony Attwood, Temple Grandin and more

Asperger's in Pink
Julie Clark

The Girl with the Curly Hair
Alis Rowe

A Mighty Girl post about autism
www.amightygirl.com/blog?p=14948

Dealing with anger and anxiety

Emotional Healing in Minutes
Valerie and Paul Lynch

The Red Beast
K.I. Al-Ghani

How to Be Angry
Signe Witson

Managing Meltdowns
Deborah Lipsky

The Huge Bag of Worries
Virginia Ironside

Starving the Anxiety Gremlin
Kate Collins-Donnelly

Books for siblings

Everybody is Different
Fiona Bleach

My Brother is Autistic
Jennifer Moore-Mallinos

Siblings and Autism
Debra L. Cumberland and Bruce E. Mills

Books for grandparents

Grandparent's Guide to Autism Spectrum Disorders
Nancy Mucklow

Your Special Grandchild
Josie Santomauro

Grandparenting a Child with Special Needs
Charlotte E. Thompson M.D.

Autism through history

Different Like Me
Jennifer Elder

NeuroTribes
Steve Silberman

A Day at the Circus

May 2004

- 7am: Stormy morning. Look out of window and see Child 1 (age 12) running round garden holding large metal ruler above head.
- Ask Child 1 to explain himself. Further investigation reveals school has been studying discovery of electricity. Child 1 has been attempting to recreate Benjamin Franklin's experiment and trying to get electrocuted.
- Carefully remove ruler and usher soaking Child back inside. #MadScientistMoment
- 4pm: Collect Children 1 and 2 (age 8) from after school club. Teacher informs me that Child 2 has attempted to throw himself from first floor window while performing complicated martial arts moves.
- Apologise to club manager and explain Child 2 is currently obsessed with Power Rangers. Have stern word with Child 2, reminding him of important safety warning: 'Do not try this at home.'
- Child 2 replies 'But I have a get-out clause: I'm not at home, I'm at after school club.' #HeHasAPoint
- 6pm: Notice makeshift trap has appeared on lawn, consisting of overturned waste paper bin propped up by stick with length of string attached. Banana has been placed under bin as bait.
- Discover Child 3 (age 5) at end of string and enquire as to purpose of trap. Has been playing video game called 'Ape Escape' and decided to catch any stray monkeys who might wander into garden.
- 6:30pm: Child 3 still lying in wait. Child 1, having heard earlier conversation, suddenly appears from behind bush dressed in full monkey suit, steals banana and chases screaming Child 3 round garden with it. #OnlyInMyHouse
- 8pm: Enter kitchen to find trail of frozen peas leading from freezer into front room. Follow trail and am confronted by scene of squashed-pea-related carnage.
- Child 2 has fallen and hit head on table. Child 1, having heard placing frozen peas on bruises is helpful, has proceeded to press large handfuls straight into his brother's head, missing crucial step of putting them in plastic bag first. #HeartInTheRightPlace

Through Darkness We Shine

'The most exciting place to discover talent is in yourself.'
Ashleigh Brilliant

A percentage of the profits from this book will be donated to my charity, Autism All Stars, so I thought you'd like to know a bit about it.

We started the charity after the tragic suicide of Dominic's best friend at the age of fourteen. His friend was an amazing boy: utterly unique and totally irreplaceable. He had many of the symptoms of autism but was never formally diagnosed, and we thought of him as an unofficial part of the family. He and Dominic were so alike it was often hard to tell where one stopped and the other began, and Dominic was totally lost without him.

To help us through our own grief and do what we could to prevent the same thing happening to other people, we decided Autism All Stars would do its best to concentrate on the positives of living with autism; acknowledging the dark times but keeping our face to the light, hence our motto: Through Darkness We Shine. We're determined to spread a message of hope and do whatever we can to make sure autistic people feel a sense of belonging, whether they've been formally diagnosed or not.

To achieve this, we encourage everyone who supports us to celebrate their differences and see them as something valuable and worthwhile, which is a great way to raise their self-esteem. The idea is to feel proud of their special interests instead of feeling like the odd one out, and use those same interests to help raise funds and awareness of autism, no matter how strange they might seem to other people.

With our love of dressing up, you won't be surprised to hear we've used our own special interest to host lots of autism-friendly character days. We also run cinema clubs and theatre performances for autistic people, with specialist sensory areas they can use if things get too much.

Living with autism is tough, so our website has plenty of helpful information for dealing with the day to day challenges it brings, and our social media pages are full of positive, inspiring stories about life on the spectrum, with a healthy dose of fun thrown in for good measure.

We're always in need of extra people to hold fundraisers for us, so do feel free to organise one of your own – the more unusual, the better.

Booking a presentation

I'm always very happy to come along and give talks on autism. As you can imagine, they're fun, lively and animated, with a detailed PowerPoint presentation to help explain things clearly. On average my talks last around one and a half hours and are followed by a question and answer session. They include information on the basics of what autism actually is, with the rest tailor-made to your specifications. I have a sliding scale of speaker's fees which you can see here: **www.autism-all-stars.org/outreach**

You can find out more about what Autism All Stars does here: www.autism-all-stars.org or by joining us on Facebook, Twitter, Instagram and Pinterest (/autismallstars).

Autism All Stars Foundation UK
Registered Charity Number 1152681

Thanks for Believing in Me

'A friend is someone who knows the song in your heart
and can sing it back to you when you have forgotten the words.'

Anon

Writing this book has been anything but plain sailing and there were more than a few dark days where I'd reach out to others for reassurance, overwhelmed by the sheer size of the task I'd set myself and considering giving up on the whole thing. To each and every person who's kept me going, I'd like to say a *huge* thank you. Every conversation, every like and comment on Facebook and every hug we've shared has helped me more than you'll ever know; without them I'd never have achieved everything I have.

Special thanks to Nigel for taking the pressure off by doing the cooking, cleaning, washing, ironing, school runs, college runs and dog walks for me whenever you could; to Dominic for your proofreading and invaluable feedback on every chapter; to Aidan for inspiring me with your courage when it comes to trying new things; to Christopher for your bravery and unquenchable spirit of adventure, and to Isabelle for keeping my spirits up with your positive attitude towards life, your kindness and encouragement about my writing skills and your reassurance that I am, in fact, worthy of the title Best Mum in the Universe.

Enormous thanks as well to my outrageously talented illustrator Jenny, who's not only an incredible artist, but is also one of the nicest, most unique people you could ever hope to meet. Thanks for 'getting' me and turning my crazy ideas into such beautiful works of art. You can see more of her creations here: www.jennystoutdesign.com – prepare to be blown away!

Last but by no means least; I'd like to thank *you*, lovely reader, for taking the time to read my story. If you've enjoyed it (which I'm guessing you have or you'd have stopped reading by now!) then I'd be extremely grateful if you'd leave me some positive feedback on Amazon to encourage other people to read it too; it really does make a huge amount of difference.

Wherever your journey takes you from here, I wish you masses of luck, love and laughter along the way, and hope you'll always remember that however tough things get, it's just my old friend Life, doing what it does, being annoying and giving you what you need, even if it's not exactly what you want.

I very much hope you've benefitted from reading this book – my own little ship sent out on the sea - I hope it's touched you, made you smile, and given you some new tools you can use to brighten your days. Most of all though, I hope it's done what it was designed to do and given you the comforting message, loud and clear, that you're really, *truly* not alone.

Coming soon...

The Ringmaster's Tale: Autism, Asperger's, Adolescence

As you can guess, life didn't get any less complicated for my family once the children started reaching adolescence. Hormones, relationships, the struggle for independence and the consumption of alcohol all started to make an appearance. Book two in the series covers some serious topics and follows our journey through the very best and very worst of times. If you'd like to be the first to hear about its release, visit **www.autism-all-stars.org/ringmaster** and sign up to my mailing list. There's a taste of what's to come on the following page...

A Day at the Circus

August 2016

- Child 3 (age 17) is terrified of bees. Husband has naturally decided his calling in life is to save as many bees from extinction as possible. Husband (age 'old enough to know better') has therefore planted wildflower 'bee garden' and put up 'bee hotel' behind house. What could possibly go wrong?

- 2pm: Folding washing. Hear hysterical screams from Child 3. On investigation, discover cloud of 15 bees happily drinking moisture from coir mat on back doorstep, thereby trapping Child 3 inside house. Husband looking at them lovingly, clearly delighted that his 'Bees Welcome' policy is such a success. Dog barking madly to come in and trying to eat several bees. Child 3 refuses to open door and goes into instant overload. Suggest to Husband that he moves doormat to another part of the garden and pours sugar water on it to entice bees away from doorway. Husband carefully moves mat. Hand Husband small glass of sugar water through gap in door while bees swirl around him like a stripy cloud. Husband pours sugar water *all over back doorstep.* Bees are delighted. More bees arrive to join in the fun. Child 3 loses his mind. On seeing my pained expression and hearing me wail 'WHY? Just WHY?' Husband mouths 'Sorry, I forgot where I was supposed to pour it.' #NoJuryWouldConvictMe

- 7pm: Working on computer. Hear HUGE crash from upstairs. Child 4 (age 9) has been jumping on my bed. Again. Entire wooden bed frame and slats now snapped clean in half. Looks like giant sinkhole has opened in middle of mattress. Child 4 hiding in bathroom. Entice hysterical Child from bathroom. Spend hour calming her down, followed by hour with Husband removing debris. Currently typing this at midnight, lying on mattress on bedroom floor. Visiting DIY shop first thing tomorrow. #ThisIsWhyWeHaveATrampoline

If you've enjoyed reading this book you can read more of my thoughts on 'Autism, the Universe and Everything' by subscribing to my blog here:

www.autism-all-stars.org/ringmaster

Printed in Great Britain
by Amazon